SCANDAL WORK

SCANDAL
WORK

JAMES JOYCE, THE NEW JOURNALISM, AND THE HOME RULE NEWSPAPER WARS

MARGOT GAYLE BACKUS

University of Notre Dame Press

Notre Dame, Indiana

Manufactured in the United States of America

Library of Congress Cataloging-in-Publication Data

Backus, Margot Gayle, 1961–
Scandal work : James Joyce, the new journalism, and the home rule
newspaper wars / Margot Gayle Backus.
pages cm
Includes bibliographical references and index.
ISBN 978-0-268-02237-2 (pbk. : alk. paper) —
ISBN 0-268-02237-2 (pbk. : alk. paper)
1. Joyce, James, 1882–1941—Political and social views.
2. Sex scandals—Great Britain—History. 3. Home rule—Ireland.
4. Sensationalism in journalism—Great Britain.
5. English newspapers—Great Britain—History. I. Title.
PR6019.O9Z5256515   2013
823'.912—dc23
2013022744

For my fathers, Russell FitzGerald and Ron Kaake

The arc of the universe is long, but it bends toward justice.
—Martin Luther King

CONTENTS

LIST OF FIGURES

ACKNOWLEDGMENTS

This book was made possible by the generosity of many individuals, groups, and organizations, all of whom I want to first acknowledge and thank collectively, as the ordering of individual acknowledgments implies a hierarchy of gratitude that does not reflect my feelings. Thank you all. The vast web of information and ideas that is the Joyce-verse is the most exhilarating intellectual ocean I ever sought to navigate, and all those acknowledged helped me to keep my head above water and saw me safely to shore.

Of those whose influence on the overall project has been most materially and logistically pervasive, my professional editor, Jeanne Barker-Nunn, has been a star. It has been my good fortune to be coached, helped, pruned, and polished by Jeanne on and off for twenty years, since she copyedited my second published article in 1992, and her work has been invaluable. Sharon Delmendo, Betsy Dougherty, Sarah McKibben, Martha Stallman, and Skip Thompson—friends, colleagues, and intellectual family—lent support that included but also far exceeded reading and responding to chapters. Their engagement with my ideas and the conditions of their production has improved every page of this book and made its writing far less lonely. My editors at the University of Notre Dame Press, Barbara Hanrahan and subsequently Stephen Little, were both, in their distinct ways, magnificent, superlative, indispensable. Kevin Dettmar and Margot Norris, the press's two external readers, supplied responses that deftly balanced praise and encouragement with essential, tactful, insightful, and readily applicable critique. Rebecca DeBoer, Beth Wright of Trio Bookworks, and indeed all those I worked with in the course of the book's production have been like Bunyanesque literary inventions created to personify rare and desirable qualities: Competency, Respect, and Kindness.

I seem to have "caught" *Ulysses* from my students, rather than vice versa. The deep and fluent thinking in theses by my advisees Sara Leonard and Austin Westervelt-Lutz first got me hooked on the novel. Krista Kuhl, Martha Stallman, Lacy Johnson, Brandon Lamson, Matthew Walker, and Doyle Taverner-Ramos have produced similarly inspiring work. I have been vouchsafed new insights through the discussion and critical writing of literally dozens of University of Houston undergraduates and graduate students, in particular those who read *Ulysses* with me, and I sincerely thank them for all they have taught me. Martha Stallman in particular has been an extraordinarily valuable interlocutor, encountering and to an astounding degree absorbing *Ulysses* in one semester, then taking on a variety of roles including protégé, entertainer, unpaid and paid research assistant, coauthor, and friend. Her help reshaping these chapters as stories, her deep knowledge of Joyce, and her gift for intellectually apt, elegant, and often hilariously filthy summary resounds throughout the book. Gevais Jefferson, Meina Yates, and Krista Kuhl were all astonishing, joy-inducing students who all became, in varying orders, paid research assistants, conversants, and friends. Every teacher should be so lucky.

A cast of dozens read individual or multiple chapters, often more than once, and supported my work with intellectual guidance and encouragement, friendship, mentorship, reassurance, humor, and kindness. My colleagues at the University of Houston have been particularly generous. Hosam Aboul-Ela and Karen Fang, Maria Gonzalez, David Mazella, and Cedric Tolliver have helpfully responded to many chapter drafts; Hosam and Karen in particular read and responded to these chapters at every stage, starting with the primal ooze from which they evolved. My generous, far-flung Irish studies writing group—Helen Burke, Elizabeth Cullingford, Susan Cannon Harris, Sarah McKibben, Paige Reynolds, and Mary Trotter—has been equally indispensable, reading chapter drafts and all kinds of related pieces of work, cheering me on, and keeping me connected to the field I love. Paige and Sarah have been especially generous, providing astute last-minute readings at moments when it cannot have been convenient to do so. Karen Steele deserves recognition alongside these other long-haul colleagues; she has been a sort of one-woman writing group and emergency interlocutor who read and guided my work as I inelegantly bumbled about in the trackless wastes of newspaper studies. Mary Jean Corbett, Philip Sicker, and Eibhear Walshe also gave invaluable feedback to chapters of this book.

I must also thank those who have welcomed me into the world of Joyce studies with a degree of warmth and openheartednes for which I continue to be grateful. Joe Schork first taught me to interpret figurative language decades before I would need that skill to follow him in the adventure of disentangling Joyce's endless figural webs. Joe Kelly introduced me to Joe Valente, Vicki Mahaffey, and Colleen Lamos— my first Joycean role models—while he and I were still in graduate school, and all have since become great friends. Joe Valente in particular has been unspeakably influential. Our joint work has shaped my thinking to a degree that cannot be accurately or adequately credited. His support for this project has been lavish; he has read numerous chapter drafts and supplied crucial feedback and guidance on little or no notice. I first read *Ulysses* for a seminar at the University of West Virginia taught by Declan Kiberd, and thus this book, like so many in Irish studies, owes a debt to this remarkable mentor, teacher, and scholar. Margot Norris has given me, in addition to an insightful reader's report, the gift of her warmth and kindness. Katie Conrad, another academic sibling and soul sister, is an influential long-time collaborator and friend who presided over my physical entry into the world of Joyce studies at her lively Bloomsday centenary conference at the University of Kansas in June 2004. Michael Gillespie, Gregory Castle, Ann Fogarty, and Paul St. Amour have been valuable and generous colleagues, while Kevin Dettmar is in a class by himself as a teacher whose heart is matched only by his vast storehouses of knowledge concerning *Ulysses* and his gifts as a seminar leader. Kevin's wise and lucid reader's report gave me what I needed to make this a better book. In addition to Karen Steele, Simon Potter has been a vastly generous native informant from the realm of newspaper studies, guiding me around the entry hall and front rooms of that vast archive. Dominique Groeneveld and Sally Connolly have greatly enriched the final stages of book writing. Natalie Houston, too, has been an inspiration and a role model. Our relationship represents a cautionary tale against too little shop talk in one's collegial friendships: if I had understood sooner how our interests intersect, this book might have been even better.

I owe more gratitude than I can ever express to the many scholars, intellectuals, and artists whose exceptional kindness and intellectual generosity enriched my study in Ireland, both synchronically, by creating an intellectual and social place for me while there, and diachronically, by guiding me on the path that got me there. This study was fundamentally shaped and influenced by all the participants in Kevin Dettmar's 2008 National Endowment for the Humanities Summer Seminar at Trinity University College-Dublin, the matrix out of which this project grew: Gregory Erickson, Georgia Johnston, Joseph Kelly, Anne MacMaster, Maria McGarrity, John McGuigan, Richard Murphy, Carrie Preston, Agata Szczeszak-Brewer, Erin Templeton, Janine Utell, Beth Wightman, Gregory Winston, and Teresa Winterhalter. In Galway, Nessa Cronin, Louis De Paor, Samantha Williams, and many others made a home for my research at the National University of Ireland-Galway's Martha Fox Centre for Irish Studies. Diachronically, Liz Cullingford, Ed Madden, Declan Kiberd, Karen Steele, Laura Lyons, Purnima Bose, Lucy McDiarmid, Jim Doan, Tadgh Foley, Lionel Pilkington, Katherine O'Donnell, Katie Conrad, Eibhear Walshe, Susan Harris, Skip Thompson, James M. Smith, and Sarah McKibben have all been indispensable to my development as an Irish studies scholar. For making my precious periods of study in Ireland productive and memorable, I owe particular, sincere thanks to Ed Madden, Katie Conrad, Sarah McKibben, Nessa Cronin, Donna Potts, Ron Savage, Vicki Mahaffey, Lionel Pilkington, Tony Tracy, Rebecca Pelan, Tadgh Foley, Maureen O'Connor, David Doyle, John Eastlake, Leo Keohane, Méabh Ní Fhuartháin, Lillis O'Laoire, Lucy McDiarmid, Noreen Giffney, Michael O'Rourke, James M. Smith, Eibhear Walshe, Paul St. Amour, Jeff Dudgeon, Enda Duffy, Harriette

Andreadis, Laura Doan, Felix Larkin, Lori Gallagher, Colleen Lamos, Moira Kelly, Kevin Barry, Jim and Kathy Murphy, and Sean Kennedy, Tina O'Toole, and Anne Mulhall. Mary Dorcey, Eveline Conlon, Colm Tóibín, and Jamie O'Neill are the nicest, most generous of contemporary Irish authors. Irish filmmaker Pat Murphy threw me a lifeline when I needed it.

Funding for a germinal year spent among the staff, faculty, and students of the Martha Fox Irish Studies Centre at the National University of Ireland-Galway was provided by the National University of Ireland-Galway and the Irish American Cultural Institute's National University of Ireland-Galway Fellowship. Long may this incredible opportunity enable the work of Irish studies scholars. My work was also supported by the aforementioned 2008 NEH Summer Seminar on *Ulysses* at Trinity College-Dublin. The University of Houston has been extremely generous at both the university and the departmental level. My original research in Ireland was supported in part through a half year of paid university research leave from the University of Houston, and the University of Houston Gender and Women's Studies Program supported the development of early chapters through a generous summer stipend. Further development, revision, and final review and copyediting of the manuscript was made possible through the 2008–2010 Houston Research Professorship, funded by the University of Houston Department of English's Houston Endowment for the Study of Literary Criticism and through a series of Houston Endowment–funded departmental research grants, and by several University of Houston research grants. Library collections that granted access to crucial materials include the British Library, the Irish National Library, the NUI-Galway library, the University of Buffalo's special collections, Houston's University of Saint Thomas's excellent Irish studies collection, and of course the amazing librarians and collections at the University of Houston. Specific, heartfelt expressions of thanks are due to my chair, Wyman Herendeen, and my department's office manager, Carol Barr; IT specialist, George Barr; and Jessica Torres and the exceptional office staff. Julie Kofford's competence as graduate advisor saved my sanity and morale from collapse prior to this book's completion. And to the staff and management of my favorite local restaurant, Zake, where so very much of the work of this book was done, thanks for the green tea and sympathy.

As always, it is the innocent who pay the most; this book was subsidized not only by my university and various other professional institutions but by my daughter, Jerilyn Backus Tennison, and my partner, Steve Tennison, who gave up countless hours of fun, togetherness, and domestic upkeep without once giving into the temptation to erase my hard drive. I would also like to thank those who helped to minimize the hardships Jerilyn endured while I wrote this: not only Steve, an exceptional coparent, partner, and friend, but also his wonderful mother, Jean Tennison. Also due thanks are the faculty and parents of the University of Houston's now sadly defunct Lab School, particularly Stephanie Phipps; Galway's Little Red Hen Creche; Galway's Scoil Chroi Iosa and their excellent principal, Sister Joan; Evelyn Conlon; Katie O'Kelly; Patsy Callanan; Moira Kelly; Carol Kelleher and the group; Houston's Garden Oaks Elementary School; Sarah Cotner; Dr. Susan Wetherton; David Santana; Principal Lindsey Pollock; Discover Gymnastics, especially Coach Joe; and HISD's wonderful Friends of Montessori. Special thanks to Dr. David Curtis and the staff of the Texas Children's Hospital STARS program and to all the friends and family who raised me up and returned me to the fray when I feared that working motherhood had me or Jerilyn down for the count: Ann Christensen, Betsy Dougherty, Moira Kelly, Sharon Delmendo, Peg Backus Wallner, Sarah Backus, Ellen Backus, Jean Tennison, and Jacqueline Hedden. It takes more than a village to raise a child while writing a book; in our case it took the best minds and hearts of two nations.

Thanks are due to all my family members: my mother, Suzanne, and my birth mother, Ellen. My fathers, Russ and Ron, and my birth father, Tim. My brother, Tom, and my birth brothers, Tony and Allan. And to all of the Backuses and the Reynoldses who have welcomed me into their families.

The last debts of gratitude are for love, support, and joy that reach deeper than words. To my best friend and comrade JoAnn Pavletich, who has, these many years, consistently given me time and space in which to return to my self. To my best friend and comrade Sharon

Delmendo, who can always be counted on to protect me even from myself when necessary. And most of all to Steve and Jerilyn Tennison, without whom my work would be ashes and dust.

Everything good about this book was made possible by those listed above. The mistakes that remain are mine alone.

Introduction

James Joyce and the Political Sex Scandal:
"The Cracked Lookingglass of a Servant"

Dante stared across the table, her cheeks shaking. Mr. Casey struggled up from his chair and bent across the table towards her, scraping the air from before his eyes with one hand as though he were tearing aside a cobweb.

–No God for Ireland! he cried. We have had too much God in Ireland. Away with God!

–Blasphemer! Devil! screamed Dante, starting to her feet and almost spitting in his face. . . .

At the door Dante turned round violently and shouted down the room, her cheeks flushed and quivering with rage.

–Devil out of hell! We won! We crushed him to death! Fiend!

The door slammed behind her.

Mr. Casey, freeing his arms from his holders, suddenly bowed his head on his hands with a sob of pain.

–Poor Parnell! he cried loudly. My poor dead king!

He sobbed loudly and bitterly.

Stephen, raising his terrorstricken face, saw that his father's eyes were full of tears.

—James Joyce, *A Portrait of the Artist as a Young Man*

1

In the mirror of [James Joyce's] art the ugliness of the Gorgon's
head may be clearly reflected, but it is cleanly severed and does not
turn the observer's heart to stone.

—Stanislaus Joyce, *My Brother's Keeper*

In his youth, James Joyce became fixated on newspapers and newspaper scandals, which in turn inspired his own notoriously scandalous writings.[1] This inspiration is obvious; even first-time readers will
usually note some of the ways in which Joyce's work is infused with
scandal. Joyce's earliest published literary prose, *Dubliners* (1914), is a
collection of naturalist short stories that often revolve around minor
scandals.[2] Something unspoken has disgraced the dead priest in "The
Sisters," and the boys in "An Encounter" meet up with a "queer old
josser" whose illicit sexual proclivities are made legible to the reader
through sexological conventions popularized by fin de siècle homosexual scandals. Eveline, in her eponymous short story, appears to
narrowly skirt abduction into the scandalous realm of "the white slave
trade." In "A Little Cloud," Little Chandler is both enticed and repulsed
by scandalmongering journalist Ignatius Gallaher's references to British and continental depravities. In "The Boarding House," scandal is
both courted and contained: Mrs. Moony places her wayward daughter Polly in the way of Bob Doran, a compliant boarder, prompting a
transgression that must be repaid in the coin of marriage.

Joyce's semiautobiographical bildungsroman, *A Portrait of the
Artist as a Young Man* (1916), is at least equally engaged with scandal,
recording the impact of newspaper sex scandals on family dynamics,
relations among Irish schoolboys, and the psyche of a maturing artist.[3] Certainly, no discussion of that novel would be complete without
noting its treatment of Victorian Ireland's greatest sex scandal, the
so-called Fall of Parnell.[4] In the novel's first intimations of a coming, precipitous decline, the great nationalist leader's scandalous affair

with "Kitty" O'Shea unleashes internecine hostilities that disrupt the home life of Stephen Dedalus, Joyce's literary alter ego.

Joyce's incorporation of scandal into his work grew more flamboyant and complex as his style evolved. In fact, the trope of the partially submerged (or brewing) sex scandal structures both of Joyce's greatest works: *Ulysses* (1922) and *Finnegans Wake* (1939).[5] In the former, Molly Bloom's act of infidelity with Blazes Boylan is only the most prominent of many incipient sex scandals around which Joyce organizes the text, while in the latter this centrifugal role is occupied by the illegibly overdetermined "sin in the park."[6] Scholars have painstakingly traced Joyce's many references to the Fall of Parnell and to the Phoenix Park assassinations;[7] more recently, applications of queer theory to Joyce's work have demonstrated its incorporation of a series of homosexual scandals, with their attendant waves of homosexual panic.[8] Nevertheless, Joyce's extensive treatment of other specific scandals and, most importantly, his fraught relationship to scandal as a genre are only just beginning to be explored.[9]

This book traces the broad impact of fin de siècle newspaper scandals, both individually and collectively, on Joyce's major works (save *Finnegans Wake*, which would call for a book in itself). While it tracks the influence of such well-known scandals and scandal figures as Phoenix Park, Myles Joyce, Dublin Castle, Charles Dilke, and Cleveland Street, *Scandal Work* focuses particularly on Joyce's incorporation of three momentous sex scandals, each surrounding a major turn-of-the-century figure who, Daedalus-like, helped create a powerful new technology—that of the modern sex scandal—and subsequently fell victim to it. The best known of these figures, Charles Stewart Parnell and Oscar Wilde, were early media celebrities who became media martyrs, undone by the British tabloid press. Although Wilde's position in Joyce's oeuvre has garnered little attention outside of queer studies circles, the following chapters show that Wilde ranks with Parnell as an iconic figure for scandal and its ills in Joyce's work.[10]

Beside these two men stands a third: W. T. Stead. Less well known today, in Joyce's time Stead was a controversial and divisive figure whose high-minded, high-impact scandalmongering made him nearly synonymous with the so-called New Journalism.[11] As editor of the *Pall Mall Gazette*, Stead was the originator of what is arguably the nineteenth century's most successful piece of scandal journalism: "The Maiden Tribute of Modern Babylon."[12] In a series of four *Pall Mall Gazette* articles, Stead exposed the world of child prostitution in London and launched a massive scandal by describing his purchase of "Lily," a thirteen-year-old virgin. Britons responded en masse to demand some rapid, decisive remediation, and in their moral panic lawmakers not only changed the age of consent for girls but also adopted the Labouchere Amendment criminalizing "gross indecency," the law that would prove Wilde's downfall.[13] Stead—in his own words— "forged a thunderbolt,"[14] but one that rebounded upon him, striking him down: though his career ultimately survived, Stead was tried, convicted, and imprisoned for his abduction of Lily's real-life counterpart, Eliza Armstrong.

Like Parnell and Wilde, Stead invoked and deftly manipulated the forces that arose with the spread of newspapers and newspaper reading, and as with Parnell and Wilde, those forces turned on him. Each of these men clearly, as David Dwan writes of Parnell, "affirmed the possibility of meaningful agency in a complex world by becoming the creator of his own myths." Each used publicity routed through and around scandal to become "the subject of the rhetoric that described him."[15] And each underwent the distinctive, scathing transformation of subject to object that the sex scandal inflicts on its victims, an ordeal that Stead alone survived. In this book I argue that Joyce made extensive use of these men's distinctive representational strategies, employing both their "scandal work" and their double identities as subjects and objects of scandal to define his own style of counterhegemonic scandal work.

JAMES JOYCE'S "NICELY POLISHED MIRROR"

James Joyce grew up and defined his earliest political and cultural loyalties in and around late-nineteenth-century Dublin during the simultaneous and closely correlated consolidation of the Irish Home Rule movement and the scandal-driven New Journalism.[16] At the intersection of and in response to these two movements, British and Irish newspapers were reinventing sex scandal as a political weapon so potent that Joyce would later deem it "moral assassination."[17] The rise of the scandal press in London and Edinburgh and the spread of penny newspapers in Ireland were also redefining the work of Irish intellectuals, activists, and writers, leaving a lasting mark on Joyce's life's work.

From an early age, Joyce perceived himself, his family, and his society as unjustly injured by a series of scandals that had been launched against nationalist leader and Irish National Party MP Charles Stewart Parnell. As Joyce's younger brother and confidante Stanislaus observed, this early perception never left him.[18] The violent disruption of the Joyce family's emotional and financial life by these Home Rule scandal wars pervasively informed James Joyce's work.[19] Galvanized by this early, traumatic intrusion of the public realm into his home life, Joyce entered into a complex, lifelong engagement with scandal, both as a genre and as a social and historical dynamic. As an adult, Joyce time and again revisited particular turn-of-the-century scandals in his reading, letters, and published writings.[20] In his most famous published works, scandal recurs continually: as a word, as a theme, in allusions to particular scandals, and, most significantly, as a subterranean organizing principle unifying and hierarchizing a wide array of disparate image patterns.[21]

Throughout his various engagements with scandal, from the thematic to the stylistic, Joyce approaches it as a locus of distortion or representational discrepancy, a crack in the sociosymbolic mirror in which we view the world. As Joyce repeatedly reminds us, the cracked mirror of scandal systematically distorts the details it reflects, diminishing or obscuring certain objects as it magnifies others. For Joyce, scandal is a crack, rift, break, or rupture that sensationally discredits a figure on one side of an implied social equation while invisibly transferring its victim's lost credibility to the scandal's author and audience on the other. As Joyce's central scandal metaphors imply, scandal affects society as it does the individual newspaper reader, eliciting a sensational affective response that redistributes representational power as well as credibility. As a speech act, scandal allocates all vulnerability, and hence shame, on the side of the exposed scandal victim, in turn eliciting a sense of pleasurable moral and scopic invulnerability on the part of the individual reader and an imagined community of such readers.[22]

In the terms of speech act theory, scandal is an illocutionary act. That is, it does something: scandal *exposes*. Scandal's illocutionary force derives from the presumed authenticity of the damaging facts it makes public. But a scandal charge's direct illocutionary act of exposure is secondary to its indirect illocutionary act of discrediting. As John Searle posits, because it is embedded in a direct illocutionary act, an indirect illocutionary act has immediate power; it is not susceptible to debate or question.[23] In the case of the political sex scandal, the unspoken conventions linking scandal's act of exposure to its act of discreditation are, as George Lakoff and Mark Johnson contend in *Metaphors We Live By*, naturalized by a strata of metaphoric associations hardwired deep in human cognition.[24] That is, the sex scandal's astonishing political potency is accounted for most fundamentally by an overdetermined neural shorthand that unconsciously converts images of "bad" sex into its socially specified metaphorical equivalents: immoral or injurious political policies.

In 1879, William Gladstone might have been describing scandal's extraordinary capacity to catalyze and energize groups when he described populism as the "political electricity [that] flies from man to man." At the time, however, the scandalmongering that was just being harnessed as a source of populist electricity was generating mere static shocks in comparison to the lightning bolts to come. Through the fields of affective disidentification they generate, modern media scandals forge contingent but compelling counterpublics, powerfully united in the creditable superiority to which each reader's estranged reactions of shock and outrage bear witness.[25] One of James Joyce's visual metaphors for scandal is a lens that leaves us "one-eyed." Fundamental to Joyce's scandal work is the drive to forcibly rebalance the subject/object split that conventional scandal forces exaggerate and reify: to restore readers' depth perception by presenting them with what he once described as a "nicely polished looking-glass."[26]

As the following chapters will demonstrate, Joyce learned from contemporary scandalmongers an array of strategies for exerting social influence through representations of transgression. In a particular sense, he was himself a scandalmonger. His own notoriously difficult and often obscene writing has frequently been the object of scandal, and as scholars have pointed out, Joyce often described his work as scandalous as a strategy for placing and promoting it, deliberately stirring up the apprehension of editors and the public concerning his work's decency.[27] In Joyce's prolonged campaign to publish *Dubliners*, for instance, he made sure to point out potentially scandalous details that had escaped his editors' notice.[28] Even though Joyce evinced a consistent, acute, and hostile awareness of scandal's destructive effects, he also used the power of scandal homeopathically, fighting the dominant scandal logic with his own alternate scandal work. Over the course of the writings examined in this study—from Joyce's earliest poetry and youthful newspaper writing through *Dubliners*, *A Portrait of the Artist as a Young Man*, and ultimately the modernist breakthrough text, *Ulysses*—Joyce developed strategies that invoke and employ the resources of the new journalist sex scandal so as to expose, circumvent, and short-circuit its broader social effects.[29]

In the following chapters I examine Joyce's relationship to scandal both as a force and as a genre, tracking through Joyce's oeuvre his characteristic use of scandal as a synecdoche for the New Journalism, English newspapers, and British print capitalism more generally. Although scholars have begun to situate Joyce's work (particularly "A Painful Case" from *Dubliners* and the "Nausicaa" episode of *Ulysses*) in the context of newspaper and commercial writing, scandal as a newspaper genre has been largely unaddressed.[30] Thus far, following Joyce's biographer Richard Ellmann, Joyceans have largely accepted the writer's penchant for scandal as another amusing and anecdoteworthy byproduct of his cranky and idiosyncratic genius. The vast critical tradition has repeatedly treated many of Joyce's shrewdest attacks against scandal as mere volleys in his war on sexual prudery, or at best as the contingent means by which he began it.[31] This book, in contrast, presents an array of evidence that Joyce's use of scandal was neither incidental nor simply a means by which Joyce entered a series of artistic or political debates, whether as a crank or a principled interlocutor. Quite to the contrary: scandal itself was one of Joyce's perennial adversaries, the focus of a lifelong project of cultural and political critique.

Joyce's interactions with scandal culture highlight a hitherto understudied origin of the modern media scandal: as a political weapon in the charged context of late-nineteenth-century British colonial relations. In this study I demonstrate how several fin de siècle scandals institutionalized modern scandal dynamics as a chronic, impinging danger for intellectuals, artists, activists, and other outlaws. Over time, Joyce developed an array of potent metaphors for scandal and its effects, all of which in various ways encode the sex scandal as a weapon or a specialized commodity. In *Ulysses* scandal is referenced through images of cutting, carving, and stabbing, of morsels, scraps, fragments, and "tit-bits"; referred to as bait, a fall, a trap, a sacrilege, a theft; represented as a soporific drug, poison, malignant magic, cannibalism; described as enthrallment, enslavement, human sacrifice, and state execution. An account of the evolution of Joyce's topical engagement with scandal, an engagement that was often simultaneously figurative and stylistic, will improve our understanding not only of Joyce's work but of its context: the rapid evolution of scandal within turn-of-the-century imperial print capitalism from counterhegemonic weapon to one of capitalist hegemony's most powerful and reliable resources.

In considering Joyce's letters, essays, and literary works as an archive of material addressing the social impact of the New Journalist sex scandal in Ireland, we can observe Joyce cumulatively theorizing scandal as a specialized, potent, destructive, and constitutive speech act within modernity. As the following chapters will show, Joyce's writing also affords a repository of successful strategies for evading scandal's pervasive disciplinary powers. Drawing on concepts endemic to the Catholicism that pervaded his youth and the Irish Revivalism so popular in his young adulthood, Joyce developed a language for describing scandal's dangerous misappropriations while reasserting the dignity and value of that which scandal degrades. And by scattering throughout his work scandalous details culled from his own and others' lives, Joyce presents us with a sequence of miniature, localized scandals, some narrowly averted (as in *Dubliners*' "An Encounter" or "The Boarding House") and others more fully realized (as in the Clongowes smugging episode in *Portrait* or Stephen's refusal to pray at his dying mother's bedside in *Ulysses*[32]), which show he not only theorized scandal but forged an uncommonly successful strategy for expressing unpopular, dangerous, dissenting opinions within a symbolic order pervaded with scandal's treacherous powers.

JOYCE AND THE MODERN POLITICAL SEX SCANDAL

A characteristic paradox of modernity is that one can often assault one's rulers by exposing their embarrassing private lives even when their public activities, however shockingly immoral, are legally and politically insulated. During a period of rapidly expanding newspaper readership, the sex scandal emerged as an inviting weapon for newly empowered groups such as women, workers, and the Irish, all of whom faced a hostile and anachronistic political terrain offering little hope for immediate reform. For political outsiders, revealing inside information damaging to rulers offered a last, desperate means to break into political conversations from which they were otherwise excluded. Using incriminating or embarrassing private details, disempowered groups could attempt, sometimes successfully, to put their oppressors on trial in the court of public opinion.

Anticolonial activist theorists like James Connolly and Frantz Fanon have argued that the "wretched of the earth," guided by their desperation to live, must be the driving force in an anticolonial movement; both predicted with terrible prescience that the native middle class, if allowed to direct an anticolonial struggle, would upon independence convert into an oppressor class little better than the previous colonial regime.[33] Though initially a powerful counterhegemonic weapon, the modern newspaper scandal's structural affinities with

just such middle-class and ruling-class interests exerted unanticipated long-term effects on the radical scandalmongering originally
developed by disenfranchised constituencies in the 1880s.[34] Owing
to the social networks on which the transmission of scandalous details depends, scandal politics had the unforeseen effect of dispro-
portionately empowering the economically advantaged and socially
well-connected within these movements. Thus, as I show, although
the rise of scandal journalism in the late nineteenth century offered
the disenfranchised a formidable weapon, in practice that weapon's
use empowered ambitious middle-class leaders at the expense of the
movements for which they presumed to speak.

Scandalmongering represents a key mechanism by which the
middle-class nationalist leaders against whom Connolly and Fanon
cautioned gained traction within the Irish nationalist movement and
unobtrusively but disastrously betrayed the disenfranchised masses.
As Klaus Theweleit notes, "truly oppressed classes attack ruling
classes because they deprive them of life (and not because of the obe-
sity of those gentlemen or the harems they keep)."[35] The dangerously
glib and entitled middle-class activists who join national movements
inspired by abstractions like cultural pride rather than compelling
need, he points out, are far too easily distracted by trifles like their
oppressors' sex lives. Fighting against both the ruling class and the
poor, middle-class-identified leaders are apt to lead entire movements
off course by substituting symbols for substance. Buck Mulligan, one
of *Ulysses*'s many scandalmongers, personifies just such an opportunistic middle-class activist and, as we will see later, provides an object
lesson in why political movements should keep such activists away
from podiums.

The class origins and educational background of movement leaders, however, is only one element of the class interests they represent.
According to Fanon, activists and even leaders from privileged back-
grounds can be an asset to an independence movement, provided they
are guided by the needs and priorities of the unpropertied.[36] Land
League and Home Rule leader Charles Stewart Parnell is an excellent
example of a ruling-class leader who, for a time, effectively represented
the interests of his nation's poor. Although Parnell was an Anglo-Irish

landowner who attended Cambridge, his political efficacy was ensured through his alliances with Ireland's landless peasantry and with working-class movement intellectuals like Michael Davitt. Parnell's privileged background nonetheless created extensive entanglements with the imperial ruling class, and these eventually overdetermined his starring role in his movement's downfall.[37]

Sex scandal itself has a class logic: while the accounts of streetwalkers may supply the raw material for scandal, only the most well-connected movement participants have access to both the embarrassing details on which scandals are based and the venues in which one can creditably publicize them. When and in what terms any such details will be publicized therefore becomes a decision guided by elite individuals within movements rather than by collective judgments and interests. The New Journalism sex scandal's relationship to the social and economic networks of British print capitalism rendered it a weapon to which only the privileged had access. Scandal is, moreover, a weapon that encourages and enables careerism among those who wield it, though its emotionally satisfying short-term effects can easily lead scandalmongers and their followers to mistake such careerism for political idealism. For these reasons, scandal is at best a dangerous and unreliable weapon, especially when deployed in the name of social justice. Joyce's work reflects both scandal's appeal and its dangers, its transgressive powers and its tendency to turn savagely on those who wield it, the latter encoded in Joyce's oeuvre in backfiring plans, self-inflicted injuries, and self-dug graves.

James Joyce grew up in the intellectually and politically progressive wing of Catholic nationalism that was hopelessly disenfranchised by the Parnell scandal. Raised in a family whose fortunes mirrored Parnell's rise and fall, Joyce came of age well aware that two elite groups were competing for the right to speak for Irish Catholic nationalists: the Catholic priests, on one hand, and the Anglo-Irish intellectuals and artists of the Celtic Revival, on the other. In response, the young Joyce angrily insisted on his right to speak, think, act, and write as he saw fit. In what amounts to an early artistic manifesto privately published in 1901, "The Day of the Rabblement," Joyce takes on not only the Catholic arbiters of nationalist morality but the

Anglo-Irish literati, condemning the Anglo-Irish–dominated Irish Literary Theatre (the forerunner of the Abbey Theatre established by Yeats, Gregory, and Synge) for its acquiescence to the conventional, scandal-averse morality of Ireland's ultra-Catholic "rabblement." Given the role of the newspaper scandal in displacing the populist movement with which his family identified and in cowing Revivalist artists while empowering church leaders, it is not surprising that Joyce repeatedly condemns newspapers, and particularly newspaper scandals, as a particularly insidious means by which those with power could silence those without it.

In his early-twentieth-century personal correspondence, Joyce frequently complained that the conventions of the New Journalism were placing an ever-widening range of human relations outside the artist's purview. In particular, the fin de siècle scandalization of nonstandard sexual arrangements was rendering subjects with which Richardson, Austen, Trollope, Thackeray, Dickens, and Eliot had dealt openly ineligible for literary representation.[38] For instance, in a 1906 letter to his editor, Grant Richards, Joyce engaged in an exuberant sparring match with Richards's printer, who had marked up pages of the *Dubliners* short story "Counterparts" to draw Richards's attention to intimations of adultery and prostitution.[39] In the letter, Joyce makes much of this printer's being English, sarcastically construing him as "the barometer of English opinion," before twice directing him "to that respectable organ the reporters of which are allowed to speak of such intimate things as even I, a poor artist, have but dared to suggest. O one-eyed printer!"[40] Joyce complains that newspapers are, through scandal, laying representational claim to all deviations from the supposed sexual norm, reducing the sexual themes permissible for serious writers to "lying drivel about pure men and pure women and spiritual love and love forever."[41]

Baldly summing up the pressures one-eyed printers were exerting on two-eyed naturalists, Joyce claims that the printer's outright refusal to print the short story "Two Gallants" reveals him to be "a militarist." In his insistence that Corley and Lenehan's urban amusements are not fit for fiction, the printer is separating scandalous sexual misbehavior from other, nonscandalous crimes, including war and other forms of state-mandated murder. By accepting warfare and other nonsexual transgressions as proper to the world of realist fiction while banishing sexual transgressions to the tabloids, the printer is defending a potent but invisible cultural cleavage that normalizes imperialist violence and expropriation by scandalizing sex.

If New Journalism narrowed the moral and political scope of serious artists' work, the political sex scandal was the paradigmatic discourse-narrowing "weapon of mass distraction" by which it did so. This mode of sex scandal is motivated primarily by politics rather than profits, although in practice the two motives are inevitably entangled; papers need profits if they want to keep publishing, and scandals launched by small, purely political newspapers can only gain traction if they are framed so as to attract mainstream readers of commercial newspapers. The political sex scandal is thus particularly representative of the New Journalism because in it the two dominant driving forces of the New Journalism—political activism and the commodification of words and shocking facts—are precariously united. This study charts the emergence of this most characteristic subgenre of the New Journalism over the course of late-nineteenth-century transnational debates about Irish tenants' rights and the question of Irish Home Rule. It describes the process by which one strand of Irish-originated sex scandal eventually displaced class and national resentments onto high-status homosexuals, culminating in the prosecution of Oscar Wilde. Most extensively, it traces James Joyce's complex response to scandalmongering's staggering powers and invidious appeal.

OBSTRUCTIVE TACTICS:
IRISH SCANDAL WORK IN THEORY AND PRACTICE

Joyce's treatment of the modern sex scandal cannot be assessed without first examining the author's positioning of newspapers and newspaper scandal within the contested colonial context in which the political sex scandal emerged. Although his earliest references to scandal journalism identified London's Fleet Street as the New

Journalism's hub, this study will show that over time Joyce moved beyond a Manichaean construction of London-based media riding roughshod over a disempowered Ireland.[42] As Joyce's understanding of scandal developed, so did his condemnation of specific constituencies within Ireland for self-servingly furthering what he describes in "The Sisters" as the "deadly work" of "paralysis" (*Dubliners*, 1). In *Ulysses* in particular, he decries the careerism of Irish writers and condemns the Irish Catholic middle class for eagerly accepting the Catholic Church as a "mighty fortress" against both more Parnell-like sex scandals and economic democratization. Above all, as we shall see, he lambastes the paired discourses of masochistic sentimentalism and sadistic, scandalized outrage that evolved in response to Ireland's disadvantaged position in the "cracked lookingglass" of the London press.

The particular subtlety of Joyce's understanding of the transnational dynamics of scandal may have originated from one peculiarity of the sex scandal's emergence as a genre in the British Isles: despite its association with the London press, key conventions of this potent new form got their start in Ireland. In fact, as discussed more thoroughly in the next chapter, the distinguishing features of the New Journalist political sex scandal can be traced to tactics adopted by Parnell and the Land League in the early 1880s. With the inescapable poetic irony of a Greek tragedy, the desperate tactics that were perfectly suited to the disenfranchised position of Irish nationalists in the early 1880s gave rise to the potent strain of political sex scandal that toppled their leader, thereby forestalling Irish independence for decades.[43] Parnellite parliamentary obstructionism used an exacting adherence to the British law and English codes of honor to disrupt colonial business as usual, eventually honing obstruction into an elaborate mode of media-disseminated political performance. As we shall see, the obstructionist tactics of Parnell and other nationalist MPs also gave rise to new forms of media activism by two other Parnellites, William O'Brien and T. M. Healy, in the Land League weekly, the *United Ireland*.

The weapon these anticolonial activists forged—the political sex scandal—used private transgressions to stir up powerful public emotions.[44] The potent public speech act that resulted had the power to morally gerrymander group formations, throwing political processes into disarray. Rhetorically, the conventions of the political sex scandal use a taboo private act unrelated to a leader's public responsibilities to discredit the aims or character of an entire group. This public disgrace enacts both the collective, visceral withdrawal of identification and sympathy from the scandalized constituency and the simultaneous affective and political inflation of that constituency's designated opponents. As the following chapters illustrate, Joyce's work repeatedly reenacts the increasingly dangerous, exposed position in which this placed Home Rule nationalists by placing his protagonists before unsympathetic audiences in exposed situations offering little or no room to maneuver.

In "The Dead," for instance, Gabriel Conroy fears that his dinner speech will fail. In *A Portrait of the Artist*, Stephen Dedalus writes an essay that his teacher pronounces heretical, leading him to be set upon by his classmates after school. In *Ulysses*, Stephen repeatedly changes tack as he attempts to explain his ideas about literature and the artist's life to members of Dublin's literary establishment in the National Library, while Leopold Bloom's failed conversational gambits in Barney Kiernan's pub culminate in violence. Here and elsewhere, Joyce recalls the treacherous (or booby-trapped) social milieu in which Parnell and other scandal victims of this period sought to speak publicly in favor of unpopular, unfamiliar, or disempowered groups and perspectives while attempting simultaneously to live reasonably fulfilling lives.[45] In a related set of image patterns, Joyce repeatedly associates Parnell's fall itself with a range of public martyrdoms, including those of nationalist martyrs Robert Emmet and the folkloric Croppy Boy, the wrongfully hanged Irish-speaking Myles Joyce, the executed Invincible Joe Brady, the "fallen" Lily/Eliza Armstrong and other illicitly sexual girls and women, and Oscar Wilde, convicted for gross indecency.

"ET TU, HEALY": JAMES JOYCE'S FIRST JOB

Biographers and critics often present Joyce's refusal while at University College Dublin to condemn Yeats's *The Countess Cathleen* during the so-called Souls for Gold controversy as his first public assertion of dissenting artistic and political principles.[46] Yet, at a far earlier and more formative moment in his political development, Joyce's first published poem registered a far more energetic dissent in response to Victorian Ireland's most politically consequential sex scandal, the fall of parliamentary party leader Charles Stewart Parnell.

Throughout the 1880s, Parnell and Katharine O'Shea's domestic arrangement at O'Shea's home in Eltham, eight miles southeast of London, was common knowledge among both Home Rule and Liberal leaders. The well-connected O'Sheas—Katharine and her estranged but doggedly opportunistic husband, William—both served as Parnell's emissaries, independently representing Parnell in negotiations with high-ranking Liberals, including Gladstone. Following the death of Katharine's wealthy "Aunt Ben" in 1891, however, William O'Shea, no longer constrained by hopes of an inheritance, brought divorce proceedings against his wife, naming Parnell as codefendant. Charles and Katharine's relationship transformed instantly from a unifying open secret to a divisive sex scandal, destroying the alliance between Irish nationalists and the Liberals that Parnell had cultivated and acrimoniously splitting the Irish National Party. In the course of the "Parnell split," the Irish Catholic hierarchy and Parnell's erstwhile lieutenant, Tim Healy, emerged as the defining voices of anti-Parnellite condemnation.

The astounding rancor of anti-Parnellite invective whipped up considerable public animus toward Parnell, making the nationalist newspapers a key site of contestation.[47] When Parnell returned to Ireland seeking to restore his status as Ireland's "uncrowned king," he was hounded by scandalmongering newspaper attacks against himself and Katharine O'Shea. The anti-Parnellites demeaningly dubbed Mrs. O'Shea "Kitty," inviting readers to assume a sexually insulting familiarity with her. In fact, Katharine was never called Kitty, either by Parnell, who called her Katie, or by anyone else.[48] One of Parnell's first acts upon returning to Dublin was to lead a crowd of supporters, crowbar in hand, in a physical battle to evict anti-Parnellites from the offices of the United Ireland, the weekly newspaper he had founded.

When the moderate nationalist daily, the *Freeman's Journal*, withdrew its support, Parnell founded a new, pro-Parnellite daily, the *Irish Daily Independent*. Parnell's stubborn, losing fight to regain his lost preeminence played out in and through the Irish and British newspapers, making for a spectacular and prolonged public fall that ended only with his sudden, remorse-inducing death on October 6, 1891.

Sometime in the year following Parnell's death, the nine-year-old James Joyce excoriated those his father condemned for Parnell's fall in a now-lost poem, "Et Tu, Healy." Based on Stanislaus Joyce's partial reconstruction of the poem, we know it reviled Tim Healy—Irish National Party MP, journalist, and inveterate scandalmonger—for using details from Parnell's private life as personally and politically disastrous weapons.[49] And we know that when the young James responded to Parnell's death with this poem comparing Healy to Brutus, John Joyce so admired his eldest son's effort that he paid to have it copied and distributed among family friends.[50] Such an act of patronage by a revered parent likely would have made a powerful impression on any child, and as we will see, there is biographical and literary evidence that in Joyce's case, it did. This lost poem is often invoked to exemplify Joyce's reading of Parnell, a reading that, in turn, has exerted a significant influence on Parnell's broader status in the Irish political imaginary.[51] As such, it might be considered one of the most influential pieces of writing ever penned by a prepubescent child.

More importantly for the purposes of this study, however, the contextual and textual features of this first poem contribute to our understanding of Joyce's oeuvre through their significant continuities with Joyce's later work. The poem responds to a sex scandal and seeks to deflect the damage the scandal has wrought back on its perceived initiator. "Et Tu, Healy" was clearly a speech act intended to "turn the knife" of an assailant back on himself by demystifying the fundamental pretense through which this form mobilizes power: its outraged insistence that the vindictive feelings it evinces proceed purely from moral considerations.[52] Thus, "Et Tu, Healy" approached scandal as a sociosymbolic operation capable of being undone, even after compromising facts have become public and their damage in the world of realpolitik seems irreparable. The juvenile Joyce's use of poetry to counter scandal hints at his later work's assumption that, if unremediated, the damage done by scandals will far outlast and exceed their most proximate political effects. The poem also constitutes the earliest expression of Joyce's opposition to the emergent norms of social purity, dating Joyce's hostility toward the social purity movement to his childhood and the political ferment of this period.[53] And as with much of Joyce's later output, the poem was motivated by ethical and social aims rather than anticipation of compensation, thus situating it outside of the system of print capitalist exchange; it had attracted his father's patronage only retroactively and by happenstance. Through the gap thus instituted between literary production and literary publication, Joyce first took up his characteristic posture of "mild proud sovereignty" (words he would later use to describe both Parnell and his own literary alter ego, Stephen Dedalus) over his own artistic output.[54]

Particularly relevant to the status of "Et Tu, Healy" in Joyce's oeuvre are his recurrent pattern of self-reference and its attendant blurring of the line separating fiction from life writing. In his mature work, Joyce cultivated paralactic effects similar to cubism's visual multiperspectivalism through the unpredictable reintroduction of earlier characters, situations, symbols, and phrases, often ones with autobiographical significance.[55] The adult Joyce incorporated fragments culled from his own childhood experiences and writings into *Dubliners*, *A Portrait of the Artist*, *Ulysses*, and *Finnegans Wake*, extending the chain of cross-temporal and intertextual associations that enrich his later work backward as far as his earliest childhood.[56] Given Joyce's mind-bendingly recursive process of rendering his life into art, the nine-year-old's impassioned response to the death of a boyhood hero represents the first of a lifetime's worth of odd jobs undertaken in response to the political sex scandal.

Stanislaus recalls the poem as ending "with the dead Parnell, likened to an eagle, looking down on the groveling mass of Irish politicians" from "the crags of Time," where the "rude din of this . . . century / Can trouble him no more."[57] In *A Portrait of the Artist*, this lofty superiority would reemerge in the proudly aloof maturing artist

Stephen Dedalus. Joyce's aquiline Parnell also prefigures *Portrait's* most central, prolific image pattern: a collection of airborne metaphors in which we see the proud, remote Parnellian eagle blossoming into vengeful eagles, birds representing consciousness, the bird girl (who unifies eroticism, spirituality, and art), bats, a bat woman, and Stephen Dedalus's final truncated flight. Even more importantly, the poem's titular theme of betrayal, arguably Joyce's greatest lifelong personal and literary preoccupation, reveals an early connection between the Joycean theme of personal and political betrayal and the emergence of the sex scandal as a treacherous political weapon. The assassin's knife, in Joyce's poetic account of the modern-day slaying of an Irish Caesar, took the form of public denunciation in the falsely moralizing mode of the political sex scandal, anticipating Joyce's continued association of both sex and journalism with betrayal. The painful personal and social pressures that wracked Dublin in the course of the Parnell split left a permanent impression on James Joyce. Through them he directly experienced the political sex scandal as a malignant force so pervasively destructive as to merit a lifelong project of countervailance.

"TO RECTIFY MATTERS A LITTLE": TALKING BACK TO THE CRACKED LOOKING GLASS OF THE BRITISH PRESS

Other of Joyce's works also show that he was acutely aware of the harm that English scandalmongering was doing in and to Ireland.[58] In his early "Ireland at the Bar" (1907), one of over a dozen journalistic essays written in Italian during his years of self-imposed exile with Nora Barnacle in Trieste, Joyce decries the London press's distorted coverage of Ireland, arguing that it unfairly represented Ireland to the rest of the world by dedicating "weeks and innumerable articles to the agrarian crisis" and publishing "alarming articles on the agrarian revolt that are then reprinted by foreign newspapers." In the article, he seeks to "rectify matters a little" by pointing out that, contrary to the representations of the London newspapers, "criminality in Ireland is lower than in any other country in Europe; organized crime does not exist in Ireland" and is so uncharacteristic that, in cases when violence does occur, "the whole country is shocked."[59] Particularly in *Ulysses*, Joyce strategically responds to the culturally fragmenting logic of the newspaper scandal by relentlessly surrounding scandal fragments—details that are, by law and convention, the property of barristers, journalists, and social scientists—with a welter of contextualizing, relativizing, and often conventionally unspeakable detail. Against the isolated, prurient evidence of courtroom testimony and newspaper writing, Joyce embeds constantly recirculating, reimagined, reinterpreted scenes of sexual exchange, whether fantasized or realized, witnessed or imagined, illegible or understood, licit or illicit, within broader social and intrapsychic processes.

Joyce's juxtaposition of the publicizable private associated with scandal and the conventionally unpublicizable specifics of private life that must, for the good of society, remain entirely suppressed dates back to *Dubliners* and the essays he published in the Trieste newspaper *Il Piccolo Della Sera* in the same years. While Joyce was documenting the cruel effects of British newspaper coverage that, like a funhouse mirror, magnified scandalous details while suppressing the larger context that would have made sense of them, he was also writing the short stories that eventually became *Dubliners* and bragging that they would show his characters' private lives in his own "nicely polished mirror." If we read Joyce's writing as structured so as to undo the distorting effects of the "cracked lookingglass" of English print culture, the progression in his writing from Italian newspaper essays condemning the distorting effects of English journalism to naturalist sketches of lower-middle-class lives and then to the more subjective stream of consciousness explorations of *A Portrait of the Artist* and *Ulysses* makes a new kind of sense, with *Ulysses* representing a further stage in a lifelong political/cultural project.

Wordplay about a "cracked lookingglass" focalizes the "Telemachus" episode—the first of *Ulysses's* eighteen untitled episodes—in which Buck Mulligan and Stephen Dedalus invoke Oscar Wilde to support opposing arguments concerning the correct role of the Irish artist.[60] "Stately" Mulligan, aspiring architect of a future independent Irish state, plays two roles in relation to Stephen throughout the narrative. He acts as a scandalmonger, dispensing private details about Stephen to anyone from whom he can hope to gain a drink, a social leg up, or a laugh, and as a pimp, treating Stephen's abilities and resources (that is, his art) as materials ripe for exploitation. Thus, he seeks paradoxically to profit from bolstering Stephen's reputation and from tarnishing it. In this early interaction, Mulligan allegorically enacts the scandalmonger's role, wielding a cracked mirror and a Wildean caption to discredit Stephen. Mulligan holds before Stephen a hand mirror "cleft by a crooked crack," stolen from his aunt's maid. After engaging Stephen's interest in his distorted reflection, Mulligan snatches the mirror away, quipping, in an allusion to Wilde's *The Picture of Dorian Gray*, "The rage of Caliban at not seeing his face in a mirror.... If Wilde were only alive to see you!" (*Ulysses*, 1.143–44). It is thus purportedly on Wilde's authority that Mulligan discredits Stephen; Mulligan allies with Wilde, another Oxford man, to dismiss Stephen as a rude, uncultured native, figuratively transforming him not only into *a* simianized caricature but specifically into *the* simianized *Punch* magazine caricature emblematic of the origins of Parnellism and the Land Wars in the First Land Act of 1870 (see Figure I.1).[61]

Stephen parries Mulligan's belittling thrust by recruiting Wilde to his own ends, citing an artfully modified epigram from *The Decay of Lying* that condemns viewers who judge art only by its verisimilitude, thereby "reduc[ing] genius to the position of a cracked looking glass." By invoking this Wildean mirror figure—the cracked looking glass in which genius is reduced to inadequacy—Stephen suavely calls attention to the malice underlying Mulligan's horseplay: Mulligan is reducing him, denying his genius, and transforming his art into an appropriable object such as the maid's mirror. In holding up a "cracked lookingglass of a servant" before an Irish artist, Stephen notes, Mulligan has unintentionally created a tableau vivant, a Wildean aphorism brought to life. The mirror is itself a "symbol of Irish art," because the scandalized position of the Irish within British print capitalism causes those who attempt to portray the world through Irish eyes to

THE IRISH "TEMPEST."

CALIBAN (RORY OF THE HILLS). "THIS ISLAND'S MINE, BY SYCORAX MY MOTHER,
WHICH THOU TAK'ST FROM ME."—*Shakspeare.*

Figure I.1   "The Irish Tempest." *Punch*, March 19, 1870. Courtesy of Punch
Limited.

seem like incompetent artists who are deviating from what the English newspaper readers and indeed most Irish readers mistake for unbiased reality.

"ODD JOBS": REPRESENTATIONAL WAR WORK AND THE IRISH ARTIST

In recalling Wilde's likening of art to a cracked looking glass, Stephen, by focusing on the crack itself rather than the distorted image the mirror reflects, is able to deflect the debate Mulligan has initiated away from his own status and worth as an artist and onto the material conditions under which Irish art is produced. Irish art, he suggests, is positioned by and within British print capitalism so that its concerns are reduced, discredited, and readily co-opted to serve the interests of others. Irish cultural representation is, in a word, distorted. Stephen elaborates further on Ireland's servitude and the crack that bedevils Irish art in an exchange with Haines, the English, Oxonian houseguest Mulligan has brought home to the tower he and Stephen share. Stephen, unhappily grounded in Dublin after his failed attempt to "fly by the nets" of national ideology at the conclusion of *Portrait*, now tells Haines that as an Irish artist he is "a servant of two masters . . . an English and an Italian" (1.638), referring to the powerful influences exerted in Ireland by British imperialism and Roman Catholicism. These institutions greatly complicate both the production and reception of "Irish art" by creating, in Joyce's complex refiguring of Wilde's two epigrams, a lens that breaks the world into two incommensurable perspectives, inaccurate both individually and in sum.

To these two wealthy and powerful masters whose influence distorts artists' attempts to depict the world through Irish eyes, however, Stephen also adds an asymmetrical third, less well-heeled master: Irish nationalism, "who wants me for odd jobs" (1.641). This simple phrase can be unpacked in several ways, the most straightforward of which is that Ireland's moribund colonial economy could supply writers only with occasional labor rather than the high-powered careers that Irish writers from Goldsmith and Sheridan to Shaw and

Wilde sought and found in London. Thus, were Stephen to embrace the "Irish Ireland" framework promoted by Sinn Fein, his future as an Irish writer would of necessity be reduced to a series of "odd jobs," like Joyce's book reviews for Dublin's *Daily Express* and the short stories that the Irish Revivalist poet A. E. ran in the *Irish Homestead*.[62] Alternatively, at a time of rising nationalism, many educated Dubliners were finding themselves doing unfamiliar and unprecedented jobs: collecting folklore and teaching Irish language classes; forming agricultural collectives and sports leagues; founding journals, newspapers, drama companies, and schools; orating, exhorting, and plotting insurrection. For writers with nationalist sympathies, these odd jobs aimed to remediate the cracked mirror of Irish art by rebutting British newspapers' representations of the Irish as either laughably ineffectual or frighteningly bestial.[63]

As Joyce well understood, the odd jobs for which Irish nationalism wanted its writers were defined in the context of an escalating representational war. In the nationalist press, goaded by the beatings the nationalists were taking in the English press, the weapons of choice were either compelling visions of Ireland as a society defined by its moral purity and religious piety or embarrassing, incriminating, and preferably "filthy" details plucked from the private lives of nationalism's enemies. As Joyce continually charged, these odd jobs were futile because they were constituted in opposition to but also reflected from a subservient position the cracked looking glass of the London press. As the soi-disant sailor Murphy in the "Eumaeus" episode of *Ulysses* contends about the Peruvian *indio* women and children on the postcard he displays, a mirror "boggles em." That is, the mirror, emblematic of imperial technology, can be used by empire's agents to redirect the attention of restless natives and thus to "keep them off" (16.486).

Like Mulligan's mirror, Joyce suggests, the London press served to keep the natives off balance by reflecting them back to themselves and to the world as grotesque colonial caricatures, as Calibans. Although the young Joyce denounced these distortions passionately and often, he was even more disgusted by his compatriots' reactions to the cracked mirror of British print capitalism, which included self-sentimentalization, cynicism, and reciprocal demonization. But even as the young Joyce repeatedly railed against the distorting mirror itself and its deleterious effects on Irish art, he was already beginning to explore representational responses adequate to the magnitude and severity of the problem. By the time he wrote *Ulysses*, Joyce was confidently emulating the fragmenting process by which the scandalmonger pilfers an enemy's private details and charges them with new and sensational public meaning.

As we shall see, his work virtuosically mimicked the procedures of scandalmongery with various defusing variations, confidently transgressing the legal and conventional boundaries separating literature from journalism with a welter of imperfect or damaged scandal fragments: nonscandalous but unspeakable private details, many presumably Joyce's own. In so doing, he also repeatedly broke the powerful bond between scandal's direct and indirect illocutionary functions of exposure and discreditation, disabling scandal's most damaging power: its seeming self-evidence. As such, Joyce's oeuvre represents an explicit and extreme alternative to the odd jobs that political and social conditions in turn-of-the-century Ireland pressed on Irish writers and intellectuals. Joyce continually blurred the distinction between journalism and fiction by radically abusing the exacting scandal logic that policed that distinction, thereby eliminating the crack in the mirror of representation upheld by laws and conventions regarding scandal and scandalously implicating us all in the filthiness of everyday life.

To better understand Joyce's representations of the New Journalist sex scandal and the process by which specific elements of the supposedly private sphere became charged with political power, the next two chapters review the scandal-related strategies employed by various leaders during the Irish Home Rule debates in the 1880s and 1890s. Against this backdrop of sex scandal as a treacherous social dynamic, subsequent chapters examine the odd jobs undertaken by various scandalmongers in Joyce's writing and by Joyce himself. Chapter 3 describes Joyce's evolving treatment of scandal, examining a few newspaper essays written in Italian during Joyce's time in Trieste, several of the *Dubliners* stories, and *A Portrait of the Artist as a Young Man.* The balance of the study comprises five chapters that each focus on a defining thematic or stylistic element in one or more episodes of *Ulysses.* This exploration of Joyce's early-twentieth-century reinvention of the New Journalism's scandalous strategies makes visible his virtuosic understanding and deployment of an array of complications, contradictions, and even opportunities latent in the scandalous speech act.

CHAPTER 1

Unorthodox Methods in the
Home Rule Newspaper Wars

Irish Nationalism, Phoenix Park, and the Fall of Parnell

---

*Writing in English is the most ingenious torture ever devised
for sins committed in previous lives. The English reading public
explains the reason why.*

—James Joyce to Fanny Guillermet, September 5, 1918

Most of the previous scholarship on the New Journalism to which
James Joyce so objected has focused on the London press, suggesting at least tacitly that the British New Journalism arose in isolation,
the brainchild of a few well-positioned English newspapermen.[1] As
this and the following chapter demonstrate, however, the defining
elements of the New Journalism actually emerged out of a complex,
interactive circuitry to which a range of metropolitan and regional
newspapers across the British archipelago and beyond contributed
facts and copy, phraseology, norms, and perspectives.[2] This network,
in turn, both influenced and was particularly influenced by a series of

Dublin- and London-based trials, internal party politics, and inter-party debates and negotiations in and out of the House of Commons.

An examination of scandal journalism's historical context and development is essential to understanding its lasting political and literary effects on the career and work of James Joyce. Many of the changes in technology, capital, the law, and literacy that enabled London-based journalists like W. T. Stead to pursue what he termed "government by journalism" in the mid-1880s also spurred similar transformations in Ireland.[3] Yet as this chapter will show, conditions specific to the colonial situation rendered the advanced Irish national-ist press especially radical, innovative, and consequential both within and beyond Ireland during this period.[4] These conditions in turn gave birth to the Home Rule scandal wars that eventually brought about the fall of Parnell, as discussed in this chapter, and set the ground-work for the "Maiden Tribute of Modern Babylon," Dilke, and Oscar Wilde scandals, which are addressed in the next chapter.

In the years just preceding the first manifestations of the new popular journalism in London, Irish politics were undergoing a rapid sea change, led by what A. M. Sullivan described at the time as "a rural generation that has grown to manhood" since the Great Fam-ine of 1845–1849.[5] Starting in 1878, Ireland's agrarian economy was rocked by serial crop failures and the influx of cheap American beef, and Ireland's rural dwellers responded to waves of agrarian scarcity and an upsurge in evictions with astonishing resolution.[6] From 1878 to 1882, Ireland's small farmers and agrarian workers, in a loose coali-tion with the remnants of the more radically nationalist Fenian move-ment, propelled Charles Stewart Parnell and the Land League into a position of unprecedented prominence.[7] The new collective agency wielded by Parnell and the Land League was in turn made possible by the spread of literacy and newspapers throughout Ireland. Although there are valid arguments that Ireland's sense of itself as a nation actu-ally preceded other European nationalisms, the growth of literacy and the proliferation of newspapers in Ireland described by Legg certainly enhanced the simultaneity of group identification and collective af-fect that Benedict Anderson attributes to a similar critical mass of newspapers and newspaper readers in other emergent nation-states.[8]

Beyond inspiring a new spirit of national cohesion and political resolve, Irish nationalist newspapers also enabled new forms of political action.[9] Whereas in the early nineteenth century Daniel O'Connell sent political messages to the London press through "monster rallies" that made their point through the vast aggregation of bodies, in the late nineteenth century Parnell was doing the reverse: sending heartening, unifying messages to his Irish nationalist constituents through newspaper coverage of his obstructive performances in the House of Commons. In short, the material and social shifts in newspaper production and consumption in Ireland during this period gave rise to new forms of political affiliation, new modes of political expression, and new structures of feeling.[10]

The Irish, in turn, exerted a strong gravitational pull on British journalism, both as individual writers and editors, many of whom only moved up the ladder to London once they had learned their craft in Irish cities, and as a collective "question" subject to pervasive and passionate debate.[11] In exerting this influence, however, Irish attempts to place their case before the British public frequently backfired, leaving them the worse for seeking justice within a system rigged against them. Because of the ambiguously transnational economic and communication networks that converged there, turn-of-the-century Dublin exhibited a labyrinthine complexity that was nicely captured in Irish Labor leader James Larkin's description of the Dublin newspaper magnate, Catholic nationalist, and union buster William Martin Murphy as an "industrial octopus."[12] Newspapers were one major tentacle system within this transnational tangle. They were also, as Larkin's figure of an Irish Catholic newspaper owner as controlling hub of a transnational industrial network suggests, a particularly apt emblem for the disguised and far-flung conflicts of interest that could covertly drive complex alliances and enmities during this period. Larkin's monstrous industrialist cum octopus extended across the British Isles and beyond through a range of economic, political, and social conduits, some more visible than others.[13]

The tense interpenetration of sometimes conflicting and sometimes coinciding economic, political, and personal interests that characterized networks connecting political leaders across the British Isles offered particular motives and opportunities for scandalmongering. Thus, as it emerged in this context in the early 1880s, the weapon of scandal was an intimate one, most commonly originating between friends, allies, or at least social equals. Parnell, the Land League's iconic leader, ultimately fell victim to this dynamic, and the echoes of his fall resound across James Joyce's work.

RADICAL SCANDALING: IRISH NATIONALISTS AND THE NEW JOURNALISM

Throughout the period 1881–1895, on which this study focuses, Irish nationalists devised a number of innovative methods to manipulate the representational discrepancies that the New Journalism was first to challenge and later to exacerbate. In Parliament, Parnell and his colleague Joseph Biggar devised new modes of political performance through an array of obstructionist tactics in the House of Commons that slowed or halted parliamentary business by endlessly providing detailed evidence concerning matters of pressing importance to the Irish but of little or no concern to non-Irish MPs. By calling attention to the incommensurability between matters in Ireland that required state attention and Ireland's disempowered position within the United Kingdom, Parnell's obstructive performances powerfully dramatized the need for an independent Irish governing body in which Ireland's most pressing concerns would not be inappropriate intrusions.

In the House of Commons, Parnell expressed with persistence and dignity an ungentlemanly and elaborate noncompliance with the collective aims of a body of British gentlemen that had, with the utmost civility, repeatedly condemned broad swaths of the Irish population to starvation and death. Parnell's use of the letter of the law to spectacularly violate the law's spirit of colonial subservience united nationalist supporters at both ends of the political spectrum and gave new agency to MPs whose numbers and disempowered geopolitical position otherwise entitled them to no power whatsoever.[14] Performatively, obstructionism also had a sort of perfect pitch, irresistibly reminding observers with its every eye-catching enactment of the bad faith in which Ireland was bound to the United Kingdom through an Act of Union that the majority of the Irish people had never endorsed. Finally, the noncompliant, aggressive, obstreperous attitude of obstructionism served to channel toward the English some of the frustration and rage that were the inevitable by-products of life under colonial rule. This quality of Parnellite obstruction, its public expression of otherwise silenced resentment, appealed to a broad range of Irish nationalists.[15]

During the long bout of intense anticolonial conflict that began with the outbreak of the Land Wars in 1878, Irish nationalists of all stripes sought new ways to set forth their grievances and counteract their negative representation in British newspapers. As the rest of this chapter demonstrates, this representational battle was largely fought in the news, propelled by several notable scandals, beginning with the Phoenix Park murders and ending with the scandal that terminated Parnell's political career. Early in this period, in 1881, two Irish National Party MPs, William O'Brien and Tim Healy, became the editorial team of the party's new weekly newspaper, the *United Ireland*. As Land League MPs, both O'Brien and Healy had observed and participated in Parnell and Biggar's parliamentary strategies for slowing, obstructing, or turning back on itself a stream of British-initiated verbal exchanges and events, and in the pages of the *United Ireland* they translated these strategies into print. O'Brien and Healy first targeted the private transgressions of colonial administrators as a weak spot in the otherwise impenetrable armature of the colonial apparatus in the *United Ireland*'s first eighteen months of existence. In so doing, in Klaus Theweleit's terms, they "substitute[d] a moral battle for a political one," thereby establishing the conventions of the modern political sex scandal.[16] This approach, one among many attempted by the hard-beset nationalists in the early 1880s, was so successful and stood up so well in court that it spawned a new scandal logic that would be purveyed well into the future, encoded in the conventions of the genre that was to define the New Journalism. By successfully compelling mainstream newspapers across the archipelago to cover an Irish grievance, this new scandal logic temporarily shifted the

English press's representations of Ireland away from its habitual fixation on Irish savagery and perfidy. It also eventually led to the scandal that destroyed Parnell and his movement, earning Tim Healy and the newspaper scandal itself the enmity of the young James Joyce.

A spirit of exuberant defiance imbues the *United Ireland*'s early issues. These issues, like Parnell's exhaustive readings of the medical conditions of Fenian prisoners before the assembled House of Commons, constituted through their very existence an implicit criticism of their larger discourse context. The earliest object of the new weekly's implicit criticism was Dublin's moderate nationalist daily, the *Freeman's Journal*, for which the *United Ireland*'s founding editor, William O'Brien, had previously worked. O'Brien's defection, coupled with the clear implication that the Land League needed a paper further advanced in its views than the *Freeman's Journal*, sent a signal to that publication's editor, Edmund Dwyer Gray: Land League leaders had noted his lukewarm commitment to the cause and would speak to the nationalist reading public through another paper if they had to. Thus was Gray's loyalty to Parnell and his movement ensured until Parnell's final downfall, since Gray feared that further criticism of Parnell might prompt the *United Ireland* to go daily and take much of the *Freeman's Journal*'s readership with it.[17]

The near-ebullient opposition that the Land League evinced during this period is vividly expressed in some of the *United Ireland*'s cartoons from the early 1880s depicting the newspaper's position of noncompliance relative to agents of British coercion. Cartoons and editorials from this period indicate that the newspaper viewed itself as holding an important position in the larger fight for improved tenant rights, land redistribution, and, ultimately, some form of Irish independence. The paper's position of courageous intransigence registers visually in cartoons depicting the gleeful children who helped to distribute the *United Ireland* defying the Royal Irish Constabulary's efforts to suppress the paper (Figure 1.1). Indeed, the newspaper's bad attitude was likely one factor influencing Gladstone's decision to imprison Land League leaders and suppress the Land League itself in the months following its establishment. In any case, the newspaper and its creators, O'Brien and Healy, expressed to a great extent the

Figure 1.1   The Royal Irish Constabulary pursue children distributing the *United Ireland*. *United Ireland*, February 18, 1882. © The British Library Board.

rebellious and brilliantly mischievous spirit of Parnell's parliamentary activities throughout the period of the Land League's suppression in 1881–1882. All of this changed radically and abruptly, however, following the Phoenix Park and Maamtrasna murders.

THE PHOENIX PARK MURDERS

Throughout the period of Parnell's rise and fall, relations between Irish nationalists and colonial authorities were tense, polarized, and subject to frequent escalations to violence on both sides. With a synchronicity of which Joyce was demonstrably aware, the two complexly interlinked societies of Ireland and Britain, deeply agitated by the new affective and social powers of the emerging mass media, were both becoming increasingly reactive, subject to particularly fraught spirals of violence into words and words into violence, a process galvanized through the proliferating newspapers and their expanding audiences. For instance, following the publication of the first issues of the *United Ireland* in 1881, a series of shocking events with significant implications for the nationalist movement unfurled. Mere months after the paper's founding, first Land League leader Michael Davitt and subsequently the rest of the party's leaders, including Parnell, O'Brien, and Healy, were arrested under a new round of coercion legislation in Ireland. Such legislation enabled British agents to shut down avenues of nationalist agitation when these nationalists pushed too effectively for concessions unpopular with British constituencies, forcibly narrowing public discourse by imprisoning leaders, dispersing or suppressing rallies and riots, and targeting advanced nationalist newspapers at will.

Predictably, the imprisonment of Land League leaders prompted outbreaks of agrarian vigilantism and protest. These, in turn, supplied London-based newspapers with a gold mine of lurid details— threatening words and menacing deeds—fueling a stream of anti-Irish bombast that effectively deferred any further reasoned discussion of the Irish question. In Ireland, the nationalist front that Parnell had held together began to polarize. Middle-class nationalists and those who categorically rejected violence sought to dissociate themselves from the mainstream press's depictions of Irish depravity by further moderating their position, while the Ladies Land League, which had stepped in to fill the vacuum created by the male leadership's incarceration, openly endorsed the ad hoc violence.[18] In early May 1882, when Parnell, Davitt, and the other Land League leaders, including O'Brien and Healy, were released from prison, the fraying nationalist front enjoyed a brief moment of reunification. Parnell had secured the leaders' release under the terms of the so-called Kilmainham Treaty, in which British prime minister William Gladstone agreed to a series of reforms, and most nationalists greeted this development eagerly, with raised expectations for land reform and new hope for progress toward some form of Home Rule. On May 6, however, this moment's fragile spirit of Liberal and nationalist cooperation was shattered by a bloody double murder in Dublin's Phoenix Park: the fatal stabbings of the newly arrived Lord Lieutenant Henry Cavendish and his undersecretary, Thomas Henry Burke, by a shadowy group of Irish radicals called the Invincibles.[19]

From the standpoint of journalistic representation, the release of the Land League leaders had afforded a brief opportunity to redress a representational imbalance that inaccurately ascribed brute violence exclusively to the Irish side. The Phoenix Park murders blew that opportunity to smithereens. For Parnell and his comrades, the Phoenix Park murders constituted an appalling crisis. Fresh out of prison and facing an internal challenge from the Ladies Land League, they needed a disciplined national movement if they were to advance their aims of land reform and constitutional independence.[20] Blindsided from within by the Invincibles' militant rejection of the Home Rule negotiations underway between Parnell and Gladstone, the Land Leaguers were also under intense fire in the London newspapers, which portrayed them as monsters and screamed for their punishment.[21] In the cracked mirror of the London press, the Invincibles now exemplified Irish nationalism, putting the rest of the movement on the defensive both morally and tactically.[22]

That the Phoenix Park murders only exacerbated an existing representational imbalance in both English and Irish mainstream newspapers is evident in a quick comparison of nationalist coverage of the Phoenix Park killings and the contemporaneous Ballina massacre.[23] On May 4, 1881, just two days before the Phoenix Park murders, children in County Mayo had taken to the streets in a spontaneous celebration of Parnell's release from prison. While they marched in the streets with pipes and drums, several were shot down by the Royal Irish Constabulary (RIC). Like the Invincibles in Phoenix Park, the RIC in Ballina had targeted unarmed individuals for purely political reasons; unlike the Phoenix Park killings, the Ballina massacre received little coverage even in the nationalist newspapers. Following the Phoenix Park stabbings, what little notice it had received was lost amid horrified effusions toward the Invincibles by nationalists and unionists alike. In effect, both sides appeared to accept British political violence in Ireland as an unremarkable fact of life, while viewing Irish violence as shameful and stigmatizing.

The key difference in unionist and nationalist coverage of the Phoenix Park murders was that pro-British papers expressed outrage, cried for vengeance, and sought to generalize guilt for the crime, whereas Irish nationalist papers expressed shock and horror, distancing their constituencies as best they could from the atrocity.[24] That the killing of the Ballina boys is hardly remembered bears eloquent witness to what registered as scandal during this period. The Phoenix Park killings remain an ambivalent touchstone in the history of Irish anticolonial violence to this day; conversely, the Ballina slayings, with their suggestive comparability to South Africa's Sharpeville massacre or to Northern Ireland's Bloody Sunday, have been virtually forgotten. Indeed, the capacity of the period's prevailing scandal logic to magnify some injuries in the press while erasing others may explain why the Invincibles, and later the *United Ireland*, chose the extreme forms of recourse they did.

In the wake of the Phoenix Park murders, Irish nationalists were politically neutralized and representationally discredited in the now-rabid English newspapers. The murders scuttled the Kilmainham Treaty, and this breakdown of cordial relations between the Land League and the Liberal Party was followed by an extended flurry of sometimes gruesome political theatre. The murderers remained at large and unknown for an extended period, allowing for a stream of scabrous speculations in Parliament and the press linking Parnell's release to the killings. When they and their accomplices were brought to trial, the Invincibles found guilty of the actual killings were executed and the others received long prison sentences (a detail that Joyce exploited in *Ulysses* by including a character whom other Dubliners believe to be Skin-the-Goat, a Phoenix Park coconspirator). The trials and executions offered nationalism's opponents additional opportunities for explicit scandal claims connecting the perpetrators to the Parnellites, further widening the Irish/English representational divide. For the Irish nationalist front, the Phoenix Park murders thus constituted an abrupt, irresistible, and far-reaching reversal.

Later that summer, another set of murders reignited this scandal process. Sometime during the night of August 17, 1882, in the remote village of Maamtrasna, five members of a County Galway Joyce family (no relation to James Joyce) were brutally murdered. Although the murders were eventually found to have been motivated by a series of land disputes and political differences, British officials were eager to read this new atrocity as a straightforward repetition of the first. Their rush to judgment culminated in what was soon uncovered as a wrongful execution of an innocent party. As Waldron notes, the British administrators' contention that the Maamtrasna murders were also the work of a radical nationalist secret society neatly provided them with both a quick verdict and further evidence of their "pet theory . . . that all Ireland's violence and mayhem was caused by Parnell and the Land League."[25] The newspaper coverage of the Maamtrasna murders took up where the coverage of Phoenix Park left off, offering various telling details, real and invented, that linked the Land League to the murders and calling for extreme, broadly applied punishment for those responsible. The widespread assumption either blatant or latent in all but the most stalwart nationalist newspapers was that Parnell had somehow been behind or benefitted from these violent events.

Soon, however, the sensational details of the Maamtrasna murders themselves were eclipsed, especially in the Irish nationalist press, by the miscarriage of justice that led to the hanging of an innocent Maamtrasna man, Myles Joyce, as one of the perpetrators. Because of inadequate translation at his trial, the Irish-speaking Myles Joyce was denied his right to self-defense and was viewed by Irish nationalists, subsequently including James Joyce, as a martyr to British prejudices, executed as an Irishman and Irish speaker rather than a murderer. Myles Joyce's wrongful execution under the auspices of Treasury Crown Solicitor George Bolton and the subsequent refusal of British authorities to conduct an official investigation into the case catalyzed the resentment of Irish nationalists subjected to daily vituperation in the pages of the British press. The rapid and shoddy administration of colonial justice in response to Maamtrasna served as a powerful counterexample to the Phoenix Park murders for Irish nationalists, who promoted the martyred Myles Joyce as a spectacular emblem of

Figure 1.2   The Ghost of Myles Joyce points an accusatory finger at George Bolton. *United Ireland*, August 16, 1884. © The British Library Board.

British injustice and a moral counterweight to the supposed savagery of the Irish (Figure 1.2).

Following Myles Joyce's execution on December 15, 1882, nationalists of all stripes laid siege to the crack in the mirror of the mainstream press. The name of the wrongfully hanged Maamtrasna man became a byword invoked as clear evidence of British injustice, an expression of rage against and a refutation of widespread media demonization of the Irish. Following Myles Joyce's execution, even the most rudimentary social intercourse between Dublin Castle functionaries and the populace they purported to govern had been replaced with a single, angry expression of collective disaffection: "Who killed Myles Joyce?"[26]

The Phoenix Park murders had infused newspaper coverage of the Irish question with new virulence. The question of whether Parnell, represented as a metonym for nationalism as a whole, had secretly instigated or approved of the murders was to generate a series of newspaper skirmishes and a final, full-scale scandal in the years to come, all focused on the symbolic question of whether the Phoenix Park murders had permanently soiled all Irish nationalism, locking all "decent" newspaper readers into an obligatory defensive identification with English rule in Ireland. The outpouring of anticolonial vituperation that followed Myles Joyce's execution was only the first in a series of countermaneuvers on the part of the misrepresented Irish. In the wake of Phoenix Park, the production of counterscandals to redirect accusations of immorality back toward the British colonial order would become a political imperative for nationalist activists and intellectuals, including Parnell's lieutenants William O'Brien and Tim Healy at the *United Ireland*.

THE SCANDAL FRAGMENT AND THE FIRST DUBLIN CASTLE SCANDAL

The rumors surrounding the sexual habits of British officials on which O'Brien and Healy would seize, along with many other personal details that took on new public vitality during this period, belonged to a new form of journalistic currency: what I term the "scandal fragment," a known or surmised private detail that journalists could detach from its private context and transport into the public sphere, where, in the name of the public good, it could be sold, bought, bartered, and used to instigate a range of public actions. The *United Ireland*'s employment of such scandal fragments in the political sex scandal that became known as the first Dublin Castle scandal would have not been legally defensible, however, without the pivotal shift in libel law that had come some forty years previously: the Libel Act of 1843.

This act marked a significant loosening of the United Kingdom's notoriously strict libel laws, under which a damaging published statement could be found libelous even if it was objectively and provably true. The Libel Act changed this, allowing proof of a statement's veracity to absolve its author or publisher of libel, but only if its publication were in the public interest. As Sean Latham observes, this loophole shifted the protections of libel restrictions from "the reputations of particular individuals" to "the good order and conduct of the larger society."[27] This seemingly minor and progressive change in libel law, however, had a range of unforeseen consequences, the most significant of which would only come decades later, in 1883 in the wake of the first Dublin Castle scandal.[28] By further opening up courtroom testimony to public recirculation, the Libel Act destabilized an earlier, more absolute division between public and private morality, constituting the beginning of the sensationalizing fin de siècle developments that Matthew Arnold would term the New Journalism.[29]

The Libel Act unsettled eighteenth-century public/private arrangements by creating a new and flexible category of private act that, owing to its exceptional depravity, merited or even necessitated public exposure—a private act that was, paradoxically, superlatively public. In such cases, existing public/private power relations were reversed, so that some private acts could now be construed as a threat to the larger society, rather than the larger society and its attentions being invariably construed as a threat to the reputation of the private individual.[30] While journalists and the reading public did not immediately grasp the wealth of opportunities afforded them by this change, by the late 1800s the new protections afforded by the Libel Act had certainly become apparent. For instance, as Latham points out, Oscar Wilde's 1895 libel case against Lord Queensberry "fell foul of the courts not when witnesses emerged confirming the charge that he was a 'somdomite' [sic], but when it was judged that the publication of such knowledge constituted a public good."[31] This breach in the levy separating the Victorian public and private spheres accorded certain details concerning the ostensibly private lives of individuals a new public status. Moreover, the entertainment value inherent in this exciting new ritual of public shaming provided an insatiably curious reading public and the print industry with a strong motivation for wholeheartedly endorsing an emerging moral logic that condemned titillating private acts as public threats.[32]

This shift in British journalism represents a logical extension of earlier trends in print capitalism. According to Michael McKeon, as the British monarchy's absolute authority devolved downward to Parliament and the courts over the course of the eighteenth century, London and Edinburgh publishers had begun publishing anonymous invective and veiled satire to punish otherwise unprosecutable transgressions emanating from this newly insulated tier in the imperial hierarchy.[33] Like the later political sex scandal, anonymous published invectives targeting public individuals and institutions typically presented fantastically shameful private behavior by functionaries and institutions as a metaphoric correlative for public actions that the law had no power to regulate.[34] In a range of post-1843 cases, including those discussed here, sex scandals came to serve a similar purpose, as a means by which the actual or supposed private behaviors of individuals served as moral stand-ins for public actions and positions that were either unregulated or outside the jurisdiction of an author's constituency.

The most significant element of this phase of political scandalmongering among the Parnellites is that the political motives behind the attack were openly acknowledged. Like eighteenth-century political satire's disparagement of repugnant policies and politicians by associating them with shit, early Parnellite invective, if anything, emphasized rather than denied the political signified behind the sexual signifier.[35] The transgressions uncovered by the sequence of Home Rule sex scandals that ensued were, as the indirect illocutionary subtext of these scandals made clear, significant not for the private wickedness they evinced but as moral allegories for a larger system of injustice. From the standpoint of Land League activists, collectively branded as murderers and monsters through the coverage of the Phoenix Park murders, branding British rule in Ireland as systemic perversion might not even have seemed particularly radical or innovative. As it happens, however, it was. These scandals radically extended both the range of scandalous details or scandal fragments by which means a scandal could be launched and the potential sources from which they could be gleaned.

The violent events of the summer of 1882 hardened feelings on both sides, leading to a marked intensification of direct hostilities between the RIC and the *United Ireland*. Besieged by the effects of new coercion legislation, including the toll taken on many of the leaders by imprisonment, and by the vitriol of anti-Irish sentiment in the English and unionist newspapers, the Parnellites, with Tim Healy in the lead, field-tested a new anticolonial weapon.[36] In 1883, with editor William O'Brien at his side, Healy led the *United Ireland* into legally and conventionally uncharted territory. While ordinary Irish citizens were expressing their outrage toward British officials with spontaneous jeers and catcalls, and their parliamentary representatives were calling attention to Ireland's disenfranchisement using the tactics of obstruction, the *United Ireland* began publishing rumors of homosexual misconduct among Dublin Castle officers.

In the period leading up to the launching of the British Isles' first modern political sex scandal, relations between the *United Ireland* and the RIC had grown increasingly antipathetic as the newspaper itself became a lightning rod for British repression. Given the official harassment directed at O'Brien and his staff, all the way down to the children who distributed the paper, the newspaper's accusations against James Ellis French, the head of the RIC, reek of understandably personal animus. As journalists just recently released from prison who had seen their printing press dismantled by French's men and who frequently had to work around police attempts to confiscate the fruits of their labors, O'Brien and Healy did not have to be rabid homophobes to find the embarrassing details of French's private arrangements an inviting target.[37] Healy, in fact, was sufficiently comfortable with male sexual variability that while once walking home from the House of Commons with radical MP Henry Labouchere, sponsor of the eponymous amendment that destroyed Oscar Wilde, he had responded to Labouchere's observation that most of the men in a given circle were "musical" (homosexual) by saying that "those who have no music in their souls are fit for treasons, stratagems and spoils."[38] This extraordinary account offers evidence that Healy's early scandal work was explicitly political, opportunistically exploiting taboos around same-sex relations as the pretext by which to put the colonial system itself on trial. The anecdote shows that Healy could, at least for the sake of a good literary pun, frame homosexuality as a beneficial component of male psychology, and he liked the resulting witticism enough to publicly recall it in his memoirs. It was presumably because he understood his attacks as allegorical, just as he understood the British/unionist newspaper attacks against the nationalists to have been, that Healy never showed any embarrassment about the obvious disconnect between his private morals, which were liberal, and his public eagerness to use compromising sexual details as vicious political weapons.

Healy once described his collaboration with O'Brien in turning out the *United Ireland* as the composition of "little salads" to which "O'Brien supplies the oils and I pour on the vinegar."[39] If so, Healy appeared to have used a heavy hand in his first unsigned reference to the "sexual irregularities" of "prominent figures in the British administration."[40] Healy's biographer, Frank Callanan, traces the first volley in the Dublin Castle scandal sequence to a row initiated by Healy in the House of Commons with RIC subinspector Cameron, who had recently put down a riot in Wexford and was thus closely associated with British repression in Ireland.[41] As previously noted, passions against the RIC were running high during this period, owing to the Land League leaders' recent imprisonment, the media catastrophe that was Phoenix Park, and the RIC's outright assaults on the *United Ireland*. Healy and his colleagues were attempting to combat these injustices in a media environment where Irish resistance was encoded as an endless series of ultrascandalous atrocities and outrages, but British aggression in Ireland was viewed as emphatically banal. To shift this scale, Healy used his position as an MP to expose Cameron by twice stating in the House of Commons that Cameron and his wife had lived together before they were married. By publicly exposing this compromising private detail, Healy used the Camerons' trivial but scandalous private transgression to symbolically put Cameron and the Royal Irish Constabulary on trial for their heinous but unprosecutable public misdeeds.

Healy's attempt to use personal details and parliamentary privilege to expand in the House of Commons the civil protections that coercion laws were restricting in Ireland earned him a string of public humiliations. On the following day, the chief secretary described Healy's speech acts as churlish and cowardly and (in Callanan's words) "refused to answer a parliamentary question from Healy relating to the Royal Irish Constabulary, until Healy withdrew the imputation he had made against the honour of a woman under cover of parliamentary privilege." The London *Times*, in a standard move, used Healy's revelation of an alleged sexual irregularity on the part of a British official to indict Healy's own implicitly Irish and gendered irregularity, condemning his violation of "that unwritten code of good breeding and good feeling which all once obeyed."

Infuriated by these public reprimands and an added rebuke from the *Freeman's Journal*, Healy launched a ferocious counterattack in the *United Ireland*, asserting his prerogative to publicize details culled from the private lives of Dublin Castle officials when, in Healy's words, such public men's "private character" was such as to "affect [their] public position." Rashly escalating the conflict, Healy declared that the House of Commons was welcome to try to "make rules to stop such questions," but that it "will not do so until the life and adventures of what is called the 'private character' of various Crown employees in Ireland, from Corry Connellan, to Detective Director and County Inspector James Ellis French are fully laid bare to the universe." Given the drubbing Healy received for purportedly insulting Mrs. Cameron, perhaps one reason changing the conversation to these particular men's "musical" activities appealed to Healy was that they involved no women whose assailed honor might provide his opponents with another round of ammunition against him. Yet the rumors that had been circulating in Dublin regarding French and some of his men also neatly leant themselves to anticolonial allegory. Homosexuality's heretofore taboo status offered Healy (and later O'Brien and others) a potent vehicle for expressing their outrage at the offenses of the RIC and the British state. By invoking transgressive acts that could be newly charged with the horrific frisson of scandal-speak, silenced Irish activists could at last give voice to the emotional consequences of British repression.

In printing these rumors, and particularly in naming names, O'Brien and Healy took an unusual, even unprecedented risk. Prior to this *United Ireland* article, sexual secrets that made their way into print were, by journalistic convention and legal precedent, taken from courtroom testimony.[42] When French and his codefendants responded by bringing libel charges against O'Brien, they therefore must have felt confident that the truth of the allegations was, legally speaking, beside the point. British libel law had traditionally weighed the damage of an accusation not against the truth of the accusation but first and foremost against the social utility of the damaging deed's exposure, and public references to homosexuality had been consistently adjudged to be socially harmful. The supreme confidence of the Dublin Castle complainants shines forth, for instance, in O'Brien's recollections of the testimony of another accused Dublin Castle official, Gustavus Cornwall, in a later trial: Cornwall "did not deign to argue, . . . delivered his answers with a majesty that seemed to fascinate the court, . . . and he left the witness stand without a break in the superb chain of his perjuries."[43]

Up to this time, as H. G. Cocks has shown, a strong social bias had favored public reticence where homosexuality was concerned, regarding volubility on the subject, whether in courtrooms or newspapers, as more dangerous to public morality than the offenses themselves.[44] The evidence gathered in Dublin by the private investigator O'Brien hired for his defense and presented in court, however, rent a hole in the veil that was, by common agreement, drawn to obscure potentially corrupting details of homosexual activities from the public. What that evidence was, we cannot know, as the grand jury, in an unusual resolution, asked the presiding judge to forbid its publication. Judge Baron Dowse did not issue such an absolute injunction but did humbly commend the grand jury's resolution "to the discretion and Christian forbearance of the Press," which, according to Morris Kaplan, "did the trick."[45]

In the course of his plea for journalistic discretion, Judge Dowse hit upon the phrase "unspeakable crimes" to describe French's transgressions, and in so doing gave to modern journalism an astonishingly utilitarian phrase by which newspapers could allude to homosexuality while at the same time disavowing any knowledge of it. On August 6, 1884, in articles that ran in Dublin's *Freeman's Journal*, the Belfast *News-Letter*, and the Glasgow *Herald*, the now well-known scandal term "unspeakable crime" appeared as a newspaper euphemism for homosexuality for the first time. All three articles use this phrase in direct quotations of the judge, who in his address to the grand jury makes an elaborate show both of not making the charges explicit and of simultaneously making them unmistakable. Dowse specified "this unspeakable crime" of which he accused the defendants not by naming it but by citing sodomy's history as "originally an ecclesiastical offence" that became punishable by death "so far back as the reign of Henry the VIII," a statute that was changed in 1862 so that the offense was then covered "under the 24th and 25th of her present majesty, and a person found guilty was punishable by penal servitude for life down to ten years."[46]

Prior to this date, the term "unspeakable crimes" had cropped up from time to time in British newspaper coverage of dreadful acts, but the phrase had invariably described acts so catastrophically violent, extreme, and far-reaching in their effects that they were impossible to articulate.[47] The purport of "unspeakable" in this prior usage was closer to "incalculable," and served to designate events like political assassination, mass killings, and insidious violence whose impact is difficult to quantify. In the journalistic lexicon, Phoenix Park was an unspeakable crime. Mass-scale abuses against the colonized, on the other hand, were also sometimes deemed unspeakable crimes. For instance, in a long letter to the editor of the *Daily News*, published on October 31, 1849, one F. C. Brown described the mass cholera epidemic that had been raging in India since 1817 owing to a widespread mineral deficiency created by the British salt tax, tolerated in British India "because it was the natives, not we, who had to writhe under it in their vitals," as an "unspeakable national crime."

From August 6, 1884 on, however, "unspeakable crimes" was converted instantly and nearly exclusively into a newspaper euphemism for homosexual acts. But it seems to have also carried with it something of the sense implied in Brown's letter to the editor, suggesting an insidious, hidden, pervasive violation underlying an ostensibly orderly and rational system governed by fair and uniformly applied rules: a hidden illness ravaging a seemingly healthy body. The term pointed to a crime at once incomprehensible and appalling, and of which it is prohibited or even impossible to speak. A few phrases from a later *United Ireland* article by O'Brien demonstrate Irish nationalists' depiction of Dublin Castle as a hub of "unspeakable" immorality as a means to direct their audience's scandalized outrage toward systemic and representational injustices for which no institutional redress existed. O'Brien described homosexual activities among Castle officers as a "system of depravity unsurpassed in the history of human crime." These activities, he contends, are specifically "English" vices and (making the political and representational context for his speech act perfectly clear) far worse than the "venial crimes . . . of the Moonlighters and Invincibles."[48]

The first Dublin Castle scandal therefore originated in response to colonial conditions in Ireland that pushed nationalists to extremes to which no analogous educated, middle-class constituency in England would have resorted. While little remembered, the scandal defined the conventions of the homosexual sex scandal and the more general rules governing homosexual representability that would prevail in both societies for decades to follow and, as Kevin Dettmar observes, "paved the way" for Oscar Wilde's prosecution under the terms of the Labouchere Amendment, passed the following year, which prohibited male homosexual activity in Great Britain and mandated a sentence of two years of penal servitude.[49]

When French's libel suit against O'Brien collapsed after a series of delays, Healy and O'Brien continued their scandalmongering in the pages of the *United Ireland*, expanding their ongoing charges against French to some of his associates. These included not only Cornwall but also George Bolton—notorious for his role in Myles Joyce's execution—whom O'Brien accused of hiding evidence to protect Cornwall. Bolton successfully sued O'Brien, but the tide turned on July 2, 1884, when Cornwall also brought charges of libel against O'Brien. A great deal of sensational testimony ensued, O'Brien's scandalous claims against Cornwall were vindicated, French was tried and convicted, the protections promised by the Libel Act of 1843 had been proven, and a new epoch of sex scandal had begun: one in which newspaper journalists, long constrained to wait for scandalous secrets to come out in courtroom testimony, were set free to pursue these secrets in the field.[50] Whereas previous scandalmongers, fearful of the real and potentially catastrophic threats posed by libel suits, had waited for scandalous details to emerge from lawsuits, where they were presented as empirical facts or evidence, Healy, in his wrath, turned to rumors of a sort that would not otherwise have reached the courts. In the process of these various contestations in Parliament, in print, and in court, Healy and O'Brien spawned the modern homosexual sex scandal and greatly contributed to the sex scandal's development as a political weapon. Journalists, politicians, and activists were liberated to seek out sexual rumors or even, as in the later case of the *Pall Mall Gazette*'s W. T. Stead, to publicize their own scandalous transactions. However, the power of the political sex scandal was simply too great to be safely contained and channeled only toward the forces of exploitation and repression, as would be made painfully evident by the spectacular fall of one of its most brilliant practitioners: Charles Stewart Parnell.

"JUICY TITBITS OF INSIDE INFORMATION": PARNELL'S OPEN SECRET

Assessed through the lens of newspapers and scandal in Ireland, Parnell's career is as significant for its early successes and relative longevity as for its eventual, explosive destruction by the media powers he had helped summon into being. In both its ascent and its final collapse, Parnell's career exemplified the scandal work of savvy Irish nationalists during this period. One excellent illustration of Parnell's skill in using the press as a weapon on behalf of himself and his movement comes from 1886, when Parnell staved off a schism in his party by channeling inside information to the *Freeman's Journal*, then the leading Irish nationalist daily newspaper.

Earlier that year, in February, Parnell had set aside the pledge of party loyalty that he required of every Irish National Party member in order to run the legal husband of the woman he considered to be his wife, Katharine O'Shea, as a candidate in a Galway by-election. To those in the know, the implications of Parnell's running William O'Shea, a conservative Whig, against Phillip Callan, the Irish National Party's blameless and pledge-bound member from Galway, were clear and damning.[51] O'Shea must have threatened either to expose or to put an end to Parnell's affair with his wife if Parnell did not secure him a parliamentary seat. Some insiders might also have sensed something amiss in Parnell's targeting of Callan, who seems to have earned Parnell's enmity by stumbling across an incriminating telegram from Mrs. O'Shea.[52] Appalled at what appeared to be Parnell's open abuse of his position, some of his closest allies, including Tim Healy, believed that Parnell's exposure was imminent and perhaps even desirable, and some Irish National Party MPs, including Callan, publicly alluded to the O'Shea affair.[53] Parnell, however, outmaneuvered his colleagues by sending a semicoded telegram to the editor of the *Freeman's Journal* arguing that O'Shea was indispensable to Irish interests because of his alliance with the powerful Liberal MP Joseph Chamberlain and that Parnell would sooner resign than do without O'Shea's behind-the-scenes assistance in Parliament. Through the resulting newspaper coverage he orchestrated, Parnell rapidly convinced his party that O'Shea's election to the House of Commons was in fact a political necessity.

In a conversation with the eminent London-based journalist T. P. O'Connor, Parnell metaphorically described his sending of the *Freeman's Journal* telegram as parrying an assassination attempt by Healy. His fellow MP, Parnell coolly noted, "had been trying to stab him in the back for years," but Parnell meant to use "the resources of civilization" against him.[54] Thus Parnell was already describing Healy and the threat of scandalmongering he embodied as Brutus to his Caesar (a sentiment young James Joyce would later echo) and his own scandal work as the fending off of an assassination attempt. An equally significant element of Parnell's description of this maneuver is his droll citation of a famous political utterance, the phrase "the resources of civilization," which had originated in an emphatically hostile speech against Parnell by Liberal prime minister William Gladstone. Still bristling from the outrages of Phoenix Park and Maamtrasna, Gladstone had identified Parnell with lawlessness, describing him, in a mixed Manichaean metaphor, as a Mosaic harbinger of the Egyptian plagues in the book of Exodus and warning him that "the resources of civilization against its enemies are not yet exhausted."[55]

From the standpoint of the imperial center, Gladstone's phrase simultaneously enacted and made light of the hypocrisy that bedeviled all British imperialism but was especially fraught in Ireland, where, owing to Ireland's constitutional but unwilling status within the United Kingdom, British institutions and investments were simultaneously domestic and alien. Gladstone's intimation that, where Ireland was concerned, "the resources of civilization had not yet been exhausted" has lived on as a redolent figure of speech that constituted an ugly threat to abandon all civilized restraint, wrapped in phraseology purporting to offer the reverse: a rational and self-disciplined application of more civilized resources. To many, the phrase captured the contradictions of Gladstone's simultaneously gentlemanly and pugnacious political personality, illustrated in an cartoon from the satirical *Gladstone ABC* depicting a dapper Gladstone "belabouring a wretched Egyptian fellah with his umbrella" (Figure 1.3). For Parnell, the *Freeman's Journal*, like Gladstone's umbrella, could be used as a "resource of civilization" in precisely the paradoxical sense that Gladstone's phrase crystallized. Both are icons of simultaneous civility and savagery, figuring the categorical confusion between imperialist and native, civilization and barbarism, that distinguished British imperial relations, especially Anglo-Irish relations, during this period. While readers of *Ulysses* have relished the scornful Joycean parody they detect in Leopold Bloom's rolled newspaper as a deflating, antiheroic correlative for Odysseus's sword, they have missed this substitution's darker implications. Like Gladstone's umbrella and Parnell's telegram, the newspaper is a civilized resource that is, for all its seeming banality, equally dangerous and double-edged.

As Parnell's description of his outflanking of Healy implies, he and other Land League leaders had learned from Gladstone and the Liberals how to manipulate the tangled imperial circuitry of which newspapers were one key system. Parnell's recycling of Gladstone's

GLADSTONE INVADING EGYPT

Figure 1.3
A dapper Gladstone
assaults an Egyptian
with his umbrella.
From *The Gladstone
ABC* (by G. Stronach).
© The British Library
Board, shelfmark:
8139.bb.22.

gentlemanly threat wryly acknowledges nationalists' participation in
a kind of hybrid, contingent communications network within which
venture capitalists and other professionals operated alongside state
and church leaders, sometimes civilly and sometimes quite savagely,
in their common pursuit of representational leverage and political
clout. The ironic involutions of Parnell's remark about the resources
of civilization encode the mutually informed and informing relationship that existed between British and Irish scandal work, recalling
Caliban's famous summation of his transformation of imperial language into an anti-imperial weapon: "You taught me language; and
my profit on't / Is, I know how to curse." In a setting simultaneously
so politically polarized and socioeconomically inbred, however, it was
perhaps inevitable that Parnell and other nationalists' new powers
of utterance would not be wielded exclusively against the imperial
enemy.

The Galway by-elections case was not the last of the small media flaps that marked Parnell's career trajectory as an Irish nationalist leader and icon. While most of these were just distractions or minor embarrassments that did not decisively shift the balance of power within the Home Rule movement, they effectively demonstrate an important truth: scandals, especially sex scandals, are rarely (as advertised) the result of some major lapse of judgment or morals on the part of their principals. Rather, the modern political sex scandal is better understood as the endpoint of an extended trajectory that progressively chips away at a target through a series of public exposures. Examining the course of these less fully realized scandal events in Parnell's career illustrates how pervasively the dynamic of scandal informed the social world of Irish nationalists during this period and helps set the conditions for Joyce's own scandal work.

While Parnell was suspected of sexual improprieties even prior to his longtime liaison with Katharine O'Shea, occasional rumors of sexual misconduct circulating among his allies caused him no trouble, and in its early phase, his affair with O'Shea was also viewed sympathetically by his inner circle. Parnell's private and public lives first came into painful conflict during his 1881–1882 incarceration in Kilmainham Prison, which separated him not only from O'Shea, the woman he already considered his wife, but also from their first-born child, a sickly daughter who was born and died while Parnell was in prison. Parnell's biographers agree that the child was Parnell's and that his distressing separation from O'Shea and their fatally ill baby rendered him eager to make terms with the British. In *Ulysses*, Leopold Bloom's lingering grief at the infant death of his sickly child, Rudy, surely echoes (among other things) Parnell's own at the loss of his daughter.

The go-between who brokered the terms of Parnell's release was none other than O'Shea's estranged husband, MP William O'Shea, who eked out a political role for himself by trafficking in what Paul Bew terms the "juicy titbits of inside information" that his status as Parnell's cuckold made available.[56] William O'Shea's self-positioning as a conduit through which Parnell could negotiate with William Gladstone and Joseph Chamberlain, on the one hand, and the Irish

Catholic hierarchy, on the other, played a significant role in several episodes in which scandalous words and details intended for private circulation within circumscribed bounds were publicly deployed as political weapons.[57]

Over the course of the 1880s, Parnell's opponents put a series of such titbits of varying authenticity, potency, and visibility on public display in order to cripple an array of Home Rule–related initiatives. One such early exposure came in the immediate wake of the Phoenix Park murders. When, a fortnight after his successor's assassination in Phoenix Park, the belligerently anti-Irish W. E. Forster resigned as chief secretary, he had compromising words from a private letter from Parnell to Gladstone read aloud before the House of Commons. The letter itself had been extracted by William O'Shea from the imprisoned Parnell on behalf of Liberal MP Joseph Chamberlain. In it, Parnell had offered to "co-operate cordially for the future with the Liberal Party in forwarding Liberal principles," and the public exposure of these private words severely damaged Parnell's image as proudly independent of English patronage. According to Robert Kee, William O'Shea had wrung these words from the imprisoned Parnell, probably through blackmail, to gain prestige with Chamberlain, who in turn was hoping to advance his own career by brokering a union with the Parnellites.[58] Although Parnell had written these words in a private letter to Gladstone, they were obviously publicly compromising and could not have come into circulation without the leverage O'Shea obtained through his access to Parnell's private life. Following Phoenix Park, the coercionist Forster used these extorted words as a weapon against the Parnellite/Liberal alliance, embarrassing Gladstone and Parnell before their respective constituencies and dancing on the grave of Home Rule's blighted prospects.

As comically reenacted by Leopold Bloom's maneuvers involving false names and hidden letters, Parnell subsequently determined to suppress written evidence by any means necessary, such suppression being essential to successfully navigating the public/private divide that his own party's contributions to the emerging New Journalism had helped to render so treacherous. His reliance on aliases in his correspondence and business dealings, which were to become a matter of public ridicule and scorn following the O'Shea divorce proceedings, served for many years to impede the transmission of details from Parnell's private life into public circulation. In one instance of hard-edged information management, in 1883 the aforementioned Phillip Callan had handed Parnell an opened and compromising telegram from Katharine O'Shea, which Parnell apparently viewed as a veiled threat. Parnell responded by opposing Callan's reelection, claiming he was a drunkard who leaked secrets to the press.[59] Although Parnell managed to use the nationalist press to reunite his party behind him, by the end of 1886 a *Central News* reporter described Parnell's emerging from the home in Eltham that he shared with Katharine O'Shea and their children. While the article detailing Parnell's presence at Eltham caused him acute embarrassment, only the British and Irish elites who were already in on the open secret of Parnell's private life understood what it meant. After 1886, though Parnell himself and his associates on both sides of the Irish Sea worked feverishly to keep his private life under wraps, it was clear that rumors and insinuations about his adulterous relationship would continuously threaten to erupt. As is the case with *Ulysses*'s ethnically and culturally alien Leopold Bloom, Parnell was a "mixed middling," an Anglo-Irish Protestant viewed in England and by unionists as an Irish extremist, too tempting a target on both sides of the channel to evade scandal's impact forever.

The next round of scandal launched against Parnell again featured that most popular of scandal fragments, incriminating letters, this time supposedly expressing Parnell's support for the Phoenix Park assassinations. Presumably because Parnell was so good at suppressing security breaches that legitimately incriminating evidence of any sort was unobtainable, the letters were forgeries. The anti-Irish *Times* publicized the first of the so-called Pigott forgeries on April 18, 1887. Subsequently, an anti-Irish but attentive committee of inquiry found the letters to have been forged by the unscrupulous Richard Piggott, who had rightly presumed the London press would pay handsomely for evidence of Parnell's Fenian sympathies. Throughout the outcry prompted by the published letters and the subsequent inquiry into their authenticity, Parnell and his supporters firmly believed that the letters had originated with William O'Shea, who did, with cautious malice, testify before the committee that he thought the handwriting looked like Parnell's. In a farcical trial scene, elements of which recur in the *Ulysses* episode "Circe," idiosyncratic elements of the letters' handwriting and spelling were traced directly to Piggott, who confirmed his guilt in court and then fled to the continent, where he committed suicide.[60]

The Pigott incident constituted a scandal in reverse, briefly but acutely embarrassing the *Times* and generally exposing increasing "tensions between accuracy and the imperative to secure a scoop" (Figure 1.4). Ultimately, however, the speed with which the paper was publically forgiven for the incident served to highlight the advantageous position of newspapers relative to private individuals.[61] The Piggott forgeries and their denouement made a particularly strong impression on the young James Joyce because, as Richard Ellmann notes, two of Piggott's sons were at Clongowes with him when the suicide occurred. The news caused "a terrible scene" when one of the other boys, against the instructions of his teachers, passed on word of Piggott's ignominious and sinful death to his sons.[62]

With the public discrediting of a sensational scandal exposing Parnell's supposed ties to the Invincibles—although Parnell's secret Fenianism was still taken for granted by many—journalistic interest began to build in Parnell's connection with Katharine O'Shea. When William O'Shea at last divorced his long-nominal wife, naming Parnell as codefendant, the array of scandalous allegations made against Parnell and Katharine O'Shea, like those that circulate around Dublin concerning Leopold and Molly Bloom in *Ulysses*, ranged from the more or less factual to the patently fancied or fabricated (Figure 1.5). The most damaging scandal fragment to come out of the O'Shea divorce case came from the testimony of a housemaid, who speculated that Parnell must have exited from O'Shea's bedroom via her fire escape so as to appear, in a pinch, as having just arrived at the front door. Remarkably, it is the very absence of scandalous evidence here that provides "proof" of the scandal's veracity, just as their lack of hard evidence only seems to fuel Dubliners' ever more lurid speculations about the Blooms's respective sex lives in *Ulysses*.

PENANCE!

"HIS HONOUR ROOTED IN DISHONOUR STOOD,
AND FAITH UNFAITHFUL MADE HIM FALSELY TRUE."—TENNYSON.

Figure 1.4 *Punch* depicts the London *Times* covered in journalistic shame
after the Piggott forgeries were exposed. March 9, 1889. Courtesy of Punch
Limited.

All of these Home Rule scandals and scandal attempts, insofar as they made it into print in the first place, demonstrate, like the stories based on Dubliners' often distorted ideas about Leopold and Molly as individuals and as types, that the sorts of scandals launched against Parnell and others connected with the Home Rule debates were overdetermined by cultural expectations. The decision to publish various allegations against Parnell was ultimately governed by editors' estimates of what seemed probable, believable, and acceptable to their readers. In all cases, the secret titbits that scandalmongers brought to light were, in effect, pre-scripted by the politics they were meant to discredit, fitting as they did with editors' assumptions about what sorts of secrets each particular target would likely be hiding.

William O'Shea's eventual naming of Parnell as a codefendant in divorce proceedings against his wife provided a thoroughly conventional and legible scandal fragment, and following the publication of the long-standing open secret of Parnell's affair with a married woman, Parnell became a divisive rather than uniting figure in the nationalist movement. Like a proverbial thunderbolt, O'Shea's divorce action—or, rather, its subsequent press coverage—thrust apart the British Liberals and the Irish National Party and further splintered the Irish side into balkanized, warring factions. As we shall see, the impact of this figurative lightning strike on the world of Joyce's childhood is clearly evidenced in *A Portrait of the Artist as a Young Man* and recurs in the literal thunderclaps that rock *Ulysses* (and later *Finnegans Wake*).

Again and again in Joyce's oeuvre, especially in *Ulysses*, the fundamental transformation of scandal is reenacted: words reify into weapons or threaten to do so. Adroit and sometimes comical steps are taken to ensure that dangerous words are, in various ways and to varying degrees, contained or neutralized. Words out of context precipitate figurative martyrdoms encoding complex references to a series of interrelated historic journalistic and physical assaults and counterassaults, culminating in the spectacular destruction of individual scapegoats, a pattern for which the prolonged and dramatic buildup to Parnell's fall over the course of Joyce's childhood supplied the original model. Even in "Et Tu, Healy," the Phoenix Park murders are recalled in the title's figurative stabbing of Parnell, which telescopes a decade's worth of media sensations into a single, violent assassination.

While the ultimate fall of Parnell marks the self-immolating nadir of Irish nationalism's engagement with the political sex scandal, the Wilde trials (discussed in the next chapter) mark nationalist Ireland's final, decisive rejection of the sex scandal as a political weapon as expressed in the blatant refusal of Irish journalists to use Wilde in accordance with the form's by then well-established conventions.[63] Irish nationalism's fifteen-year participation in an ultimately catastrophic scandal sequence shaped Joyce's repeated engagements with the Phoenix Park murders, the Parnell scandals, and the other three monumental Victorian scandals discussed next: "The Maiden Tribute of Modern Babylon," Dilke, and Oscar Wilde scandals. Moreover, the political activities of both the parliamentary obstructionists and the New Journalist scandalmongers, whose work drove the Home Rule scandal wars, bear more than a passing resemblance to specific obstructive or "difficult" textual strategies employed by James Joyce, whose childhood social world their work defined. As the following chapters demonstrate, Joyce, alert to ways that British print culture could appropriate the inventiveness of Irish expressivity while disempowering Irish artists and the Irish as a whole, found in Parnell, Stead, and Wilde suitably multifarious objects of both identification and dis-identification, emblems not only for Irish nationalist martyrdom but for the broader range of sexual, political, and artistic dissent that Joyce resented scandal dynamics for stifling.

CHAPTER 2

Investigative, Fabricated, and Self-Incriminating Scandal Work

*From "The Maiden Tribute of Modern Babylon"
to the Oscar Wilde Trials*

---

*It is through Art, and through Art only . . . that we can shield
ourselves from the sordid perils of actual existence.*

—Oscar Wilde, "The Decay of Lying"

*Wilde's early epigrams . . . show an instinctive understanding of
the paradoxical nature of the modern subject, whose chief goal is
to become a work of art and exist in a realm of beauty. However,
as Wilde's career as a speaker and writer make plain, this goal
entails a devil's bargain with the external world, for the artist of
the self inevitably places himself on the art market.*

—Gregory Castle, *Reading the Modernist Bildungsroman*

As outlined in the previous chapter, nineteenth-century changes in
British libel law allowed for the emergence of sex scandal as a potent

political weapon, a development in many ways fundamental to what has been termed the New Journalism. The Dublin Castle scandal and its attendant fallout unsettled established relations between libel law and print capitalism, producing a new category of fungible private detail that I am calling "the scandal fragment." This development, in turn, enabled the sensational newspaper writing for which the terms "the New Journalism" and "scandal journalism" became interchangeable. The scandal fragment reconstitutes real or presumed details of a private act as proof of a culpable secret necessitating public exposure. Exposed, such shards of damning evidence—like the proverbial smoking gun—appear self-evident; they seem to speak for themselves. As a direct illocutionary speech act, a scandal exposes, an exposure that itself turns embarrassing personal trivia into crucial evidence of an urgent social problem. As an indirect illocutionary speech act, scandal does not merely discredit the scandal object; it transfers that object's credibility to those groups and political aims that the scandal narrative situates in symbolic opposition to it, thereby converting the prurience and schadenfreude of both the scandalmonger and the duly scandalized reader into creditable public spiritedness. Scandal's fundamental form, then, is that of a Manichaean moral equation that keeps its authors and readers on the credited side and its victims on the other.[1] And, as some enterprising public intellectuals were discovering, while scandal fragments on which new moral and political boundaries could be established might still come out by chance or in court proceedings, they could also be created.

The late-Victorian media's initial encounter with the scandal fragment, a powerful new fusion of word and thing, was marked by an outbreak of do-it-yourself scandalmongering. By the spring of 1885, new forms of scandal work in the London press were sending shock waves through the British social order. The originators of the New Journalism's most influential sex scandals—from "The Maiden Tribute of Modern Babylon" through the Dilke scandal, the Cleveland Street scandal, and the Oscar Wilde trials—created or obtained their scandal fragments in various ways, but all had imbibed the new entrepreneurial approach to scandal that began with Parnellite obstructionism and the first Dublin Castle scandal. Like those of the

Parnellites and the anti-Parnellites, the political agendas motivating the earliest of these well-known New Journalist scandals were straightforward, though the scandals' results were not. Eye-catching instances of shocking sexual transgression started as flagrant, apt metaphors for larger social ills, but in the public imagination these transgressions rapidly displaced the systemic ills against which they were deployed, transforming into paramount social evils in their own right.[2]

This chapter examines the development of the scandal fragment into an autonomous force in British society, elaborating on moments and dynamics in the history of the political sex scandal that Joyce would rework in his own scandalous writing. The "scandal work" first undertaken in Dublin by Parnell, Biggar, O'Brien, Healy, and the Land League migrated to the British publishing capitals of London and Edinburgh, where its practices were initially incorporated into a largely class-based series of contestations. In particular, the New Journalism's putative founder, W. T. Stead, is frequently credited with moving his influential newspaper, the *Pall Mall Gazette*, in politically progressive and economically lucrative directions through the incorporation of scandalous sexual secrets. Stead, according to Walkowitz, "introduced human interest stories that exposed the secrets of the rich and incited sympathy for the poor, . . . thus constructing sexual issues as news."[3] Quite rapidly, however, the New Journalism's conflicted pursuit of both progress and profits generated a series of London-based sex scandals that refigured sexually scandalized men and boys from all classes as both emblems of and scapegoats for the ills of unregulated capitalism. These scandals, like the Phoenix Park, Myles Joyce, Dublin Castle, and Parnell scandals, would become touchstones throughout Joyce's oeuvre.

The late-nineteenth-century shift in moral focus from economic exploitation to sexual transgression that the sex scandal facilitated contributed to the abrupt consolidation of modern homophobia that Eve Sedgwick describes and to the widespread loss of traction among socialists and militant labor organizers that followed.[4] A review of the political sex scandal's genesis, from its inception in the pages of the *United Ireland* and its spectacular introduction into mainstream print capitalism by W. T. Stead through its apotheosis in the Wilde trials, shows both the how and the why of James Joyce's transformations of the scandal genre. As a writer, Joyce is known for the peculiar materiality of his words. As we shall see, the distinctive involutions of the scandal fragment—both word and deed, speech act and fungible commodity—afforded Joyce a model for the ritual power of words as things when words that are emphatically private (that is, taboo) traverse the highly charged boundaries cordoning off the private from the public. Given the social and sexual unconventionality of Joyce's private life, the pervasive threat that sex scandal posed to all public figures who espoused unorthodox views provided him with a powerful motivation to engage in some preemptive scandal work of his own.

INVESTIGATIVE SCANDAL WORK: "THE MAIDEN TRIBUTE OF MODERN BABYLON"

The contribution of the Dublin Castle scandal to the conventions of the modern sex scandal, and thus the claim that the genre originated at the economic periphery in Ireland and only subsequently migrated into the imperial metropolis, is evidenced by the timing of W. T. Stead's definitive New Journalist sex scandal, "The Maiden Tribute of Modern Babylon."[5] The first in a series of newspaper articles in which Stead, the editor of the *Pall Mall Gazette*, would expose his own experiences in London's brothel district appeared on July 4, 1885, following the failed libel suits and subsequent convictions of some of those implicated in the Dublin Castle scandal in the second half of 1884. Such precedent-setting libel trials would have been closely followed by editors and journalists across Great Britain, so that their timing relative to the Maiden Tribute scandal strongly implies a connection between the speech acts that the courts found to be within O'Brien's right to publish and the new mode of investigative scandal that Stead launched the following year.

Prior to the *United Ireland* libel cases, Stead's masterful unleashing of the scandal fragments he gathered during four weeks of "exploring the London Inferno" would have been unthinkable. No editor would have exposed a prominent, large circulation daily newspaper to the extraordinary financial risks to which the notoriously rash Healy had exposed his party's small weekly. By Stead's own account, his multipart sensation was intended to decisively alter the rules of scandal, but this was possible only after the failure of the libel charges against the *United Ireland* rendered the sex scandal a more usable weapon. As the result of his efforts to protect young girls from rape by exploiting the libel loophole opened by O'Brien and Healy, Stead injected the sex scandal directly into mainstream British journalism and politics.

Stead asserted that many of the conditions he was reporting had already been revealed in evidence taken by a House of Lords committee three years earlier, in 1882, when venerable MPs, after listening to descriptions of practices with which many were undoubtedly personally familiar, dismissed the data before them as out of date and therefore unreliable. Determined to pierce the representational barrier that protected "the sturdy innate chivalry and right thinking of our common people" from coming to grips with the "strange, inverted world" of "the streets and the brothel," Stead began his own firsthand explorations of London's child sex trade. In the first of four investigative articles on the induction of prepubescent girls into prostitution, Stead explicitly attacks the status quo whereby the press "reports verbatim the scabrous details of the divorce courts [but] recoils in pious horror from the duty of shedding a flood of light upon these dark places, which indeed are full of habitations of cruelty." The Maiden Tribute series, a decisive volley in Stead's larger campaign to (in the words of Linton Andrews and Henry Taylor) "use the press as the true and only level by which thrones and governments could be shaken and the welfare of the masses improved," introduced into popular print (and thus in a new way into the public view) the young prostitutes many Londoners stepped past or over on their way home every evening.[6] Like the Dublin Castle scandal (and the later and better-known Dilke and Cleveland Street scandals), the intended argument of Stead's sensational account of the sexual and physical abuse of the poor at the hands of the profligate rich was that a politically and representationally insulated elite was abusing its power. The revealed sexual details, in addition to representing the literal abuse of young girls, thus also emblematized a far broader range of class-based abuses.

Although part of Stead's motivation in publishing the Maiden Tribute articles was undeniably financial—and in that way enormously successful—his investigation was also legitimately progressive, as evidenced by his close collaboration with feminist activist Josephine Butler and a network of affiliated feminists working to protect poor and working-class girls and women from violation by both individuals and the state. In the 1870s and 1880s, Butler played a leadership role in the campaign to repeal the Contagious Diseases Acts, which made women deemed prostitutes liable to compulsory inspection for venereal disease and, if infected, to forcible incarceration.[7] With the help of Butler's contacts—former prostitutes who had retained ties with others still in the profession—Stead both staged and documented a series of transgressions that he could employ as scandal fragments: as appalling evidence of sexual secrets with which to launch a political scandal over the coerced recruitment of poor girls into prostitution.

Through Rebecca Jarrett, a reformed procurer affiliated with Butler, Stead offered a destitute mother five pounds in return for her thirteen-year-old daughter, Eliza Armstrong, to whom he gave the *nom de scandal* Lily. Stead documented every step in the process of procuring Eliza, beginning with Mrs. Armstrong's indifference concerning the actual employment for which her virginal "Lily" was destined. (As we will see, Lily's physical and emotional vulnerability is recalled in *Ulysses* in the ambiguous, sexually exposed status of the Blooms' daughter, Milly.) Removed from her family by Jarrett, Armstrong's virginity was confirmed through a gynecological examination conducted by a corrupt midwife (an event commemorated in Buck Mulligan's gynecological examination of Leopold Bloom in "Circe"). Jarrett then took Armstrong to a brothel, chloroformed her, disrobed her, and put her to bed. Stead himself went through all the motions enacting her final, forcible initiation into prostitution "short of consummation" so as to document her fear and powerlessness to summon help or resist and followed this up with another medical examination to document her continued technical virginity.[8] Finally, Stead oversaw Armstrong's removal to France, documenting his freedom from police interference at every stage.[9]

Physically violated and psychologically traumatized, the thirteen-year-old Armstrong's experience was arguably little better than that of the average abducted slum girl, and it eventually led to Stead's being tried, convicted, and sentenced to three months in prison. Yet Stead and his colleagues sincerely believed that he had rescued Armstrong. Although their belief in the utter benevolence of these activities may have stemmed in part from the Victorian emphasis on the hymen as the sine qua non of female virginity, Butler and Stead's background as staunch opponents of the Contagious Diseases Acts indicates that they knew perfectly well that forced gynecological exams and involuntary confinement were injurious. Clearly, their moral compass had shifted, magnetized by what Kali Israel terms "the power of melodramatic sociosexual scripts."[10] Stead's activities and reportage created a powerful scandal equation that defined Armstrong as "rescued," unlike those "sacrificed" girls whose immoral victimization Stead and Butler had set out to expose and prevent. In any case, Stead's meticulous documentation of these proceedings produced a stunningly successful political sex scandal. The Maiden Tribute articles marked the apogee of late-Victorian scandal journalism, unleashing vast public outrage and formally initiating what has been termed "the journalism of exposure."[11]

A close reading of the Maiden Tribute articles reveals that Joyce was influenced by Stead not just thematically but stylistically as well. Although Stead describes his extraordinary actions as a desperate counter to parliamentary obduracy, his account of the events that led him to adopt these extreme measures is confusing almost to the point of incoherence. Whereas Stead's writing in the series is otherwise memorable for its elegance, precision, and rhetorical punch, on close inspection the passage in which he first explains to readers how he came to find himself wandering around the red-light districts notably prefigures Leopold Bloom's incoherence when, in the "Circe" episode, he is discovered in a similar position:[12]

When the Criminal Law Amendment Bill was talked out just before the defeat of the Ministry it became necessary to rouse public
attention to the necessity for legislation on this painful subject.
I undertook an investigation into the facts. The evidence taken
before the House of Lords' Committee in 1882 was useful, but
the facts were not up to date: members said things had changed
since then, and the need for legislation had passed. It was necessary to bring the facts up to date, and that duty—albeit with some
reluctance—I resolutely undertook. For four weeks, aided by two
or three coadjutors of whose devotion and self-sacrifice, combined with a rare instinct for investigation and singular personal
fearlessness, I cannot speak too highly, I have been exploring the
London Inferno.

The tautology of the "necessary . . . necessity" of legislation, the mys-
teriously unnamed "painful subject," the confusing movement between Stead's recent investigation and the investigations of the House
of Lords three years earlier, the oxymoronic stance of reluctant resolution, and Stead's curious uncertainty about whether he had two or
three devoted, self-sacrificing, and fearless coadjutors all bespeak a
certain caginess as to the timing, motivation, and execution of his
investigative scandal work.[13] At a minimum, this explanation is symptomatic of his uncertainty not only about how to address a newspaper
audience on this awkward topic but how to position his work relative
to familiar public debates on the subject, leaving aside the murkier
and more banal concerns of legality and liability.

    In the context of his demonstrated ambition for the *Pall Mall Ga-
zette* and his own editorial reputation, Stead's deliberate vagueness
as to his timing and motives hints at an imperfectly sublimated lust
for social power and economic success that rendered his ambiguous
victimization/rescue of a thirteen-year-old slum dweller as much a
bid for prominence and power as for social justice. This sort of intrusion of personal ambition into supposedly altruistic or artistic aims so
angered Joyce that he repeatedly associated it with simony: the sinful
trafficking in sacred objects for worldly gain, most notoriously in the

sale of the purported body parts and personal effects of Jesus, the disciples, and various saints.

The organizing allegory in which Stead couched his scandal fragments will be strikingly familiar to readers of Joyce, whose biography and writing demonstrate that he was familiar with Stead and the Maiden Tribute articles.[14] Most centrally, Stead describes his transactions with Eliza Armstrong as taking place within "the Labyrinth of Daedalus," in which, according to Greek mythology, youths and maidens sacrificed by Athens in a forced annual tribute to their Cretan conquerors wandered "hopelessly lost," only to be "devoured by the Minotaur, a frightful monster, half man, half bull, the foul product of an unnatural lust."[15] This labyrinth, as Stead describes it, is "as large as a town," and the maw of the creature that lurks at its center is "insatiable." Those who wander lost in its interior have no "'hope of rest to solace' . . . save for the poison anodyne of drink."[16] Stead, like Theseus, enters this "strange, inverted world" with heroic intentions, though upon entering the labyrinth he soon finds himself lost. The logic of this paradoxical space is, he tells us, irreconcilable with "the world of business and the world of politics," not because it is the opposite of this daytime world but, more bewilderingly, because it is both "the same and not the same": "I heard of much the same people in the house of ill-fame as those of whom you hear in caucuses, in law courts, and on Change. But all were judged by a different standard, and their relative importance was altogether changed." As a result, "after a time, the eye grows familiar with the foul and poisonous air, but at the best you wander in a Circe's Isle, where the victims of the foul enchantress's wand meet you at every turn." In later chapters I will examine the classical images that Joyce, like Stead, associated with brothels: Circe, the minotaur, the labyrinth, maiden sacrifice, potions, and magical, bestializing transformations. Here, however, Stead's use of these tropes not only demonstrates their rhetorical power within an extended speech act mapping an unknowable elsewhere at the heart of London itself, but also foreshadows how this new rhetoric would take on a life of its own, contributing to results far beyond Stead's original declared aims.

It appears that Stead, like Healy, was intoxicated by the new powers of the press that his scandal work summoned (and not, as his enemies claimed, overtaken by his unconscious sexual preoccupations, which in any case would have been, as Joyce maintained concerning his own soul's "sexual department," much the same as the next man's).[17] Like Parnell and Healy, he mobilized the powers of scandal by working across scandal's constitutive subject/object divide. Stead harvested scandalous details by becoming both the scandal victim/object and the moral subject of the morality play he scripted, and his position at the center of the transnational psychodrama he precipitated appears to have induced a level of exhilaration akin to mania.[18] Stead's states of scandal-induced grandiosity are perhaps best illustrated by his well-known headline likening his scandal work to that of Zeus hurling bolts of lightning: "We knew that we had forged a thunderbolt."[19] The affective energies Stead unleashed through his journalism were clearly collective rather than individual; the great emotional and psychological power of his central metaphor of children sacrificed to a frightful monster that embodies "unnatural lust" stirred up a massive public outcry for new legislation. Yet Stead's narrativization of this powerful figure, brought to life by means of the scandal fragments he had produced, also foretold with precision the disastrous course of the energies he unleashed.

In his initial, emblematic image of Daedalus's labyrinth into which Athenian "youths and maidens" were flung, Stead encodes not only the fate of maidens sold or coerced into "white slavery," but also of "youths" like the telegraph messenger boys in the later Cleveland Street affair whose activities in the London labyrinth would become emblematic of the fate of the poor at the hands of the dissolute rich. In Stead's narrative, however, the question of the sexual exploitation of boys also invoked in the sacrificial "youths and maidens" is quickly discarded. When Stead transposes the Cretan labyrinth to modern London, the youths evaporate. As Laurel Brake argues, Stead took advantage of a powerful cultural script when he emphasized the endangerment of virginal girls.[20] Yet Stead's abrupt exclusion of endangered and exploited boys would not have been possible had it not also conformed to another late-Victorian script concerning homosexuality.

The disappearance of the Athenian boys upon the sacrificial chil
dren's arrival in London would have seemed natural to the *Pall Mall
Gazette*'s relatively affluent, public school–educated readership of
what Eckley calls "gentlemen, radical freethinkers, and field preach-
ers,"[21] who would have been familiar with both homosexuality (if only
from their Greek and Latin schoolbooks) and its routine exclusion
from public representations of contemporary society (or, as the Dublin Castle scandal had made newly possible, its inclusion under the
cloak of highly coded terms).

The underlying logic by which Stead's initial assault on child
exploitation would later morph into an assault on male homosexuals made to stand in for a culpable aristocracy can be traced to the
Maiden Tribute's close genealogical links to the Dublin Castle scandal
and Stead's use of the terms that scandal was newly transposing into
a highly recognizable and inflammatory code for male homosexuality. Words like "unnatural" were now the shadowy vehicles through
which homosexuality could obtrude into public signification. Thus,
Stead's regular use of the terms "maiden tribute," on the one hand,
and "unnatural lust," on the other, has the effect of ushering his symbolically freighted fourteen-year-old virgins in two different directions. As the figure of the Cretan labyrinth shifts from its original
setting to modern-day London, its victims cease to be referred to as
"young men and maidens." Instead, they become a specifically femi-
nized "maiden tribute." The maidens also proliferate, with Stead insisting that "this very night in London, and every night, year in and
year out, not seven maidens only, but many times seven . . . will be
offered up as the Maiden Tribute of Modern Babylon." The imperiled
girls thus emerge as the scandal's center, as the "facts" with which
Stead confronts his fellow Londoners. At the same time, its boys dis-
appear into the article's political unconscious, cropping up only in
the murky allegorical vocabulary of homophobia that Healy, O'Brien,
Judge Dowse, and subsequent newspaper coverage of the libel trials
had established: unnatural lust, atrocities, outrages, and, of course,
"unspeakable" and "unnatural crimes."[22]

In a shrewd (if unduly optimistic) attempt to harness the forces
he was unleashing, early in his first article Stead included a subsection

titled, with the deliberate baldness of a political flyer, "Liberty for Vice, Repression for Crime." In it, he sides firmly with the sex radicals of his time and our own by stating that he is not calling for "any police interference with the liberty of vice," arguing that adults should have "absolute liberty to dispose of their persons in accordance with the principles of private contract and free trade." Nonetheless, the murky, euphemistic language that was becoming associated in newspapers with homosexuality begins to blur the very distinctions Stead is anxious to make. Even the word "crimes," when applied in a sexual context, had already been linked to homosexuality through the Dublin Castle scandal and its coverage. Stead's caveats that sexual immorality should be tolerated when it is not "guilty of [any] outrage on public morals" and that "the relations between man and woman [are] an affair for the moralist" both tacitly invoke homosexuality and leave its status ambiguous, allowing Stead to stir the heated emotions such words engendered but to redirect them toward his cause of ending child prostitution (a cause that had thus far garnered mostly yawns from the public at large). As homosexuality is not "between a man and a woman," it may be an "outrage on public morals" despite its status as a vice between adults.

Stead's list of acts he believes should be criminalized includes the sale, purchase, and violation of children; the procuring of virgins; the entrapment and ruin of women; the international slave trade in girls, and "atrocities, brutalities, and unnatural crimes." Out of the ensuing rounds of marches, demonstrations, petitions, and legislation that Stead's scandal work elicited, the Maiden Tribute scandal's most lasting social effect would be in regard to the most open-ended of these items: the one in which his scandal work had no explicit investment. This strange evolution from the protection of underage girls sold as sex slaves to the persecution of consensual sex acts between men offers an exemplary and perhaps originating instance of Kevin Ohi's now widely observed rule of sex scandal: the impetus for a sexual transgression typically devolves onto the nearest sexual deviant.[23] If the New Journalist sex scandal struck, metaphorically speaking, with the rapidity and power of a lightning bolt, sexual deviants rapidly afforded its intended targets with a protective lightning rod.

In his first article in particular, Stead describes his investigations in language as memorable for its stately allusiveness as for its sensational modifiers and lurid euphemisms lifted from the conventions of the gothic novel.[24] Providing more than mere ornament, this language imbues the facts of the article with moral significance that directs the scandal toward specific targets. For instance, Stead adapts his Circe's isle metaphor by noting that the spectacular external transformations of Odysseus's men are, within the London metropolis, invisible and private: "Whereas the enchanted in olden time had the heads and the voices and the bristles of swine, while the heart of a man was in them still, [brothel patrons] have not put on in outward form 'the inglorious likeness of a beast,' but are in semblance as other men, while within there is only the heart of a beast—bestial, ferocious, and filthy beyond the imagination of decent men." Stead's allegory emphasizes the indistinguishability of brothel patrons from upstanding gentlemen, necessitating his work of investigation and disclosure while legitimating its targeting of the wealthy and powerful. At the same time, it broadcasts a potent subliminal threat to any who might oppose him: since the unspeakably vicious are, in their public appearance, indistinguishable from "other men," any man who objects to Stead's investigations or his conclusions will doubtless be a member of this hidden constituency. Conversely, however, Stead also constrains the invisible network of contaminating black magic that he has exposed by defining it in opposition to what is properly "English": as a "Moslem hell" in which sojourners are forced to "drink of the purulent matter that flows from the bodies of the damned," a concluding metaphor that temporarily affords his readers a needed escape from the universally contaminating implications of his scandalized map of London's brothels.

Yet Stead's scandal fragments are presented in a substructure of metaphor that emphasizes entrapment in a labyrinth constituted by a vast system of misrecognition. Thus, he claims, his goal is "not to secure the punishment of criminals but to lay bare the working of a great organization of crime"—to render perceptible differences that are hidden under a veneer of superficial sameness. Much of what makes the labyrinth, Circe's wand, and the horrifically hybridized minotaur so sinister, after all, is that all defeat rational interpretation or comprehension. Ultimately, Stead's response to the problem of deception, coercion, and rape within the market of vice is to claim that they are caused by a sort of epistemological miasma, a kind of bad magic that renders outsiders unable to discern between the vicious and the criminal, the human and the bestial. His solution is paradigmatically that of the Victorian imperialist: a commission should be formed, evidence should be gathered, and lists should be drawn up identifying various activities that happen in brothels and categorizing them under binary rubrics distinguishing between the licit and illicit. Nonetheless, the very horror that Stead evinces at the incomprehensible world of the brothel district also casts some sexual activities— most specifically homosexuality—deeper into unknowable darkness. Every vague reference to atrocities and outrages serves to energize an intense if inchoate fear and loathing of nameless acts that, by implication, cry out to be identified, dragged into the light, and punished. The power of Stead's Manichaean allegory, moreover, allocates considerable moral credit to those readers most shocked by the figuratively unspeakable "worst" of the crimes to which he alludes.

Stead's relationship to the London labyrinth is reminiscent of Fanon's description of the colonizer's paradoxical relationship to the native shantytown, the labyrinthine space that is both inaccessible to and the by-product of the logic and linearity of the settler's village.[25] Both Stead's labyrinth and Joyce's representations of Dublin's brothel district similarly present a space both outside of and constitutive of British rationality and oversight. But if Joyce had Stead's labyrinth in mind when he crafted his own recurrent references to virgins, prostitution, brothels, and Nighttown, his life history would have led him to identify with the Maiden Tribute's sacrificed youths and maidens rather than either the quixotic Stead or the ravenous minotaur. As we shall see, the use that Joyce made of Stead's scandal work was enabled by his identification with Lily as an emblem for the Athenian boys as well as their sisters. Certainly, Stead's description of the Athenian youths and maidens as the "doomed fourteen" would have gotten Joyce's attention, for it was at the age of fourteen that Joyce, by his own account and that of his brother, Stanislaus, first entered the

Dublin brothel district. Stead introduced but then shied away from the fate of the young teenaged boys flung into the labyrinth by a conquering power; Joyce's *Portrait of the Artist* and *Ulysses* are the testimony of one of those who made it through to the labyrinth's heart.

"THE NEAREST DEVIANT": THE DILKE SCANDAL

If the Dublin Castle and Maiden Tribute scandals unleashed new energies in language, newspapers, and politics that were far in excess of their aims, it was in part because of the intense emotions that scandalmongering stirred up for the instigators as well as their audiences. In the heat of these verbal and legal battles, the compulsion to hurl the next thunderbolt often overrode both tactical and ethical considerations. Like Tim Healy, for whom scandalmongering became a compulsion that increasingly operated apart from the interests and aims of the party it ostensibly served, Stead was also a serial scandalmonger whose moral outrage took on a life of its own. Although Stead's espoused politics were progressive and sympathetic to Irish Home Rule, he unknowingly set the groundwork for and personally facilitated a particularly cynical political sex scandal that would deliver the single greatest setback to Irish constitutional aspirations in the years between the Phoenix Park murders and the fall of Parnell. What has become known as the Dilke scandal was a documentably fabricated media event and the most devastatingly effective political sex scandal prior to Parnell's spectacular fall. It also represents the most decisive shift in the media scandal's transformation from a weapon of opposition into one of reaction. Whereas individual career interests had compromised Healy's and Stead's early scandalmongery, it was in the Dilke scandal that Theweleit's observation about the dangers of the middle-class preoccupation with sexual morality was fully borne out.

In May 1885, Liberal MP Sir Charles Dilke traveled to Ireland to promote a plan for Ireland's pacification conceived by his friend and ally in the Liberals' radical wing, MP Joseph Chamberlain. The Liberal government's plan was to placate the nationalists with a sop: an expansion of local government overseen by the Irish Catholic Church, setting up the church as the British state's surrogate in Ireland. In the Irish Catholic Church, Chamberlain believed, the British state had a made-to-order comprador bureaucracy, conservative in its political and social outlook and beholden to the British state for its authority. Chamberlain, using serial scandal instigator William O'Shea as his intermediary, aimed to bypass Parnellite nationalists by handing over certain internal responsibilities to the church, a shift that had already begun in the allocation of the national schooling of Catholic children to the church in the late 1870s.[26] While in residence at Dublin Castle, however, Dilke found British governance in shocking disarray; in the wake of Myles Joyce's execution, the lord lieutenant was being ostracized by the whole of the Irish people.[27] Confronted with what he now understood to be a catastrophic breakdown in governance, Dilke instead embraced the Parnellite agenda, returning to London from Dublin committed to Home Rule for Ireland. Whereas Dilke had meant to sell moderation to the Irish, the Irish had instead sold Home Rule to Dilke.

Thus Chamberlain found his ingenious sectarian scheme unexpectedly snubbed by both the Irish and his closest ally. When the Irish nationalists emphatically rejected Chamberlain's plans, he took emphatic umbrage (and would, in fact, go out of his way to punish the ungrateful Irish throughout the rest of his career). According to the circumstantial evidence outlined by Roy Jenkins, Chamberlain also conceived a grudge against Dilke. Shortly after Dilke's conversion to Home Rule in July 1885, Chamberlain apparently arranged a scandal that destroyed the career of his former friend and colleague, who was also his only competitor for the position of Gladstone's anointed successor.[28] Certainly, someone arranged for false and highly sensational allegations against Dilke to be made by the young wife of a newly elected MP, a Mrs. Crawford, with whom Dilke was barely acquainted. In response to an anonymous series of insinuating letters, Mr. Crawford had his wife watched for several days before confronting her. Upon learning of her husband's receipt of one further, decisive epistolary accusation of her engagement in unspecified sexual improprieties, Mrs. Crawford broke down and accused Dilke of having led her astray in a number of unusual and newsworthy ways. In the divorce coverage that ensued, the scandalous power of Mrs. Crawford's confessions derived from her status as an aristocratic lady. That such a well-bred young woman should have done such things at all was itself only just (if thrillingly) imaginable to the *Pall Mall Gazette*'s largely middle-class readership, but that she might claim to have done them when she had not was inconceivable. While no evidence emerged to show that Dilke and Mrs. Crawford had ever been alone together, one meeting that did emerge from the Crawford divorce trial was with another virtual stranger, Joseph Chamberlain, two days before the most incriminating letter's delivery.[29]

Neither Crawford nor Chamberlain ever explained the reason for this meeting, but the most probable explanation for Crawford's visit to Chamberlain and her false accusations against Dilke is that Chamberlain, armed with knowledge of a very indiscreet affair, told Crawford what to say when her husband received a letter exposing her adultery. Jenkins makes the case that Mrs. Crawford was threatened with her lover's exposure but promised that he would be shielded if she named Dilke as her seducer and ascribed real sexual details to the fabricated affair. In due course, the letter arrived, Mrs. Crawford wept and confessed her many exotic transgressions, and the bewildered and humiliated Mr. Crawford named Dilke in divorce proceedings.

The British press was happy to acquaint the newspaper-reading public with Dilke's supposed activities, including, most sensationally, what Kali Israel describes as a "Frenchified taste for lesbian eroticism" that led him to "violate the boundaries of class" in a ménage à trois with Mrs. Crawford and a housemaid.[30] Stead in particular was relentless in his denunciation of Dilke's depravity. Doubtless still suffering from the ill effects of three months in prison for abducting Eliza Armstrong, Stead may have been goaded by Dilke's supposed impunity in comparison to his own admirable self-denial, especially as his own restraint had not spared him from penal servitude.[31] Certainly his attitudes concerning consensual vice had discernibly hardened. Stead responded to Dilke's purported "Franco-eroticism" by obsessively denouncing "the horrors of 'unnatural' male desire."[32] Under the pressures of this new sociosexual script, Stead's avowed broad-mindedness evaporated along with his gallantry toward working-class girls and women. In a later comparison of Dilke's crimes to those of Parnell, he insisted that Parnell was less odious than Dilke in that he never "force[d] Mrs. O'Shea to endure the humiliation of passing the night with an Irish Fanny."[33] Although the accusations against Dilke were insubstantial, a decree nisi issued by the judge found against Mrs. Crawford and permitted Mr. Crawford to divorce her. In the court of public opinion, this result proved Dilke's guilt, thereby soiling his name, largely neutralizing his influence, and radically altering the course and pace of the Irish Home Rule debates.[34]

The Dilke scandal, like the previously discussed Piggott forgeries that soon followed, reveals a powerful reversal in the relationship between sexual and political transgression that the early New Journalism had sought to establish. Both of these fabricated scandals demonstrate the important role that the prior assumptions of individual editors and the press as a whole played in the creation and perpetuation of particular scandals. By 1885, "deviant" politics were presumed to correlate with and lend credence to dirty secrets, rather than "dirty secrets" symbolizing and calling attention to dirty politics. In this respect, Ohi's scandal-attracting "nearest deviant" was gradually emerging in the guise of "the homosexual," but also (as embodied in Dilke and Parnell) as the political deviant whose suspect foreign sympathies, class privilege, and unconventional politics all signal and make loathsome his probable sexual deviance.[35] Stead presumed that Dilke's radical and therefore deviant politics made him a highly probable practitioner of French vice, just as Parnell was presumed by the *Times* to be secretly in league with violent Fenianism. In both cases, the secret titbits that scandalmongers brought to light, while false, did real damage because they fit with editors' assumptions about what sorts of secrets certain people were likely to be hiding.[36]

In the Dilke scandal—a dress rehearsal for the fall of Parnell— letters and infidelity once again supplied scandal fragments radically damaging to the prospects for Home Rule. Unquestionably, the period's accelerated production and circulation of coerced or falsified evidence helps explain Leopold Bloom's extravagant care with regard to letters and writing. In the "Sirens" episode, for instance, Bloom muses on the dangers of putting one's lecherous thoughts into letters, which could end in their being "read out for breach of promise" (11.1078–79). Joyce depicts other Dubliners noting Bloom's extreme caution about signing things and shows Bloom employing a false name (Harry Flower) in his epistolary affair with Martha Clifford. Bloom's careful, evasive measures are a form of modern prophylaxis meant to thwart contracting this new and especially virulent sort of social disease. These evasive maneuvers fail spectacularly, however, in both the "Cyclops" and "Circe" episodes of *Ulysses*, in which Bloom is put on trial on the basis of falsified evidence. The repeated dramatic failure of Bloom's elaborate precautions calls attention to the inescapability of scandalous misappropriation for stigmatized individuals and groups within the modern social order.

In this and other ways, as we shall see, Joyce connects scandal-mongering to the category of hostile folk magic known in Ireland as "pishoguery": the use of discarded, trivial body parts such as hair or fingernail parings to gain secret power over enemies so as to destroy them at a distance. Bloom is particularly vulnerable to such malicious misappropriations because of his status as an ethnic outsider. Like Jewish victims of the blood libel—the widespread European folk belief that Jews used the blood of Christian children in their rites— Bloom is already viewed by his neighbors as a likely practitioner of secret abominations. Thus, as Margot Norris concludes in her reading of the politics of conversational exchange in "Circe," Bloom is a man on the edge of a social precipice, fighting a losing battle to stay out of the ranks of the explicitly stigmatized, of those flagrantly mentally or ethnically deviant Dubliners who, like Dennis Breen, Reuben J. Dodd, and Cashel Boyle O'Connor Fitzmaurice Tisdall Farrell, are already established "nearest deviants" whose supposed private oddities serve to divert scandal's destructive bolts wherever the storm clouds of scandal are gathering.[37]

THE ART OF SELF-INCRIMINATION: THE OSCAR WILDE SCANDAL

Homosexuality's emerging status as the epitome of sexual transgression and class-based abuse of power was consolidated in the course of the so-called Cleveland Street affair (1889–1890), which, virtually anomalously among the major late-Victorian sex scandals, seems to have been triggered by a purely accidental disclosure.[38] Police, investigating an unrelated theft, found that some telegraph messenger boys with unexplained money in their possession were working as male prostitutes at 19 Cleveland Street. Had this discovery occurred early rather than late in the 1880s, it would surely have followed the time-honored script of complete suppression or of quietly punishing the prostitutes and discreetly suppressing the identities of their patrons. In neither case would newspapers have reported anything beyond a short, oblique entry among their coverage of court cases. As the prosecutions of the Cleveland Street prostitutes got underway, however, a range of newspapers—most famously the radical *North London Press* and Henry Labouchere's *Truth*—followed the new script established by Healy, O'Brien, and Stead. New Journalists seized on the high status of some of the alleged Cleveland Street patrons, making the house's hidden, scandalous sexual activities emblematic of the general class advantages and protections of the wealthy. Stead himself justly complained of the gross class inequalities evident in the differing treatment of "two noble Lords and other notable persons in society who were accused by witnesses of having been principals in the crime" from that of their "wretched agents" who "are run in and sent to penal servitude."[39]

Once again, however, what the press intended as a mobilizing metaphor rapidly solidified into a superlative atrocity, the horror of which eclipsed the social inequities it originally invoked.[40] Wedded to the gothicized, homophobic discourse that had characterized the modern sex scandal from its inception, Stead, Labouchere, and the radical press succeeded only in suturing together in the public imagination the qualities of male aristocracy and homosexuality. Although the Labouchere Amendment had already criminalized male homosexuality, it was in the course of the Cleveland Street scandal that homosexuality was refigured, through the language of scandal, as class privilege's most appalling and characteristic excess. Thus, over the course of various scandals, social movements addressing national, age, gender, and class inequities coalesced into a powerful media front, the greatest and most lasting if unexpected achievement of which was retrogressive legislation and enhanced social prejudice against homosexual men.

Although the connections between Oscar Wilde's fate, the Labouchere Amendment, and the Cleveland Street affair have been much discussed, the relationship between Wilde's career and the more general scandal milieu in which his public persona was formed has not. To understand Wilde's underexplicated influence on Joyce's art, we must first consider Wilde's scandal work as evolving within a broad scandal context. Wilde, who launched his public career prior to the first Dublin Castle scandal, when homosexuality was decisively outside the scandal lexicon, had early adopted visibility as a reliable form of self-defense. Over time he developed a sort of homeopathic relationship to Britain's rapidly evolving scandal culture by using what could be termed "self-scandalization" to make himself untouchable.

In effect, prior to the mid-1880s, public disclosures of defaming personal details, whether voluntary or involuntary, were protected against by an aura of privacy that rendered them illegible. This was particularly and emphatically true as regards homosexuality. The trope of unspeakability that H. G. Cocks explicates in *Nameless Offences* had served to make Wilde's playful self-revelations a highly serviceable defense against a Victorian culture that could only respond to a gentleman's public avowals of sexual irregularity as an elaborate hoax. (Of course, as shown by public perceptions of Mrs. Crawford during the Dilke scandal, rules for ladies were different.[41]) As the danger of involuntary public exposure in the newspapers grew, Wilde's voluntary public disclosures became, if anything, more incomprehensible. Ever the provocateur, Wilde made such speech acts in various ways on a regular basis and showed every sign of enjoying himself while doing so.[42]

Thus it was at Wilde's own instigation, in the routine pursuit of this strategy of self-scandalization, that the scandal fragment initiating his downfall entered public circulation. The misspelled "somdomite" scrawled on the back of a calling card left for Wilde by the Marquis of Queensberry, the father of Wilde's lover, Lord Alfred Douglas, was the incipient scandal fragment that prompted Wilde, like Dublin Castle's French and Cornwall before him, to initiate ill-considered libel charges, thereby allowing for the transposition of more private details into the public view in the course of three trials and the circulation of their proceedings in the media. As Wilde's biographers and critics often lament, Wilde should have understood that the Cleveland Street affair signaled a radical shift in the late-Victorian symbolic order. His friends certainly did. But the evidence indicates that Wilde stayed the course to his destruction in continuance of a highly serviceable strategy that for quite some time had afforded him both celebrity and safety.

Famously, when pressed either to own or to deny his homosexuality in a court of law, Wilde owned up, though in a circuitous and evasive manner.[43] As Lucy McDiarmid shows, however, Wilde's most celebrated act of self-incrimination had been well rehearsed in his earlier writings.[44] In an impromptu public address following the publication of *The Picture of Dorian Gray*, according to Neil McKenna, Wilde had similarly owned and lauded the love between men after George Curzon, the future viceroy of India, directly accused him of homosexual activities before the Crabbet Park Club. In response, Wilde made an "amusing" and "articulate defense of the love between an older and a younger man, virtually the same rousing speech he was to utter in his second trial,"[45] leaving the disconcerted club members claiming to be wholly convinced of his innocence. Although Wilde's refusal to publicly deny or even hide his desire for other males is frequently cited as the cause of his downfall, it should also be noted that Wilde's public expressions of homoerotic feelings and activities had for an extended period actually served to protect him by rendering unthinkable the signified toward which such signifiers gestured.[46] Oscar Wilde was, in other words, a writer who sought to cope with the growing scandalous visibility of an array of private acts and expressions by publicly associating himself with those acts. Defying the late-Victorian presumption that no one genuinely associated with such activities would voluntarily say so, Wilde employed a pattern of strategic, playful self-exposure as a means to manage his society's growing obsession with the exposure of secrets. As we shall see, it is in this respect, more than any other, that James Joyce, who utilized a similar but exponentially intensified strategy of shameful self-exposure, surely identified with Wilde.

As William Cohen has argued, one key link between the sex scandal and the Victorian realist novel is that many of the best-loved Victorian novelists, including Charles Dickens and George Eliot, themselves lived scandalous lives that set them at odds with their era's paramount codes of respectability. For such writers, Cohen suggests, "literature compensates for or recasts their scandalous lives."[47] But the manner in which literature served to recast a scandalous life was obviously quite different in the work of Wilde than in that of Dickens or Eliot. Whereas Wilde still drew on earlier Victorian strategies of forging a decorous persona in literature and as a cultural commentator in compensation for his indecorous private life, long before his court case he was already intermingling his lofty role of Oxonian cultural arbiter with a plethora of homosexual references, from the green carnation and use of the name "Earnest" (slang for homosexual) and the suggestive term "bunburying" in *The Importance of Being Earnest* to the only lightly coded references to homosexuality in *Dorian Gray* and the occasional public avowal. In this respect, Joyce appears to have followed Wilde, his single hesitation being that Wilde did not go far enough. Inspired by Wilde, Joyce's literature responded to his life scandals in a way that was not only deliberately libelous but also, as Latham argues, deliberately and explicitly self-libeling.[48]

As we shall see, Joyce would repeatedly and extravagantly play on the Wilde trials' most sensational scandal fragment as an emblem for his own literary self-disclosures. Most notably, in the fantastic "Circe" trial scene, Joyce presents Bloom defending himself against a highly evocative piece of evidence: an excrement-stained newspaper sheet. Wilde's cause was lost in the court of public opinion when the newspapers published the damning "Savoy hotel evidence," the centerpiece of which was a chambermaid's testimony that she had found shit stains on Wilde's bed sheets.[49] In the "Circe" trial scene, Bloom is hauled into court on a charge that reenacts this imploding convergence of irreconcilable codes governing private and public decorum: during his morning trip to the jakes, he has defiled Philip Beaufoy's prizewinning story, *Matcham's Masterstroke*, by smearing the sheets of the paradigmatic New Journalist organ, *Titbits*, with "the hallmark of the beast" (15. 844–45). The entire courtroom fantasy in "Circe" pointedly recalls Wilde's public discreditation through the sensational public display of shit-marked "sheets." By coding Bloom's violations as artistic as well as bodily, these proceedings also gesture toward the ways in which Wilde's own writings, both public and private, were transformed into "shit-marked sheets" when they were used against him in court. In this multivalent image of a filthy newspaper, Joyce comically conflates the process by which scandal logic sensationally isolates fragments of the private and gives them new and sensational public meaning with charges against artists who cross the same public/private boundaries with details drawn from private life that are adjudged tasteless and inappropriate for publication.

Bloom, publicly accused of plagiarism he did not commit, embodies both Wilde's and Joyce's position as artistic scapegoat, vulnerable to charges of shameful shit-smearing not because the specifics of their own private lives were any more untoward than those of Bloom in the outhouse, but rather, as Joyce earlier explained, because Wilde's crime, like Joyce's in writing *Ulysses*, "was to have caused . . . a scandal."[50] In other words, Wilde was punished not for his private activities but for drawing attention to them in his art, social life, refusal to flee, and the courts.[51] As I have argued elsewhere, through the figure of the scapegoated Bloom, Joyce suggests a connection between the crimes of Oscar Wilde, who caused a scandal by refusing to cover up his private life when a stray piece of it entered into circulation, and his own scandalous publications.[52] Through scandal work that both emulates and hyperbolically exaggerates that of Wilde, Joyce launched a preemptive attack of the sort that Katherine Mullin finds across his corpus, ridiculing in advance those who would surely claim that his writing was simply an ill-bred assault on the tasteful sensibilities of his betters.[53] Thus through his later scandal work James Joyce made good on Oscar Wilde's conviction that it is "through Art, and Art alone, that we can shield ourselves from the sordid perils of actual existence."[54]

Although Wilde's nondenial of his homosexuality was certainly part of his scandal, ultimately his downfall can be understood as the culmination of a trajectory set in motion by scandals as varied as the Phoenix Park and Maamtrasna murders; the hanging of Myles Joyce and the first Dublin Castle scandal; the Maiden Tribute, Dilke, and Parnell scandals; and the Cleveland Street affair.[55] As we shall see, both the figure of Parnell and the figure of Wilde serve Joyce as resonant markers for the destructive convergence of the private and the public in the context of the political sex scandal and for the accumulated effects of a series of scandals that catalyzed two decisive and seemingly abrupt shifts in the discourse of the time. In the first of these shifts, the fall of Parnell marked the Irish Catholic Church's ideological capture of nationalism (and thus of most nationalists), while the convergence of Parnell's private affairs and his public activities constituted a disastrous collision of the private and public that terminated what had been a promising nonviolent path to Irish independence. In the second such shift, Wilde's third trial and guilty verdict marked the institutionalization of male homosexuality within British scandal culture as the paradigmatic scandal secret, readily available as a symbolic substitute for any other moral failing.

The Oscar Wilde trials are frequently seen as what Brian Lacey calls "the birth of a new kind of consciousness about a particular aspect of the human condition," instituting the visibility of male homosexuality, particularly among middle- and upper-class English men.[56] But within the context of this study, which places Dublin rather than London at its epicenter, the scandalous airing of Oscar Wilde's dirty laundry over the course of the trials signifies quite differently, as the last in a series of political sex scandals that had its start in what was arguably the most significant and abrupt reversal faced by Irish nationalists over the course of the famine-ridden nineteenth century: the Phoenix Park murders. By the time Oscar Wilde brought suit against the Marquis of Queensberry for libel, Healy and O'Brien's innovative use of homosexuality as an anticolonial weapon in the subsequent Dublin Castle scandal had changed the discourse environment in which both the Irish nationalist movement and homosexual men operated. From Joyce's perspective, Oscar Wilde was a last, belated casualty of the Home Rule scandal wars.

To interpret the Parnellite sex scandal as a mode of political allegory is not to reject the commonly accepted psychoanalytic position that bourgeois Irish nationalism exhibited, in Joseph Valente's words, "a racially inflected will to purity" but rather to acknowledge the legal and political power relations through which such a "will to purity" came into being.[57] This new mode of scandal and its defining contribution to the New Journalism more generally was democratizing in its aims, even as it had the simultaneously undemocratic effect of discrediting and silencing sexual dissidents both within and beyond the Irish nationalist community. Most disastrously of all, the new scandal logic unleashed by the first Dublin Castle scandal set at odds private sexual proclivities, coded as deviance, and public political dissent, coded as violence, in a fragmenting and escalating internecine struggle for a mutable, ever-receding moral high ground. It is this reorganization of the body and its capacities for political resistance and erotic surrender into shaming and morally opposed and competing fragments that Joyce attempts to disrupt in his own scandalous writing.[58]

In Joyce's view, as we shall see in the following chapters, the British press had martyred not only Parnell and Wilde but, through them, the broad constituencies they represented: the Irish in the case of Parnell and sexual, social, and political dissidents and artists in the case of Wilde. By conflating the sex scandal with political martyrdom, especially in *Ulysses*, Joyce capitalizes on the new relations of private to public enabled by the New Journalism even as he vigorously contests its scandalizing of collective public identities through the publication of individuals' decontextualized private acts. As we shall see, the strategies by which he does this in his later and best-known works actually originated in his earlier work. Just as Wilde "rehearsed" his speech from the dock in his writing and public utterances well before he delivered it in the form we all now recognize, Joyce's scandal work in *Ulysses* at times draws nearly verbatim from earlier letters and newspaper essays in which he decries the treatment that the Irish and Wilde received at the hands of the British press and employs stylistic strategies he began developing in his earlier newspaper writing, short stories, and *A Portrait of the Artist*. As with other genres that were subject to Joyce's particular brand of appreciative aggression (including sentimentalism and high literary realism), over the course of his development as a writer Joyce both savagely parodied and shamelessly exploited the sensationalizing techniques of the New Journalist political sex scandal.

CHAPTER 3

James Joyce's Early Scandal Work

"Never Write about the Extraordinary"

The pink edition extra sporting of the Telegraph *tell a graphic lie lay, as luck would have it, beside his elbow and just as he was puzzling again, far from satisfied, over a country belonging to him . . . his eyes went aimlessly over the respective captions which came under his special province the allembracing give us this day our daily press.*

— Joyce, *Ulysses*

Let us pry.

— Joyce, *Finnegans Wake*

In both his personal correspondence and his published writing, James Joyce, like many high modernists, deplored the artistically standardizing effects imposed by Britain's commercialized print culture. Owing at least in part to his position as a déclassé, urban, Irish-Catholic outsider, Joyce found the political and aesthetic constraints embedded in print capitalism's prime directive—to "give the public what it wants"—artistically deadening and ethically abhorrent.[1] Indeed, Joyce's hostility toward the press, popular audiences, and commercial writing runs through all of his early writing and thinking.[2] In his earliest published essay, "Ibsen's New Drama" (1900), and in a subsequent private letter, Joyce lauded Henrik Ibsen's magisterial detachment from commercial considerations, while his self-published essay, "The Day of the Rabblement" (1901), castigates W. B. Yeats, Lady Augusta Gregory, and J. M. Synge for placating the conservative Catholic masses. Though George Russell, editor of the *Irish Homestead*, had offered Joyce in 1904 the chance to gain "easily earned money" for something rural and sentimental, cautioning him only to "not shock his readers," Joyce gave him "The Sisters," "After the Race," and "Eveline," stories that provoked a flurry of complaints from shocked readers and lost Joyce the *Homestead* as a venue and income source.[3]

For Joyce, the years following this episode were distinguished by simmering resentments against unresponsive editors and debates and rows with those editors who did take an interest. Throughout his career, Joyce's "mild proud sovereignty" repeatedly offended editors, reviewers, readers, and sometimes even friends and benefactors.[4] He terminated his run as a book reviewer for the *Daily Express* when, having earlier pushed his luck by "slating" Lady Gregory's "drivel to Jaysus" (as Stephen is accused of doing in *Ulysses*), he insulted the newspaper's publisher in a subsequent review. Characteristic of the wrath that Joyce could stir up, his editor not only sacked him but reputedly threatened to assault him.[5]

Following his 1904 removal to the continent, the venue with which Joyce maintained the longest association was the Triestene daily newspaper *Il Piccolo della Sera*, a leftist organ that routinely covered the period's nationalist movements and gladly published Joyce's reflections on Irish culture and the Irish independence struggle.[6] Joyce produced his most explicit reflections on the effects of newspaper and commercial writing in and on Irish society in a series of editorials written for this politically broad-minded and geographically and linguistically detached venue. During these years, Joyce was also completing work on *Dubliners* (1904–1907), fighting to get the collection into print (1905–1914), and revising *Stephen Hero* into *Portrait of the Artist as a Young Man* (1907–1914).[7] Although his early collection of poetry, *Chamber Music*, appeared in print with comparative ease in 1907, the period from 1907 to 1914 was, for Joyce, a difficult one, as the dire implications of his refusal to make terms with the literary marketplace became increasingly clear. Throughout this period, Joyce was incessantly, painfully aware of the ease with which print capitalism's representatives could and routinely did ridicule, scandalize, lock out, and starve artists who lacked what they considered to be the right priorities. As he increasingly recognized the New Journalism's use of scandalous words as weapons and as a means to control artistic output, Joyce started developing a literary praxis capable of wielding those same words as a means of self-defense.[8]

In an exchange with Djuna Barnes, another extravagantly self-libeling modernist, Joyce summarized the counterintuitive strategy he was developing for countering the sensationalizing pressures of print capitalism: "A writer," he asserted, "should never write about the extraordinary. That is for the journalist."[9] If the New Journalist labored to sensationalize the quotidian, Joyce claimed for himself and other serious writers the obverse mission: to reclaim as normal the supposedly shocking. Joyce's representations of various ways in which an author's written words may be used as weapons by and against their creator evince, among other things, his concern for writing's sociosymbolic efficacy, its use value. As we shall see, even in his early work Joyce reflected extensively on the new scandal journalism's use of its victims' own words to discredit them, whether in the court of public opinion or in a court of law. The counterstrategy he was developing in his own scandal work was one that would allow him to unleash some of scandal's social power without his work's instigating or lending itself to hostile diversion into scandal wars not of his choosing.[10]

"ONLY A PAUPER. NOBODY OWNS."

Joyce evinced repeated, even systematic concern for the ways in which words operate in the world, depending on whether they are circulating in the first place as commodities or whether their primary function is expressive. Thus in Joyce's case concerns about protecting his freedom of expression from the commodifying forces of scandal apparently inspired the same tortuous writerly strategies that appealed so powerfully to high modernist arbiters like Ezra Pound and T. S. Eliot, for whom, according to John Wilson Foster, literature was "a taxing and exiguous affair and its proper and deserving readership a select, indeed elite one."[11] That the motivations driving Joyce's predilection for certain kinds of complexity were so different from those of his contemporaries might account for Joyce's ultimately bewildered response to Ezra Pound's ever having welcomed Joyce's "magic flute" into his "big brass band."[12] True, Joyce's youthful complaints against the "rabblement," whose unrefined tastes he perceived as driving not only the newspapers and penny novels but the Irish Revival, closely resemble other modernists' rants against the masses. But as his art evolved, Joyce took his analysis of writing's economic context far beyond the idle exercise of sneering at popular writing and readers from the lofty perch of his rarified work. As Stephen Dedalus repeatedly reflects in *Ulysses*, words produced in exchange for money can often be misappropriated to ends inimical to their writers' interests. Joyce's acute sensitivity to the dangers such hostile misappropriation posed to marginalized writers distinguishes his approach from the haughty suspicion of popularity and commercialism held by most high modernists, whose dread of being seen as what Virginia Woolf termed "middlebrow" had less to do with a fear of depoliticization than with old-fashioned elitism.[13]

As Richard Ellmann bemusedly notes, Joyce was quite complacent about his own and his father's insolvency.[14] In the context of the larger opposition Joyce posits between the exchange value and use value of writing, however, his approving definition of himself as a bankrupt and the son of a bankrupt would appear to be more of a political and artistic manifesto than a mere eccentricity. Throughout his career, Joyce, unlike most modernists, took elaborate steps to avoid writing directly for pay, producing his work within the distinctly anachronistic alternate economic arrangement of patronage. From an early age, James Joyce paid for his own—and later his family's—upkeep with monies obtained from patrons rather than through commissions from publishers or the sale of his completed work. He established his career as an author on this precarious footing despite the extreme poverty it imposed and despite the more remunerative options that were often available to him.[15] Even in his famous and sometimes stunning expressions of ingratitude toward his benefactors Joyce repeatedly emphasized the use value over the exchange value of his artistic output. In *Ulysses*, Joyce repeatedly hints that liberty is abjection's political and existential corollary. His youthful counterpart, Stephen Dedalus, tells Leopold Bloom that he is going into the world to "seek misfortune," while the middle-aged Bloom melancholically reflects, "only a pauper[,] nobody owns" (6.333), as he watches an illegitimate slum child's mourning coach pass by. Later, thinking of his father's suicide, Bloom muses again, "nobody owns" (6.365).

Joyce's equation of principled poverty with freedom complemented his lifelong conviction that writing for pay was simoniacal, amounting to the exchanging of things of the spirit for things of the world. This view apparently began to crystallize as early as 1891, when John Joyce started circulating copies of "Et Tu, Healy." John Joyce's status in the Joycean imaginary as a fulcrum complexly conjoining the freedom afforded by patronage with the worldly snares of simony is evident in his transformation in *Portrait* and *Ulysses* into Simon Dedalus, whose Christian name underscores the simoniacal threat posed to Stephen's art by Simon's alcoholism, which puts the whole family under pressure to pawn or sell (rather than cultivate) any available resource. Joyce's notion of art as sacramental, particularly evident in Stephen Dedalus's evolution from aspiring Catholic priest to artist in *Portrait of the Artist*, reflects Joyce's feeling at this time in his career that, according to his brother Stanislaus, it was "imperative that he should save his real spiritual life from being overlaid and crushed by a false one. . . . He believed that poets . . . were the repositories of the genuine spiritual life of their race, and that priests were usurpers."[16] Joyce emphasizes the spiritual distinction between the instrumental and the expressive in Stephen's ambiguous interaction with the English dean of studies in the final book of *Portrait* (162–66). Refusing Stephen's offer to help him start a fire in his office, the dean tells the young aesthetician, "There is an art to lighting a fire. We have the liberal arts and the useful arts. This is one of the useful arts." Stephen's response—"I will try to learn it"—suggests a decisive early step in the direction of Joyce's mature artistic style, refiguring the Promethian exchange of the eminently useful but also beautiful substance of fire as a claiming rather than a receiving.

The metaphysics underpinning this opposition between the priest and the writer corresponds to the opposition between journalism and "writing" implied by Joyce's comment to Djuna Barnes, perhaps explaining his occasional conflation of journalism and religion, journalists and priests. *Portrait*, for instance, gradually delineates an obverse distinction between the sacralizing functions of the Catholic Mass and of the kind of writing to which Stephen aspires, the former enforcing an absolute distinction between body (profane) and spirit (sacred), the latter incorporating the spirit in the body.[17] *Portrait*'s celebration of Joyce's/Stephen's monistic writing, in which the sacred and the profane commingle, calls attention to the profanatory function of both the church and the newspapers' Manichaean rituals: the Mass deprives ordinary bread of its sacral dimension, while words produced for profit reduce the sacred, transpersonal act of communication to a competitive, individualist quest for "daily bread." It is this profane usurpation of the sacred role of art that Joyce ridicules in *Ulysses* in the quip, "give us this day our daily press" (16.1237–38).

"THE LACONIC ASPECT OF THE INTERPRETER": "IRELAND AT THE BAR"

Produced during a crucial period in Joyce's development of a defensive scandal work, Joyce's Triestene newspaper essays on the Irish question have posed a problem for Joyce scholars because their straightforward use of the sensationalizing conventions of nationalist journalism differs so much from the complex and ambiguous formulations of the same issues in *Ulysses* and *Finnegans Wake*.[18] But if we acknowledge that in both contexts Joyce is ferociously attacking the work of scandal by using elements of scandal discourse, his shift from outraged virtue in his nonfiction writings to the iconoclastic anarchy in much of his fiction becomes ideologically coherent. When we realize that the targets of Joyce's outrage are the formal strategies that rendered Irish nationalists voiceless in the first place, we see, for example, how Joyce's description of the trial and execution of Myles Joyce in "Ireland at the Bar" bears a surprisingly close resemblance to the black comedy of the dying Croppy Boy in the "Circe" episode of *Ulysses*.[19]

Viewed within this trajectory, "Ireland at the Bar" (1907) and "Oscar Wilde: Poet of *Salomé*" (1909), which both appeared in *Il Piccolo della Sera*, demonstrate Joyce's earliest attempts to extend his youthful outrage on behalf of Parnell and the Parnellites to the subject of scandal itself. These essays eulogize two Irish martyrs to the New Journalism: Myles Joyce, wrongfully executed in 1883, and Oscar Wilde, convicted in 1895 of Labouchere's new crime of gross indecency. The following examination of the intricate intertextuality of these two essays shows Joyce uniting and critiquing the scandal figures of the lawless Irish defendant and the scandalous sex pervert "before the bar" of the court and the London press, initiating the tropes connecting newspaper scandal, silencing, entrapment, commodification, and martyrdom that would come to infuse his fiction as well.

Joyce's focus on silencing in these two essays was prefigured, however, in his best-known commentary on the Irish question, the first of the three lectures he delivered at the Università Popolare, Trieste, his 1907 "Ireland: Island of Saints and Sages." Like "Ireland at the Bar," written later that year, "Saints and Sages" focuses on ritualized enactments of socially imposed silence. In his account of the spectacle of Queen Victoria's carriage ride through Dublin "in the midst of a silent people," for instance, he repeatedly condemns the role of the English press, which he lists alongside "the battering ram, the club and the noose" as factors maintaining an insuperable "gulf" between Britain and Ireland (119). He dismisses the supposed "difference of temperament" between the Irish and the English that had become "a commonplace among the columnists of Fleet Street" (118), pointing instead to the crucial role of the press in reasserting these differences whenever understanding and cooperation might threaten to break out.

Although both "Saints and Sages" and "Ireland at the Bar" describe an epistemological breach that, Joyce argues, fatally distorts British audiences' understanding of conditions in Ireland, it is the later "Ireland at the Bar" that systematically examines newspapers' specific role in imposing and sustaining this epistemological disparity. In this essay, Joyce sarcastically inventories the unaccountable ways in which England "proceeds with excellent judgment disposing of the most complicated questions of colonial politics" and concludes that truly, "there is no question more entangled" than the inability on the part of the English to accurately perceive the Irish and of the Irish to accurately represent themselves across a media-generated "abyss" (146). It is with this account of Myles Joyce's trial, written for an Italian audience twenty-five years after the fact, that James Joyce therefore begins to define and formally respond to key conventions of the scandal wars that had shaped the world of his childhood.

In "Ireland at the Bar," Joyce describes in detail an intricate, irrational, and ineffective set of colonial procedures that entrap an Irish-speaking man within a labyrinth of fatally distorting "legal ceremonies" (145). Joyce's account of Myles Joyce's trial merits quotation at length (145):

> The magistrate said:
> 'Ask the accused if he saw the woman on the morning in question.'
>
> The question was repeated to him in Irish and the old man broke out into intricate explanations, gesticulating, appealing to the other accused, to heaven. Then, exhausted by the effort, he fell silent; the interpreter, turning to the magistrate, said:
> 'He says no, your worship.'
> 'Ask him if he was in the vicinity at the time.'
>
> The old man began speaking once again, protesting, shouting, almost beside himself with the distress of not understanding or making himself understood, weeping with rage and terror. And the interpreter, once again replied drily:
> 'He says no, your worship.'

In this depiction, the defendant is trapped and rendered incomprehensible within a labyrinth of words. He is made physically vulnerable by his inability to represent himself despite (and in a sense even owing to) his frantic attempts to make himself understood by a hostile and culturally alien audience.

In case the reader should miss this account's allegorical dimension or the culpability of the press, Joyce explicitly glosses them, declaring that

> the figure of this bewildered old man, left over from a culture which is not ours, a deaf-mute before his judge, is a symbol of the Irish nation at the bar of public opinion. Like him, Ireland cannot appeal to the modern conscience of England or abroad. The English newspapers act as interpreters between Ireland and the English electorate which, though it lends an ear every so often is finally irritated by the eternal complaints of the Nationalist deputies who, it believes, have come to their House with the aim of upsetting the order and extorting money. (146)

Joyce thus equates the "laconic aspect of the interpreter" with the English newspapers' ceremonial display of sensational evidence cherry-picked to reinforce a pre-specified narrative. Whereas Joyce's characterization of Myles Joyce as "left over from a culture which is not ours" corresponds to the racialized, imperialist version of history that Ann McClintock, for instance, has critiqued, it can be argued that Joyce rhetorically recruits his readers into an imagined, shared modernity so as to expand rather than dismiss the political/cultural significance of Myles Joyce's Irishness.[20] By focusing on the language question, Joyce recasts Myles Joyce's trial as a dramatic example of the dangers the tabloid press poses to not only Irish speakers but all Irish *speakers*—i.e., those Irish who speak out publicly in any tongue—if they should lose control over their words.

Joyce informs his Triestene readers that occurrences in Ireland are covered in the English press only when "some trouble breaks out," at which point the shocking details are disseminated across the globe by London newspapers exhibiting "some of the laconic aspect of the interpreter mentioned above" (146). While Joyce describes the voice of British hegemony as at once terse and powerful, he characterizes Myles Joyce by his excessive but failed attempts to communicate. Unlike Parnell, who maintained his much admired self-possession in his dealings with the British state through his famous taciturnity, Myles Joyce is not silent but silenced: he has clearly lost control of his speech and, by analogy, of how he is perceived by the colonial gaze he cannot escape. The premise that absolute verbal self-mastery represents the only means by which an Irish subject can enter the British symbolic order without losing representational control is a cornerstone of Joyce's writings. Indeed, in *Portrait of the Artist*, Joyce's best-known expression of his artistic values, Joyce asserts his determination to maintain artistic and semantic control through a policy of strategic withholding, in a striking *ars poetica* decisively forsaking all weapons save silence and its geographic and intellectual equivalents, exile and cunning (213).[21] An examination of "Ireland at the Bar" shows that some of Joyce's most striking techniques for employing this artistic strategy actually found their start in his nonfiction writing and were developed in direct response to the scandal work of the New Journalism.

"SILENCE, EXILE, AND CUNNING"

Joyce's most characteristic literary deployment of silence has come to be known as the Joycean epiphany, a startling, sometimes violent image or moment whose connection to the preceding narrative is not immediately clear, and "Ireland at the Bar" concludes with a stunning and revealing instance of this trope. For years, Joyce had been experimenting with ending pieces with a tone of abrupt, embittered stoppage. An early example appears, for instance, in his final book review for the unionist *Daily Express*, written in 1903. Although Joyce's review admires this "little, slender starveling of a story"—T. Baron Russell's *Borlase and Son*—he concludes the piece with a sudden jab at Longworth, publisher of both Russell's book and the *Daily Express*, by noting that "the binding of the book is as ugly as one could reasonably

expect" (99). In response, not only did Longworth stop paying Joyce
for book reviews, but the newspaper's editor was said to have "threatened to kick Joyce downstairs if he ever came to the newspaper's offices
again."[22] This enraged reaction to Joyce's seemingly mild provocation
suggests that the editor sensed great danger in Joyce's terse distinction
between Russell's *writing*, presented as an admirable, useful creation,
and Longworth's book, described as an unappealing commodity.
While Joyce further developed the biting non sequitur in subsequent
lectures and newspaper essays, including "Ireland: Island of Saints
and Sages," "Fenianism: The Last Fenian," and "Home Rule Comes
of Age," it is in "Ireland at the Bar" that Joyce's signature conclusion
reaches its full maturity.

Just as the jarring, ambiguous insinuations of the Joycean epiphany supply the antidote to the New Journalist sex scandal's tidy, facile
conclusions, so too does Joyce's treatment of scandal victims work in
opposition to scandal logic's discrediting aims. The figure of the silenced Irish speaker Joyce used in his essay was a common trope in
English-language writing, generally used to authorize a Stead-like act
of gallantry on the part of an English-speaking author who graciously
steps forward to speak on behalf of a purportedly declining and disappearing Irish-speaking community.[23] Although Joyce's representation of Myles Joyce does reproduce a familiar sort of sociocultural
melodrama, staging the victimization of a silenced and abjected Irish
speaker to endorse its claims, Joyce (unlike Stead and other imperial
would-be do-gooders) clearly identifies with the victim whose plight
his essay laments. Through his portrayal of Myles Joyce's wrongful
conviction and execution, Joyce makes visible the double binds be-
setting all "Irish speakers," including himself. In Joyce's account of
Myles Joyce's trial, the Irish-speaking man's fate epitomizes the strictures in which the scandals of the late nineteenth century bound
Irish nationalists: they were either unheard or, if they resisted their
silenced position, construed as linguistically, emotionally, and physically excessive.[24] Early in "Ireland at the Bar," Joyce explicitly defines
his aim in writing it: to "rectify matters a little" so as to be "useful"
(147)—to produce writing with social value. The notable modesty of
this aim contrasts strikingly with the grandiosity of what in *Ulysses*

Joyce would term the "scurrilous effusions of the O'Brienite scribes" (16.1503).

Having established his credibility with this persona, whose humble, reasonable tone eschews both the melodramatic laments of the social savior and the bombastic strains of the scandalmonger, Joyce cunningly subverts the conventional English newspaper discourse that casts Ireland as a land of excessive, irrational violence. In the final paragraphs of the essay, Joyce comments on the distortion created by "the telegrams sent out by London" that suggest to the world that "Ireland is going through a stage of exceptional criminality." At first conceding that "there were, it is true, two violent deaths in Ireland in the past months," he then immediately explodes the readers' expectations by adding that these were "at the hands of English troops" who fired without warning on an unarmed crowd in Belfast. In a parallel construction, Joyce then addresses the other fixture of the newspapers' image of Ireland: the agrarian outrage. Again he concedes that "there were attacks on livestock," then dryly notes that these "did not even happen in Ireland" but in "Great Wyrley in England, where barbaric, insane criminals have been rampaging against livestock for six years." The essay ends on a stunning detail that simultaneously conforms to the rules of New Journalist scandal discourse regarding Irish politics, which frequently gravitated to gore, and egregiously violates them, since the events described happened not in Ireland but in England: "Last week two horses were found dead with the usual cuts to the base of the stomach and their guts spilled out over the grass" (147). By ending with an image so fierce and unexpected that it fully arrests the reader's ongoing dialogue with the writing, Joyce produces an effect directly opposed to that of the tabloid scandal, which seeks to generate in readers the sort of "outrage" or emotional excess that compels an immediate and heated further response. James Joyce, through his choice of a deliberately inapropos scandal fragment, one that is deeply shocking but falls outside the range of scandalous details authorized by the period's scandal discourse, is able to do what Myles Joyce could not: he effectively interrupts the flow of destructive scandal talk before it reaches its foreordained conclusion.[25]

The impossible position of Myles Joyce served James Joyce as a figure for the impossible position of the Irish people as a whole, faced with a campaign of rabid scandalmongering in the English press. Like the Parnellites, whose verbal strategies forged the weapon with which their movement was ultimately destroyed, Myles Joyce's attempts to speak are not just ineffectual but ultimately self-destructive. The defendant's efforts to break out of the cracked looking glass in which he is reduced and distorted only bolster the conviction of his impassive judges that he is emotionally and culturally alien and contemptible, liable to uncontrolled effusions such as the ones of which he stands accused. By telling Myles Joyce's story using rhetorical strategies developed specifically to counter the scandal logic that condemned him to death, James Joyce seeks to shield not one Irish speaker but all Irish speakers from the moral assassinations of the British New Journalism.

"LITERALLY ELECTRIFYING EVERYBODY"

"Ireland at the Bar" thus represents an early theory of scandal and public speech that Joyce further developed in his next essay in *Il Piccolo della Sera*, "Oscar Wilde: The Poet of *Salomé*." Both Myles Joyce and Oscar Wilde were simultaneously overrepresented and underrepresented in the cracked mirror of the British press, and their experiences supplied Joyce with case studies whereby he could examine the function of the mirror itself. The logic that the 1843 changes in libel law had built into British scandal discourse demanded that a subject must first be rendered elusive, secretive, or culturally liminal before that subject's private practices could safely be presumed to demand public-spirited investigation and disclosure.[26] In his Triestene essays, Joyce is beginning to delve into the discourse conditions through which scandal victims are made to appear silent, invisible, and incomprehensible, an exploration that he continues to pursue across a range of categories, including scandalized sexual practices and Irish religious and ethnic identities. Joyce's yoking of the doomed Irish speaker with the invisible homosexual through the figures of Myles

Joyce and Oscar Wilde calls attention to how the representational assertion of absence, silence, or secrecy onto a marginalized subject position constitutes a prerequisite to scandal.

As in his earlier depiction of Myles Joyce's trial, Joyce's depiction
of Wilde in "The Poet of *Salomé*" focuses on ways in which an Irish
subject was reduced to an inchoate, humiliated, and distressed object,
a dehumanized shorthand for the failings of the Irish as a whole. In
both of these essays, Joyce was beginning to investigate a strange form
of harm that he would later term "lovemaking damages," a political
weapon that is (as Bloom reflects in "Eumaeus") one way "of bringing
off a coup" (16.1289). In both, Joyce's focus is the figurative lightning
strike, the moment when scandal's social energies are unleashed—the
moment, as Bloom thinks of it, when the revelation of a "fact" sends
"a thrill . . . through the packed court literally electrifying everybody"
(16.1374). As we have seen, in "Ireland at the Bar," Irish folk culture
itself is metaphorically humiliated, rendered mute, and subsequently
martyred in the person of Myles Joyce, whose designation as "the pa-
triarch of the miserable . . . tribe of the Joyces" suggests an element of
identification on James Joyce's part (145). A similar identification is
betrayed in "The Poet of *Salomé*" by Joyce's emphasis on the young-
adult Wilde's poverty, his inability to support his wife and two children, his having to pawn his "medals, trophies of his academic youth,"
and his obligation to take on demeaning writing jobs of the sort that
Stephen is constantly tempted with in *Ulysses* (149).[27] Moreover, from
the outset of "The Poet of *Salomé*," Wilde is figuratively sutured not
only to Joyce but to precolonial Irish culture. Joyce asserts that Wilde's
elaborate name, Oscar Fingal O'Flahertie Wills Wilde, "symbolizes
him," linking him to the "nephew of King Fingal and only-born
of Ossian," who was "to meet his civil death while sitting crowned
with vine leaves at table and discussing Plato," and to "O'Flahertie, a
fierce Irish tribe whose destiny it was to besiege the gates of medieval
towns," wild Irish holdouts whose names "struck terror into peaceful
men" (148).[28]

Having established Wilde and his art as personal and Irish cultural avatars, Joyce describes Wilde's final trial as a shattering lightning strike that reduced Wilde's beautifully civilized life and art to

ruins. Like Myles Joyce, Parnell, and Ireland itself, Wilde was transformed by British legal and representational processes into an inchoate object of contempt:

> His fall was greeted by a howl of puritanical joy. On hearing of his
> condemnation, the mob that was gathered in front of the court-
> house began to dance a pavane in the muddy street. The newspa-
> per journalists were admitted into the prison and, through the
> window of his cell, were able to feed on the spectacle of his shame.
> White bands covered over his name on theatre billboards; his
> friends abandoned him; his manuscripts were stolen while he un-
> derwent his prison sentence of two years' hard labour. His mother
> died under the shadow of shame; his wife died. He was declared
> bankrupt, his belongings were auctioned off and his sons were
> taken away from him. When he came out of prison, thugs under
> the instructions of the noble Marquess of Queensberry were lying
> in wait for him. He was driven, like a hare hunted by dogs, from
> hotel to hotel. Hotelier after hotelier drove him from the door,
> refusing him bread and board, and at nightfall he finally ended
> up under his brother's window crying and blubbering like a child.
> (149–50)

Whereas Wilde's extravagant loss of physical and emotional control
in this final image resembles that of Myles Joyce, his hunted, hounded
figure also converges with that of Parnell, whose fate Joyce describes
in "The Shade of Parnell" (another *Il Piccolo della Sera* essay, published in May 1912) as "hounded by the Irish press," forced to flee
"from country to country, from city to city, 'like a hunted hind'"
(196). Above all, the specific details foregrounded here make clear
that Wilde is not just one isolated victim but, as the most recent of the
Irish scandal martyrs invoked by Joyce, an emblem for precolonial
Irish culture and resistance. Wilde's cultural productions are stolen.
His community and his family are broken up; his loved ones die while
he is helpless to save or comfort them; his wealth is confiscated; his
children are lost to him. He is driven from place to place and refused
"bread and board" (150) in a society overflowing with surplus, just as

in "Ireland at the Bar" Joyce describes the Irish as seeing "pastures full of well-fed cattle while an eighth of the population is . . . without the means of subsistence" (147). As in that earlier essay, Joyce in "The Poet of *Salomé*" uses narrative strategies specifically calibrated to neutralize scandal's inflammatory, dehumanizing effects: his description of the crowd's puritanical howls and dance in the muddy street symbolically transfers the shameful, dirtying effects of the Wilde scandal from its object to its audience.

A person less similar to a wild O'Flahertie than Wilde would be hard to imagine; Oscar Wilde's well-known preference for Paris and Rome over Kilkenny and Dingle exceeded even that of Joyce's Hiberno-averse Gabriel Conroy. Joyce's transfusion of wild Irishness into his representation of Wilde is thus a flagrantly textual construct, one that reflects Joyce's own sense of himself as a persecuted artist liable to being silenced and dismissed because of his Irish subject position. As he did in his characterization of Myles Joyce, James Joyce makes the story of an Irish speaker persecuted by newspapers both personal and national. This construction of Wilde allows Joyce to develop and extend his critique of newspapers, and specifically newspaper scandals, as keeping him, Ireland, and the Irish as a whole in a marginalized and silenced position.

In both "The Poet of *Salomé*" and "Ireland at the Bar," Joyce presents the London press as a distorting lens through which only part of an otherwise inaccessible story is visible. In "Ireland at the Bar," Myles Joyce is depicted as obscured both through time and distance: "left over from a culture which is not ours," he has been shorn of the dense network of private specificities within which the known details of his life might have made sense. These specifics have been trebly screened out, first by the "laconic interpreter," then by the exclusively Anglophone reporters, and finally by the attenuation imposed by both cultural and geographic distance. Most graphically, Joyce figures this distance as traversed only by "the dispatches received from London which, while they may be lacking acrimony, have some of the laconic aspect of the interpreter mentioned above," and which arrive at the doors of "the real sovereign of Ireland, the Pope . . . like so many dogs in church; their cries, weakened by so long a journey, hav[ing] almost died out by the time they reach the bronze door" (146).

Similarly, in "The Poet of *Salomé*," the reader watches as Wilde is transformed by the courts and the newspapers into a sensationally commodified figure: "The newspaper journalists were admitted into the prison and, through the window of his cell, were able to feed on the spectacle of his shame" (149). Joyce repeatedly describes English reporters viewing and depicting Wilde in a manner that misappropriates Wilde's scandalous, self-created celebrity as their own "daily bread." In Joyce's account, the English press views Wilde through an aperture, delivering him up as a static and partial spectacle of shame to their equally rapacious readers without any explanatory context. Ultimately, this passage counters the British press's scandalous representation of Wilde as an aristocratic monster of perversion by reframing him instead as an Irish artist who, like Myles Joyce, was martyred by the British press. In the essay's culminating tableau, Joyce compares the scandal journalists who discredited Wilde to the Roman soldiers who gambled for Jesus's clothes, suggesting that to Wilde's tombstone should be added a line from Psalm 22, "they divide my garments among them and cast lots for my clothes" (151). In this economical final image, Joyce introduces what will become a recurrent trope for scandal in his later work. He imagines the New Journalists picking through dirty laundry as simoniacs exchanging things of the spirit for things of the world and as thieves or pishoguerists seeking gain through the malicious misappropriation of their victim's personal effects.

"TO LOOK UPON ITS DEADLY WORK": JOYCE'S EARLY FICTION

In these essays for *Il Piccolo della Sera*, we can therefore see Joyce beginning to work out solutions to problems he had been addressing in his creative writing since the age of nine: why, how, and under what circumstances words can do violence and how dangerous words can be deflected, defused, or undone. The New Journalist sex scandal offered Joyce not only an illustration of how words become weapons but a repository of strategies for redeploying dangerous words in self-defense. In *Dubliners* and *Portrait of the Artist*, Joyce further developed both his theory of and practical responses to scandal, devoting extensive attention to scandal's subtle power to reorder social relations. The representational crack that divides people's lives as they are lived from people's lives as they can be discussed, even in private conversation, troubles the young characters in the earliest *Dubliners* stories, while the collection's later stories increasingly focus on the specific problems this divide poses for adult writers and artists. It is precisely this crack that Joyce sought, in the *Il Piccolo della Sera* essays, *Dubliners*, and *Portrait*, "to rectify a little" and later, in *Ulysses*, to disable entirely.

While newspaper readers no doubt enjoyed the unprecedented access to embarrassing private details that the emergent scandal journalism afforded them, Joyce's representations of his Dubliners' inner lives continually remind us that newspapers were also arousing new anxieties concerning the safety of the private sphere (as shown in Figure 3.1). In *Dubliners* and in *Portrait*, Joyce both explores and combats the effects of newspaper culture on Irish consciousness, answering the sensationalizing quality of the New Journalism with his own mode of "scrupulous meanness." The resulting narratives ostentatiously suppress the conventionally scandalous while faithfully reporting all that remains: the improperly private. By producing what are, in effect, scandals with the scandal fragments omitted, Joyce created stories full of scandal-like rituals and speech acts that do not carry the malignant force of scandal. Through this strategy of obverse suppression—a distinct alternative to the sensational scandal work of Parnell, Healy, Stead, and even Wilde—Joyce forged a representational strategy calibrated to substitute his own "nicely polished mirror" for the "cracked lookingglass" of the New Journalism. Both *Dubliners* and *A Portrait of the Artist as a Young Man* direct our focus away from sensational scandal fragments and onto their characters' gnawing unease concerning their own and others' potentially scandalous but unspecified private transgressions.

Figure 3.1   A man suffering from the paranoid delusion that Oscar Wilde is hiding in his bedroom plunges through his bedroom window. *Illustrated Police News*, April 27, 1895. © The British Library Board.

Through the leitmotif of the "brewing scandal," in *Dubliners* Joyce explores the paranoid semipublic, semiprivate self-consciousness of the citizens of the New Journalism's empire, particularly at the economic and regional outskirts of respectability.[29] From the outset, the stories render in minute detail how scandalous narratives are both communicated and suppressed by the conventions of polite middle-class discourse.[30] The "strangely-sounding" terms "simony," "paralysis," and "gnomon" with which the protagonist in "The Sisters" is preoccupied serve as appropriately esoteric keys to understanding the stories as thematizing partly occluded scandals. "Simony," as we have seen, was for Joyce epitomized by the commodification of art and sexuality.[31] Joyce's image patterns treating scandal as a transgressive—even sacrilegious—theft operate along precisely these lines, converting what might be sacred rites within the realm of human relations into desacralized commodities.

The other two terms are no less evocative. Read in the context of scandal, "paralysis," *Dubliners'* most extensively explicated trope, illustrates the entrapment and loss of agency that Joyce first examined in the figures of Myles Joyce and Oscar Wilde. The panic fueled by scandal culture underlies some of the collection's most memorable moments of paralysis, particularly in "Eveline," which ends with both the title character and the reader frozen, unable to rationally weigh the relative risks of staying in an abusive situation or of escaping to a world the newspapers depict as teeming with disguised "decoys" on the prowl for girls to sell into sex slavery (or, like Jack the Ripper, to eviscerate).[32] Similarly, the child protagonists of "An Encounter" are confronted with a man who appears to be an escapee from the tabloids, a "queer old josser" who in his very person serves as a warning against straying outside the narrow moral and physical bounds endorsed by the New Journalism. The ambiguous but central relationship in "The Sisters" between a deceased priest and a young boy serves as an object lesson in the paralyzing, silencing effects of scandal culture on middle-class discourse: the boy himself has no means to assess, let alone convey, the significance of their bond, while the adults around him are constantly referring to it in a way that arouses his anxiety without articulating their specific concerns. "Clay's" Maria, too, is in some way trapped in a Magdalene laundry, perhaps (as Martha Stallman has argued) to atone for an early transgression such as an extramarital pregnancy.[33] Viewed this way, "Clay" becomes a story of a woman for whom paralysis was the only alternative to scandal. "The Boarding House," in turn, recounts the story of a passive young couple manipulated into marriage in order to stave off a sex scandal, an attempt to "fly by the nets" that (as we learn in *Ulysses*) will spawn a new array of discrediting open secrets.[34]

The term "gnomon," too, is suggestive of scandal's operations. Its geometrical meaning refers to a shape that is missing a piece of precisely the same shape in miniature, one that may also denote the answer to a riddle.[35] As such, the figure of the gnomon serves as the representation of a signature formal strategy in Joyce's early narratives: conveying everyday scandals from which one key piece of evidence has been removed. These stories create their odd effects specifically through their suppression of key information without which a reader is morally and epistemologically hobbled or paralyzed, unable to assess with certainty what has happened, what it means, or whether certain characters or actions are good or bad.[36] For instance, in "An Encounter," the Old Josser's presumed masturbation can never be proven or disproven; textual confirmation of its occurrence is withheld even as its presumed occurrence insistently colors the rest of the story. Read in this way, these accounts are the opposite of sensational news items: rather than forcibly reorienting the reader's moral perspective with a decontextualized, deplorable detail—a scandal fragment—Joyce's stories confront us with the practical limits of our competency to judge and act in the face of information that is inevitably, like a gnomon, incomplete.

As Joseph Valente and I have argued, in both *Dubliners* and *Portrait* specific moments of sexual initiation—instances when a subject absorbs unfamiliar sexual information at the emotional, physiological, or intellectual level—supply a lens through which Joyce staged the traumatic incommensurability or crack between private experience and public accounts of the said experience.[37] In *Dubliners*, this disjunction is first invoked in the oft-noted ellipses in the second paragraph of its opening story, "The Sisters," which place under erasure elements of private experience that deviate too scandalously from permissible public accounts of priests' lives. A similar discrepancy, this time between courtly love and consumer capitalism at the colonial periphery, is mapped out in "Araby," while apparent but unspecifiable discrepancies between popular romance narratives and real-life encounters between the sexes are limned in "Eveline," "The Boarding House," "An Encounter," "Clay," "Two Gallants," and "A Painful Case."[38] As numerous critics have noted, in all of these cases, the smooth surface of polite social narrative insisted upon and reified by scandal culture is broken by symptomatic interruptions or incongruous, inassimilable details hinting at an alternate story obstructed by the surface account.[39]

As he did in "Ireland at the Bar," Joyce closes several of the stories in *Dubliners* with shocking, seemingly incongruous images of ambiguous meaning, fragmentary evidence of unspoken crimes that nicely parody the scandal fragments prized by New Journalists and their readers. This trope appears in the form of the broken chalice in "The Sisters," the gold coin in "Two Gallants," and even the tritely sentimental poem read by the journalist Joe Hynes at the end of "Ivy Day in the Committee Room." These are impotent scandal fragments, supplying empirical proof of improprieties that are unspecifiable at least in part because they are not among the conventional synechdoches for particular transgressions employed by the New Journalist newspaper scandal (such as a hotel receipt, a poem, or dirty sheets) that were so readily understood by contemporary newspaper readers, critics, and juries.[40]

While an understanding of Joyce's stylistic responses to scandal is crucial, it is equally important to note that many of the stories in *Dubliners* also engage with the subject thematically. In "A Little Cloud," for instance, the affective politics of British print capitalism are made painfully explicit in the would-be writer Little Chandler's slavish and unsuccessful attempts to solicit the approval of his former colleague, Ignatius Gallaher.[41] Little Chandler, for whatever reason, cannot produce the sort of misty Celtic poeticism he knows English editors want, filling him with a frustrated self-hatred he directs outward toward his infant son, while Gallaher, in a moment of self-disclosure, complains of exhaustion brought on by endless pressure to dig up "copy"—scandal fragments—so as to have "something new in your stuff" (61). In "Counterparts," Little Chandler's ominous older alter ego Farrington is a nightmarish rendition of the Irish writer who stays in Ireland, mindlessly copying the words of others while living for the perpetually receding future moment when he can triumphantly assert his own viewpoint and have it affirmed. In the final passages of "Ivy Day in the Committee Room," the hardened careerism that, in Joyce's view, defined post-Parnellite Irish politics is protectively veiled by the noble sentiment with which Joe Hynes commemorates Parnell. "A Painful Case" juxtaposes the obscure complexities surrounding a failed sexual overture with a brief news report concentrating all blame for the "painful case" of Mrs. Sinico's sordid death onto the woman herself. The facile moral summation of this casually sensationalizing newspaper item brilliantly dramatizes the vast moral distance between quotidian life and the conventions of contemporary print capitalism.[42]

In "A Mother," the social power of scandal is embodied by Mr. O'Madden Burke, a journalist for the *Freeman's Journal* who, in both this story and *Ulysses*, serves as a figure for the nationalist press. The story's protagonist, Mrs. Kearney, worries that her daughter, Kathleen, will not be fully paid for accompanying the singers at a concert series sponsored by the local nationalist committee. As Valente and Patrick Bixby have noted, Mrs. Kearney's downward trajectory reenacts Parnell's descent, brought on by a trial in the court of public opinion.[43] As Mrs. Kearney becomes increasingly frantic on finding herself stonewalled, O'Madden Burke declares her use of the Parnellite tactics of obstruction and boycotting against the male organizers as "the most scandalous exhibition he had ever witnessed" (126), reducing her attempt to participate in the nationalist movement on her own terms to a scandal fragment, a shocking and stigmatizing deviation from Irish norms of gendered middle-class gentility. In what will become an intertextual joke in *Ulysses* when Myles Crawford condemns the innocently outraged Tim Healy as "a sweet thing in a child's frock," Mrs. Kearney's scandalous fall occurs when a character named Healy, a sweet thing in a frock, flirts with O'Madden Burke, then usurps Kathleen's position as accompanist so that thereafter it is she who will call the nationalist tune.

But it is the collection's final story, "The Dead," in which suppressed private details pose a constant threat to established social orders, that represents the culmination of James Joyce's early scandal work, incorporating stylistic strategies of counterscandal and references to real-life scandals and culminating in the surfacing of a long-suppressed sexual secret. Like Joyce, the short story's Europhilic protagonist, Gabriel Conroy, has written book reviews for the Dublin-based unionist *Daily Express* and is subtly compared to Parnell and W. T. Stead. Joyce alludes to the Maiden Tribute scandal by assigning to an obscurely damaged young maid the name of Lily, the false name

Stead had ascribed to Eliza Armstrong, the impoverished "maid" whom he abducted. Lily the caretaker's daughter resembles her scandalous namesake in age, class, and sexual vulnerability; her response to Gabriel's intrusion into her personal affairs, that men are "all palaver and what they can get out of you," recalls the nature of Stead's accounts of his transaction with Armstrong, in which the altruism purported by his purple prose belied his willingness to take advantage of her for his own political and commercial ends.

The Parnell scandal also surfaces in "The Dead." Immediately prior to the moment Miss Ivors confronts Gabriel with her discovery that he is the "G. C." who reviews books for a pro-unionist newspaper, Gabriel notices a decorative needlework picture of the "two princes being stabbed in the tower." This image both recalls the assassination of Caesar figured in "Et Tu, Healy" and reminds Gabriel of a needlework vest covered with heads of foxes, an allusion to Parnell's most notorious alias, the Healyite scandal fragment "Mr. Fox." Like Tim Healy and the anti-Parnellites, Miss Ivors embarrasses a political opponent by confronting him with an alias he has used to maintain a safe distance between his public and private activities and uses the newspapers to enhance her own social standing by discreditably exposing another.

It is also through Miss Ivors that the normally taboo topic of Gretta's Galwegian origins, which Gabriel's "West Briton" mother has permanently designated shameful, is dragged into the open. Gretta's childhood in Galway has been so habitually denied and repressed by the couple that when Miss Ivors asks directly if Gretta is from Galway, Gabriel responds that her people are (coldly denying even the existence of Gretta's youth, a phenomenon that Jane Elizabeth Dougherty describes as a widespread cultural repression of Irish girlhood in much of Irish literature). This time, however, we see how the machinations of the media scandal can be confounded by earlier, counterhegemonic scandal forms: in this case, the broadside ballad. Bartell Darcy's singing of "The Lass of Aughrim," in which a seduced and abandoned woman laments the faithlessness of the lord who gave her a ring that had no value, represents a scandal involving women's sexuality, Irishness, and class from the perspective of the scandal

Figure 1.5   Charles Stewart Parnell as "the Crowbar King." *Saint Stephen's Review,* December 27, 1890. © The British Library Board

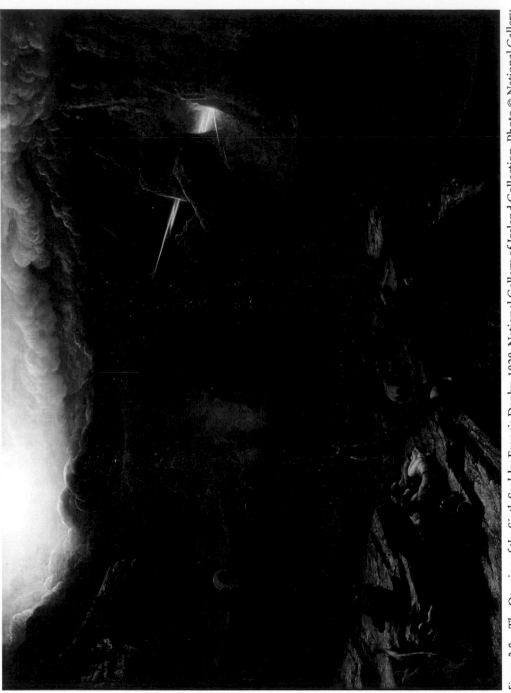

Figure 3.2 *The Opening of the Sixth Seal*, by Francis Danby, 1828. National Gallery of Ireland Collection. Photo © National Gallery of Ireland.

victim. This powerful and moving expression of an earlier folkloric moral framework leads Gretta to reassert the importance of a long-suppressed scandal fragment of her own: her youthful love affair with a poor Galwegian boy, Michael Furey. Whereas Gabriel has responded to the threat of scandal with the fear and secrecy that such threats both demand and use as tautological evidence, Gretta has found in Irish art the language with which to reclaim a valuable memory that she had disavowed.

When Gretta finally speaks of this split-off, shameful fragment that she has kept submerged to protect her marriage, the quiet breaking of this smallest of possible scandals within a community of two finally discredits in Gabriel's eyes the Anglicized middle-class norms to which he has hopelessly aspired and to which he has sacrificed his wife's (and presumably his children's) individual and cultural specificity. Thus in "The Dead," we see Joyce's first counterscandal, in which he inverts the power of sex scandal to maintain or even radically extend middle-class norms. Here the emergence of a suppressed sexual detail—one drawn, importantly, from Joyce's relationship with Nora Barnacle—discredits the regionally and culturally unmarked middle-class propriety that Gabriel and Gretta have struggled to sustain at the expense of her very sexual subjectivity.

"THERE IS ANOTHER WAY": *A PORTRAIT OF THE ARTIST*

While the radical discrepancy between the discourse of newspaper scandal and lived personal experience had already structured the short stories in *Dubliners*, Joyce further emphasized this highly interactive cleavage in his largely autobiographical coming-of-age novel, *A Portrait of the Artist as a Young Man*. In the context of this study, we can see that the explicit story of Stephen Dedalus's heterosexual development in a society rocked by the Parnell scandal is shadowed by a more elusive narrative arc that maps Stephen's silently growing awareness of heterosexuality's unspeakable twin, homosexuality, against the backdrop of the Dublin Castle, Cleveland Street, and Wilde scandals. Stephen's emerging consciousness of the many possible nuances and colorations that inform relations between males in a simultaneously patriarchal and homophobic society extends from the much-discussed Clongowes smugging scandal to Stephen's unspoken decision to put a few national borders between himself and Cranly following Cranly's declaration of romantic interest, the latter an implied narrative of erotic self-positioning in post-Wilde Ireland that Joyce elaborates on in *Ulysses*.[44]

In *A Portrait of the Artist*, Joyce extensively deploys the strategy of palimpsestic overlay established in *Dubliners*, in which an array of scandalous improprieties lurk beneath the surface of his seemingly straightforward and even banal scenes of lower-middle-class life. As Dettmar has argued, the panic that spreads among the boys at Clongowes in response to rumors surrounding the smugging episode early in the novel makes visible the wider panic that homosexual scandals unleashed in Ireland while simultaneously establishing a covert counternarrative concerning the specific fears of an artistic male youth in the wake of the Wilde trials, a scandal that had powerfully conjoined the public identity of the male artist/aesthete with particular proscribed sexual desires and acts. Even prior to the smugging episode, waves of similarly acute anxiety had broken out in Stephen's home in response to a series of miniature scandals described in *Portrait*'s first chapter. In the earliest of these, Joyce depicts a small-scale riot in Stephen's household in response to his revelation of a forbidden desire: his scandalous pronouncement that he will grow up to marry the Protestant Eileen Vance.

The little boy's imaginative exploration of growing up and marrying precipitates a frenzy on the part of his female caregivers calibrated to traumatically obliterate any such future possibility. When he attempts to escape them, he is chased, as in Joyce's descriptions of both Parnell and Wilde. As he hides under a table, his nurse, Dante, threatens him with a fate reminiscent of Stead's thunderbolt: if he does not recant, she claims, eagles will pull out his eyes.[45] In addition to the classic Freudian significance of the threat to Stephen's eyes,[46] this image and others in the scene include some of Joyce's characteristic figures for scandal. The eagle associated in "Et Tu, Healy" with Parnell's heroic impassivity in the face of scandal is here refigured as the obscure but terrible retribution elicited by unsanctioned sex acts. It is significant that the threat of this Jovian punishment comes from Dante, who was modeled on Joyce's childhood governess, Mrs. Conway. Conway was undoubtedly the origin for Joyce's conception of thunder and lightning as expressing the wrath of a scandalized God: according to biographer Peter Costello, she frequently took the young Joyce children to the National Gallery on Merrion Square to look at Francis Danby's *The Opening of the Sixth Seal*, an enormous, sublime rendering of the apocalypse in which lightning gives spectacular form to God's wrath (Figure 3.2).[47] *Portrait*'s first representation of sex scandal as a ubiquitous and terrifying threat thus prefigures the later Christmas dinner table scene in which Dante hurls another figurative lightning bolt, the fire and brimstone sermons that terrify Stephen into confessing, and the moment in *Ulysses*'s "Oxen of the Sun" when Stephen is once again terrified by the roar of thunder.[48]

The earliest pages detailing Stephen's arrival at Clongowes, the boarding school for sons of the Catholic gentry in which he (like James Joyce) is briefly enrolled, record this period's social anxieties concerning the protection of other males' privacy when Stephen's father, Simon, cautions him "never to peach on a fellow," that is, never to pass on discrediting evidence.[49] Stephen's first brief encounter with the other boys whose private activities he had been instructed to protect enacts not only a form of playground pishoguery but the impact of society-wide debates concerning private sexual morality on Irish subjectivity. When Wells, acting as an investigative reporter for this small society, demands to know whether Stephen kisses his mother good night, Stephen is subjected to a form of hazing in which his private practices are unexpectedly brought to the attention of his classmates. Stephen anxiously seeks to formulate a publicly acceptable answer, stating first that he does, earning him jeers, and next that he does not, earning further jeers. This instance of schoolboy meanness calls attention to the fundamental incommensurability of private acts with public norms. Private acts are shaming ultimately *because* they are private, and by definition not to be exposed in the public realm; it is this very categorical transposition that lends to the publically exhibited private act its power to fascinate and to shame.

Within the context of this period's intense representational warfare over Irish manliness that Valente describes, if Stephen says he does kiss his mother, then he is too soft or effeminate, whereas if he says he does not, he is barbarous. In either case, the humiliating burden of Irish Catholic masculinity is, for this moment, his to bear on behalf of the group as a whole.[50]

The cruel double bind in which Stephen is trapped when questioned about kissing his mother is followed by two additional and escalating acts of bullying by Wells, both of which are suggestive of scandal. In the first, Wells attempts to dispossess Stephen of an emblem of his genteel origins—his snuffbox—in exchange for a "seasoned hacking chestnut," expecting Stephen to pretend to accept what is actually a theft as a trade and thus to be complicit in his own exploitation, as writers must when they trade away power over their own words in exchange for subsistence wages. Stephen refuses, and the coercive nature of Wells's purportedly fair proposition becomes plain in the consequential incident in which Wells, in retaliation, literally dirties him by shouldering him into an open cesspool.

After undergoing, like Parnell, a series of raids on his private life and a defiling fall, Stephen becomes sick "in his heart" (25) and winds up in the infirmary, where he is befriended by Athy, whose superior knowledge of the world is demonstrated through both his familiarity with newspapers and his ability to negotiate access to them. He recommends newspapers to the young Stephen for their bounty of information about "accidents, shipwrecks, sports and politics," but adds, in a reference to the Parnell split, then in full cry, that currently the newspapers are "full of politics." Yet, as Vicki Mahaffey observes, in his explanation of the "old riddle" he poses to Stephen, Athy also hints that there is another answer: it is possible to respond effectively to double-binding assertions and to resist scandal's power to arbitrarily cleave the world into light and darkness.[51] In what is surely a double entendre for the polite, chaffing homoerotic banter of which Athy, prefiguring Buck Mulligan, is a confident master (it will later be Athy who supplies the most complete and satisfactory explication of the smuggling scandal), he tells Stephen, "There is another way, but I won't tell you what it is" (35).

Joyce's goal of aquiline ascendance above the note of print capitalism, first registered in "Et Tu, Healy" when the martyred Parnell/Joyce surveys the world from a lofty perch far above the "rude din" of scandal journalism, was sincere, artistically valuable, and doomed from the start. Indeed, the elaborate self-ridicule Joyce inscribes in the discrepancy between Stephen's Daedalean "flight by the nets" at the end of *Portrait* and the implied Icaran crash that has landed him back in Dublin at the beginning of *Ulysses* specifically encodes the young Joyce's inability to consistently maintain his preferred stance of lofty economic and aesthetic independence.[52] Thus the neat division between journalism and creative writing implied in Joyce's advice to Barnes belies his works' complex and extensive interplay between commercial speech acts authorized by "extraordinary" sensational fragments and serious "unsensational" writing that respects the sacred mystery of all life, despite their seemingly opposed representational, aesthetic, and ethical imperatives. As suggested by the failure of Stephen's first attempt to simultaneously soar beyond and raise himself up by means of the newsprint labyrinth in which Ireland was debilitatingly hemmed, Joyce's artistic efficacy was both threatened and enabled by the reifying forces of print capitalism.[53] As Joyce learned young, to soar high like Icarus, as had Parnell, Stead, and Wilde, was to court a disastrous fall. The Daedalean strategy he began to refine in response was to fly low, alert and responsive to conditions on the ground. As we shall see, it is in *Ulysses* that Joyce most fully works out the connections between Ireland and scandal journalism that he first explored in his early writings, stylistically and narratively invoking the figures of Parnell, Stead, Wilde, and other scandal martyrs to contest scandal's destructive cultural, political, and ethical effects.

CHAPTER 4

Reinventing the Scandal Fragment

"Smiling at Wild(e) Irish"

Butter, that's a thing that's much meddled with. On the first of May before sunrise it's very apt to be all taken away out of the milk. And if you lend your churn or your dishes to your neighbour, she'll be able to wish away your butter after that.

—Quoted in Lady Gregory, *Visions and Beliefs in the West of Ireland*

'Twas rank and fame that tempted thee, 'Twas empire charmed thy heart.

—*The Rose of Castile*, Act III, quoted in *Ulysses*

Although the figure of Oscar Wilde may not frame all of *Ulysses* in the same fashion Parnell frames *Portrait of the Artist*,[1] his appearance in the early pages of the novel signals the central role that Wilde, as artist and as symbol, will play in this, Joyce's most extended critique of scandal. In the opening episode, "Telemachus," Joyce's artistic alter ego, Stephen Dedalus, is obliged continually to defend himself against the simoniacal or, more accurately, pishogueristic encroachments of his housemate, Buck Mulligan. Whereas Joyce's likening of scandal to simony, taken from Catholicism, evokes scandal's transformation of the sacred into the profane for profit, his likening of scandal to pishoguery, a cultural practice drawn not just from Irish folklore but specifically from the folklore collections of Revivalist cultural arbiters like Lady Gregory, emphasizes the means by which those sacred fragments are obtained and distributed. In "Telemachus," Mulligan's repeated attempts to pick through Stephen's personal effects and private life in search of shameful fragments that he can sell draw the imagery of scandal as simony, established at the end of "Oscar Wilde," into the thematics of middle-class pishoguery that emerge in *Dubliners* and *Portrait* and proliferate throughout *Ulysses*. This episode dramatizes the dilemma of the Irish artist by linking the efforts of Mulligan and Haines to make Stephen their pishogue through a series of petty misappropriations to scandal through both explicit and stylistic references to Wilde.

Within the Irish oral tradition, pishoguery is a sort of malignant magic that is brought about through or enables the movement of private effects outside of their proper sphere. In Irish folk culture, pishoguery covers a wide range of sociosymbolic activities; "pishogue" can designate either pishoguery's practitioner or its victim, or even the benevolent healer called on to undo its effects. It may also denote the bit of private matter—for instance, hair or fingernails—used for the purpose of malign magic.[2] Joyce's work makes clear that he was quite aware of this tradition. In *Ulysses*, for instance, he invokes pishoguery by name twice: in the "Cyclops" episode, when the Citizen describes Bloom's counterpart, Dennis Breen, as a pishogue, and in "Circe," in which Molly dismisses Bloom using the same term. In one sense, Joyce uses the odd term "pishogue" in his work in much the same way (as Kevin Dettmar observes) that he uses "smugging": as a flagrantly opaque scandal term that is all the more potent for its indeterminacy. During the Parnell split, Tim Healy had openly gloried in the power of nonsensical name calling, categorically refusing to engage Parnell and his supporters on the more precarious terrain of reasoned debate.[3] This should alert us to the recurring significance of flagrant opacity in the many quasi-scandalous rites of discreditation and exclusion in Joyce's work, from casual pub gossip to elaborate curses and rituals. But Joyce also uses the *concept* of pishoguery in his writing, illustrating the sorts of petty, mean pilfering that unleash the wrathful thunderbolts that strike down scandal victims like Oscar Wilde.

That Joyce had long pondered his own artistic aspirations in light of Wilde's fate is elegantly demonstrated by a letter Joyce wrote to his brother Stanislaus in 1906, three years before the publication of "Oscar Wilde: Poet of *Salomé*." Joyce's reflections on the personal and artistic implications of Wilde's simultaneous invocation and obscuring of scandalous bonds between men in this letter prefigure the meditation in "Telemachus" on the murky and vacillating line between respectable and deviant male bonds. As in "Telemachus," in this letter Joyce probes the characteristic scandal-induced social and literary question that Eve Sedgwick famously elaborates in *Between Men*: In a power structure predicated on close bonds between definitively heterosexual males, how close is *too* close? In this letter, as in "Telemachus," Joyce's then-disintegrating friendship with Oliver St. John Gogarty supplies the test case, while Wilde supplies the standard against which Joyce measures his own and Gogarty's respective attempts to manage their intimacy—as men and as artists—in a perilous and unpredictable habitus.

In the two years since they had cohabited in the Martello Tower in Sandymount, south of Dublin, in the summer of 1904, Joyce had fallen out of touch with the real-life counterpart of *Ulysses*'s Buck Mulligan. To Stanislaus, Joyce expresses hurt, or at least annoyance, that Gogarty had married without bothering to inform him, adding that he assumed Gogarty "wouldn't dare present me to his wife." Although this presumed fear could betoken general class snobbery or a more specific wish on Gogarty's part to put their days of shared drinking and whoring behind him, it is suggestive that Joyce immediately follows this reference to Gogarty's marriage and reluctance to introduce Joyce to his wife with a discussion of the masked references to homosexuality in Wilde's *The Picture of Dorian Gray*. "I have just finished Dorian Grey [*sic*]," he tells Stanislaus, and "can imagine the capital which Wilde's prosecuting counsel made out of certain parts of it. It is not very difficult to read between the lines." While Joyce credits Wilde with having "had some good intentions in writing it—some wish to put himself before the world," he nonetheless finds Wilde's reticence disappointing: "If he had had the courage to develop the allusions in the book it might have been better." This he follows with a complaint that both Wilde and "his Irish imitator"—Gogarty—produce verses that are stylistically "reversed" or backward, creating art at odds with their private lives and values.[4] This passage of the letter then abruptly culminates in a classic Joycean epiphany, with Joyce's revelation that "I am troubled every night by horrible and terrifying dreams: deaths, corpses, assassinations in which I take an unpleasantly prominent part."[5]

Whether deliberately or accidentally, in this letter Joyce has identified the dangers to which his own writing might expose himself and others, dangers that seem to drive Gogarty's supposed fear of introducing Joyce to his wife. While Joyce is certainly annoyed that Gogarty seems anxious to rewrite the past and to pose as a more upstanding citizen than Joyce knows him to be, he may also be angry that Gogarty has burdened Joyce with a tacit directive to keep the details of their time together buried, converting them into shameful secrets. Such a burden would force Joyce to decide whether to follow Simon Dedalus's injunction "never to peach on a fellow" at the expense of his own art or to include a full and honest account of their one-time relationship in his art and risk causing harm to another.

In this letter, it is clear that both Wilde and Gogarty serve as negative examples for Joyce, representing artists unwilling to openly acknowledge their private practices in their public writing and therefore producing what Joyce deems to be inferior art, "crowded with lies and epigrams."[6] By projecting fearful reticence onto Wilde and Gogarty, Joyce nerves himself up to write "better" than either man despite his own fears, which are suggested by his "horrible and terrifying dreams." The assassinations Joyce dreamed of as he grappled with

Gogarty's perceived betrayal and mused over *Dorian Gray*'s use as evidence for the prosecution belong to a broad network of metaphors in Joyce's oeuvre that figure scandal as, in Joyce's own terms, "moral assassination."[7] This metaphor originates in "Et Tu, Healy," recurs in the Triestene essays, shapes Joyce's depiction of the Parnell scandal in *Portrait*, and, as we shall see, saturates *Ulysses*. That Joyce does not specify the nature of his role in these dream assassinations suggests that he was afraid not only of becoming the victim of scandal, like Parnell and Wilde, but of himself becoming the standard kind of scandalmonger, like Healy and Stead: one who charges the costs of scandal to others. Joyce's reflections to Stanislaus betray his fear not only of *being* morally assassinated like Wilde but of *performing* a moral assassination, of doing to Gogarty what the simoniacal London journalists had done to Wilde. In this letter, as in his story of Stephen Dedalus's attempts to find his way as an Irish artist in *Ulysses*, Joyce was unquestionably struggling with the real dangers run by an artist seeking to craft a new scandal logic. Thus it is perhaps unsurprising that in the very first episode of *Ulysses*, Joyce returns to the key figures of this letter: Wilde, as himself, and Oliver St. John Gogarty, in the guise of the unsinkable Buck Mulligan.

"HE THAT STEALETH FROM THE POOR LENDETH TO THE LORD"

From the outset, the "Telemachus" episode counterposes the public sex scandal against the discreet sounding of sexual interests and intentions that would have been a common feature of close relations between intellectually ambitious university men in the post-Wilde epoch. In this it also addresses the culminating preoccupations of Joyce's earlier account of Stephen's development as an Irish writer, *A Portrait of the Artist*, joining a figurative debate on the subjects of sex, scandal, nationality, morality, and art. Against Stephen's triumphal flight "by the nets" at the end of *Portrait*, his at-first unexplained presence back in Dublin implies an ignominious and deflating fall, an image that will figure the damage created by scandal throughout

Ulysses. In comically sexualized terms, one might say that Stephen ends *Portrait* on top and begins *Ulysses* on the bottom, summoned to "come up" by the ascendant Mulligan.

Stephen's youthful expectation of sensational success is further comically deflated with every new detail of his bodily, social, and mental disarray. Cranly, Stephen's loyal confidante in *Portrait*, has in *Ulysses* been unceremoniously replaced by the roughly playful, competitive, demeaning, and opportunistic Mulligan, whose seductive advances are both sneakier and cruder than Cranly's. Stephen must repeatedly reject the entanglement with British hegemony that a continuing bond with Mulligan would entail. Determined to keep Stephen on board, Mulligan repeatedly asserts his presumably accustomed mastery through ridicule, flattery, and seduction. The depressed and conflict-avoidant Stephen thus finds himself breaking up with Mulligan—through a series of gestures too tactful for Mulligan to register—not once, but several times within the novel. Indeed, in "Scylla and Charybdis," the episode in which Stephen fully, consciously acknowledges Mulligan's youthful appeal, we will learn that he has even tried to break it off by telegram.

Joyce describes Mulligan, as seen through Stephen's eyes, in terms that emphasize his body as powerful, attractive, and potentially dangerous.[8] Mulligan's every particular, as Len Platt notes, emphasizes his positional superiority in comparison to some corresponding detail betokening Stephen's economic, emotional, and physical disarray.[9] The Anglophilic Mulligan is "stately" in contrast to the cosmopolitan Stephen's statelessness. Mulligan is plump and voracious, while Stephen is malnourished, indifferent to and even irritated by the demands of his "dogsbody" (1.137). Stephen likens Mulligan's sleek, confident bearing to that of a cultural and political arbiter, "a prelate, patron of art in the middle ages" (1.31–33), while he himself, badly in need of a patron, is "a server of a servant" (1.312). Mulligan's well-tended white and gold teeth contrast with Stephen's rotten ones (1.25–26); his "strong wellknit trunk" with Stephen's verminous, poxy, unclean, rotting dogsbody; his physical bravery with Stephen's cowardice (1.162); and his robust, manly ablutions with Stephen's aversion to water (1.475).

The detailed physical description Joyce devotes to Mulligan's person is, at minimum, uncharacteristic. Haines, the irritating English snob whom Mulligan has just installed in the tower and whose presence Stephen finds intolerable (for reasons that, in the next section, we'll discuss in greater depth), attracts no such lingering gaze. Through Stephen's attentiveness to Mulligan's physique runs an indirect current of physical desire, one that charges moments like Stephen's brief reflection in "Proteus" on his foot in Mulligan's shoe (3.447–48). Stephen's acute awareness of Mulligan's body implies that his repeated renunciations are costly and thus principled. Indeed, from "Telemachus" through "Scylla and Charybdis," Stephen repeatedly refuses a dangerous entanglement with a selfish Oxonian "lord" who, as Haines's nightmare and his private conversation with Mulligan in "Wandering Rocks" reveal, regards Stephen (with titillated fear) as a "black" or racialized panther (1.57). Thus, over the course of *Ulysses* Stephen is, among other things, actively evading his own Wilde scandal. By repeatedly declining all invitations to "feast" with Mulligan and Haines, Stephen is symbolically refusing to play either the part of Wilde or that of the rent boys Wilde and Lord Alfred Douglas pursued in tandem. He will not join with an ambitious and attractive second-rate Oxonian poet in the lighthearted pursuit of Haines and his Fleet Street contacts, construed by Mulligan as ignorant and tasteless others easily "touched" by anyone with the real Oxford manner. Neither will he allow Mulligan to pander him to an Oxonian lord as the kind of youthful lumpen proletarian "panther" that Wilde and Douglas enjoyed hunting.[10]

Mulligan first invokes what Stephen later contemptuously terms the "tame essence of Wilde" (9.532) when he claims that his own, domesticated version of Wilde would want Stephen to develop himself along the lines Mulligan specifies (134, 143–44). Mulligan uses Wilde, in other words, to propose himself as Stephen's mentor or patron, a proposal Stephen rejects. Following each of Stephen's several demurrals, which commence when Stephen responds to Mulligan's proposal that they go together to Athens by asking whether Haines would accompany them (1.42–43), Mulligan becomes explicitly seductive. Calling Stephen "my love," Mulligan tells him "my name for you is the best. Kinch, the knifeblade" (1.48–55). Mimetically, Mulligan's nickname for Stephen is deliberately flattering, praising Stephen's knife-like intellect. "The knifeblade" also recalls the knife that figured scandal in "Et Tu, Healy" and that will figure scandal as a political weapon in "Nestor" and "Eumaeus," again hinting that Mulligan, like Lord Alfred Douglas, is out to embroil a superior artist in an ill-chosen sex scandal.[11] Through these endearments and pet names, Mulligan ritually lays claim to Stephen; in particular, by this "best" nickname, Kinch, Mulligan lays hold of Stephen as one would any useful tool: for his own purposes. Mulligan again expresses his desire to get his hands on Stephen when, in a bawdy Oxonian double entendre, he offers to teach Stephen "the Greeks . . . in the original" (1.79–80).[12] Mulligan unintentionally reveals the economic interests underpinning his sexualization of Stephen, however, every time he offers Stephen to Haines. Twice commanding Stephen to "touch [Haines] for a quid" (1.290–91),[13] Mulligan is acting as the consummate economic go-between, the pimp, and constituting Stephen, the impoverished artist, as prostitute.[14]

Joyce explicitly introduces the theme of middle-class pishoguery, a term that, like simony, aptly describes scandal's unholy transformations, when Mulligan reaches into Stephen's pocket without permission, removing, using, and deprecatingly displaying his dirty "rag" (1.69–74). Through this forcible penetration into Stephen's orifice, Mulligan unapologetically "steals from the poor," as he does repeatedly over the course of the novel. Indeed, Mulligan often figuratively picks the pockets of the poor so as to "len[d] to [a] lord," as when he urges Stephen to give Haines his epigrams. Mulligan continually emphasizes Stephen's impoverished status, another way in which Mulligan credentials himself by discrediting Stephen. He emphasizes Stephen's shabbiness, for instance, by picking over his clothes—more rags—and offering him cast-off shirts and handkerchiefs and trousers. He subtly eroticizes these transactions by telling Stephen "you look damn well when you're dressed" (1.118–19), a line that simultaneously compliments Stephen's looks, asserts a proprietary desire to dress him, and slyly implies his knowledge of Stephen's appearance when he is undressed.

As he performs his discrediting seductions, Mulligan attempts to recruit Stephen into his state-building project, repeatedly advising him to affiliate himself with the Oxbridge intelligentsia. He asserts that Stephen should use his "real Oxford manner" (1.53–54) to gain favor and financial backing from the Oxford-educated Haines, heir to an imperial fortune that his father has amassed, Mulligan notes, through a sort of imperial black magic, selling jalap to Zulus "or some bloody swindle or other" (1.156–57).[15] Throughout these passages, Mulligan is emphatically positioning himself as a middleman, attempting to gain Stephen's labor for Haines and Haines's patronage for Stephen while presenting himself to each as the other's agent. While he clearly places great importance on staying in Haines's good graces by treating Stephen as an asset he can bring to the table, Mulligan insists to Stephen that it is the two of them who are united against Haines. He emphasizes his loyalty to Stephen in contrast to Haines's snobbery when he tells Stephen (twice) that "the oxy," Haines, "thinks you're not a gentleman" (1.51–52; 1.155–56). In this masterful double-dealing, Mulligan condemns Haines and the English upper crust more generally for their inability to conceive of a penniless Irish Catholic genius, denies his class pretensions and pride in his own Oxford affiliations by calling Haines "oxy" as a term of derision, congratulates himself for his own superior insight, and reminds Stephen of his social inferiority, all in a few economical speech acts.

That Joyce is figuring Mulligan's and Haines's opportunistic plunderings as pishoguery, and that Stephen is attempting to intervene in such routine ritual misappropriation, is made explicit in the transaction a few pages later between Mulligan and the milkwoman who makes a delivery to the tower. As a visiting female neighbor who traffics in milk and whom Stephen imaginatively romances into a witch (1.401), the milkwoman is the sort of figure against whom Irish peasant informants had long cautioned roving antiquarians. In this exchange, however, it is the neighborhood witch who comes off the worse in an interaction with a coven of educated folklorists. Haines declares, "We had better pay her," but threatens to send her away empty-handed when he unreasonably demands a written bill (1.440) at the same time that Mulligan is making away with the butter, cramming "a crust thickly buttered on both sides" into his mouth (1.446–47). Stephen is also initially unsympathetic to the milkwoman, whom he inwardly dismisses, drawing on the vocabulary of sex scandal, as Haines's and Mulligan's "common cuckquean" (1.405). He takes her part, however, when Mulligan tries to short her of payment she is due. When Haines appropriates the neocolonial role of the so-called honest broker, graciously instructing Mulligan to "pay up and look pleasant" (1.449), Mulligan reaches into his own pocket and produces a coin, pronouncing it "a miracle" (1.453). But it is Stephen who places the coin in the milkwoman's "uneager hand," and it is he who notes what Haines and Mulligan seek to deny through their silence: that some of the money owed has been withheld. Resisting this latest attempt by local "lords" to "steal from the poor," Stephen assures her, "We'll owe twopence" (1.458).[16] Joyce will also associate Haines with pishoguery in "Wandering Rocks," in which Haines's strange protectiveness of his cream pointedly implies that folklore collecting is itself a form of pishoguery whereby English "lords" may project onto the Irish their own propensity for insidious forms of misappropriation. While enjoying yet another hearty meal served by attentive Irish hosts, Haines asks the doubtless bemused Mulligan to confirm that his cream has not been meddled with, explaining that he does not want to be "imposed on" (10.1094–95).

Pishoguery, even more than simony, is an activity that for Joyce captures scandal's temptations as well as its risks. As illustrated in the County Fermanagh folk stories concerning witches who steal their neighbor's cream that Henry Glassie has glossed in *Passing the Time in Ballymenone*, the pishoguerist is inevitably unpopular but eats well, and Joyce spent much of his life hungry. When Stephen expresses to Haines his disdain for the tawdry "odd jobs" offered him as an Irish artist and intellectual, his disdain is tinged—like his disdain for Mulligan—with a measure of longing. Stephen's refusal to participate in the attempted pishoguery of the milkwoman, or in Mulligan's multifarious scandalizing of both himself and Haines by turns, constitutes his refusal to be relegated to the only odd jobs offered him by the New Journalism: to be either scandal's author or its object, to be either victim or moral assassin.

"THE GAPING WOUNDS WHICH THE WORDS HAD LEFT"

After Stephen bests Mulligan in a verbal duel over Wilde (a contest of wills and wits that, as we will see in the next section, exposes both Mulligan's and Stephen's most deeply held artistic and political concerns), Mulligan changes his seductive tack and "suddenly link[s] his arm in Stephen's" and "walk[s] with him around the tower" (1.150–51). Once again shifting from competitor to solicitous defender, Mulligan apologizes "kindly" for teasing Stephen and declares that he prefers Stephen to "any of them" (1.151). Registering this shift as another volley in Mulligan's ongoing campaign, Stephen thinks of his own verbal facility as his only weapon, though a formidable one, reflecting that Mulligan has "parried again" because "he fears the lancet of my art," just as Stephen fears Mulligan's "lancet" (1.152–53). Stephen overtly notes the parallel between Mulligan's seductiveness and Cranly's earlier overture when he thinks to himself, "Cranly's arm. His arm," a momentary tactile memory that calls attention to the structural and categorical parallels between the two scenes (1.159).[17]

Mulligan lays claim to Stephen as Cranly once sought to, assuring Stephen that he is "the only one who knows what you are" (1.160–61). He demands to know why Stephen is drawing away from him and threatens to "rag" Haines "if he makes any noise" (1.162–63). Mulligan's threat to give Haines a ragging worse than the apparently oft-recalled ragging of Clive Kempthorpe at Magdalen College, Wilde and Douglas's college at Oxford, summons to Stephen's mind a scene conjoining the Joycean scandal tropes of rags, breaking news, stolen clothing, humiliating exposure, pursuit, cutting, and ritual sacrifice: "O, I shall expire! Break the news to her gently, Aubrey! I shall die! With the slit ribbons of his shirt whipping the air he hops and hobbles round the table with trousers down at heels, chased by Ades of Magdalen with the tailor's shears. A scared calf's face gilded with marmalade" (1.166–70). Thus Clive Kempthorpe's ragging provides Mulligan with charged private details that, like the gold coin Corley receives from the slavey in "Two Gallants," may be publicly exposed in a manner that not only betokens but generates social power. Here, Mulligan deploys this quick reference to the sexual humiliation of a man Stephen does not even know so as to reassure Stephen that he can and will protect him from other men while subtly reminding Stephen—in what can be construed as both a threat and a come-on—that he has forcibly torn men's trousers off as well as graciously supplied them.

Immediately following their verbal duel and Mulligan's seductive parries, Stephen admits that Mulligan has wounded him. When Stephen had first visited Mulligan at his aunt's home following Stephen's mother's death, Stephen reminds him, Mulligan called up to his aunt, who supplies Mulligan with money and dislikes Stephen, that "it's only Dedalus whose mother is beastly dead" (1.98–99). Mulligan thus had reduced Stephen's bereavement to a glib headline, using wording that prefigures *Ulysses*'s most repulsive tabloid headline, lauding an American lynching in "Cyclops": "Black Beast Burned." Not only did Mulligan treat Stephen cruelly when he most needed comfort, but moreover, like Judas, the simoniacal soldiers that rifled through Jesus's clothes, and contemporary scandalmongers, he did it for money, in the form of his aunt's continued support: "The aunt," he tells Stephen, "thinks you killed your mother. That's why she won't let me have anything to do with you" (1.88–89). Mulligan's cutting language so wounds Stephen that he is still "shielding the gaping wounds which the words had left in his heart" (1.216–17) when he makes his retort. Mulligan's wielding of words as offensive weapons for personal gain resembles the simultaneous commodification and scandalization of words within the New Journalism. In contrast, Joyce depicts the reticent Stephen's verbal resistance to Mulligan, and by implication his own scandal work, as a parry: as legitimate self-defense against words capable of doing real harm.

Mulligan's breezy endorsement of his aunt's matricidal indictment is but one of a series of scandalous charges that Mulligan brings against Stephen over the course of the episode, highlighting the codependence of Mulligan's economic opportunism and his scandal-mongering. By charging Stephen with having murdered his mother, Mulligan represents Stephen's dissenting beliefs as both criminal and sinful, while empowering the aunt who supplies him with funds and her rigidly conformist Catholicism. Joyce thus constitutes the power struggle between Stephen and Mulligan as a competition between the intellectual and aesthetic powers of the artist and the sensationalizing simony of the middle-class scandalmonger. In addition to his claim that Stephen has committed ritual matricide, Mulligan notes that a psychiatric specialist of his acquaintance says Stephen has GPI, psychosis brought on by late-stage syphilis (1.127–29), and then sweeps a hand mirror "a half circle in the air to flash the tidings [of Stephen's GPI] abroad" (1.130). Thus, in the book's first four pages, Buck acquaints Stephen, the reader, and even international audiences with two highly scandalous charges against Stephen that are circulating in Dublin, presumably with Mulligan's encouragement. Mulligan functions here as does the London press in "Ireland at the Bar," internationally transmitting ("flash[ing] abroad") the same sort of sensational charges against Stephen that Joyce claims London newspapers use to silence the Irish. Despite their friendship and shared nationality, the ambitious Mulligan depicts Stephen as one of the stereotypically Irish "unbalanced, helpless idiots about whom we read in the *Standard* and the *Morning Post*" ("Ireland: Island of Saints and Sages," 167)—that is, as abhorrently violent, depraved, and psychotic.

When Mulligan literally and then figuratively exposes Stephen's dirty "nose rag," just as in the case of the New Journalist news rag, it is the scandalmonger, like the pishoguerist, who transgresses—violating his victim's person and public standards of decency—but it is the scandal victim, or pishogue, who is discredited. By conveying these proceedings through the slippery conventions of the roman à clef, however, Joyce further twists the already paradoxical logic of sex scandal. Through the evident erotic tension between Stephen Dedalus and Buck Mulligan—a tension that becomes increasingly compromising to Joyce with every liberty Mulligan's words and actions appear to ascribe to Gogarty—Joyce establishes a pattern that will only grow more complex over the course of *Ulysses*. Beginning in "Telemachus," Joyce exposes what were plausibly his own youthful follies so as to indict neither himself nor Gogarty, but rather to disclose the uncongeniality of the treacherous terrain where both were learning to wield the lancets of their art in response to the scandalous, scandalmongering opportunism of an ambitious Irish middle class.

"IF ONLY WILDE WERE ALIVE TO SEE YOU!"

The misappropriations of Mulligan as an apprentice middle-class scandalmonger are not, however, limited strictly to wounding words and sleazy come-ons. By claiming the endorsement of such a power-ful artistic figure as Oscar Wilde, Mulligan attempts to beautify the inherently ugly machinations of scandal politics. Through Stephen and Mulligan's debate in "Telemachus" over Wilde's cultural signifi-cance, Joyce both invokes Wilde as a figure for scandal and indicts those who scandalized him, just as he did in "Oscar Wilde: The Poet of *Salomé.*" Because Stephen Dedalus and Buck Mulligan are the most central characters in *Ulysses* with specific, identifiable real-world counterparts[18]—Joyce in the case of Stephen and Gogarty in the case of Mulligan—the interactions between them, in their duel over Wilde and elsewhere, contain some of the most potentially libelous and self-libeling of the novel's numerous quasi-scandalous disclosures.[19] As we shall see, in "Telemachus" Joyce uses these artfully crafted exchanges to recreate the philosophical, aesthetic, and personal conflict with Gogarty that served as a whetstone for the principles that would guide his future work, work that would improve on and offer an answer to the scandal work of the New Journalism.

Stephen and Mulligan's fight to win Wilde's hand occurs, signifi-cantly, in the context of another politically charged domestic squab-ble, this one over the continued presence of the culturally tone-deaf Haines. Haines, whose night terrors include loud threats of violence (1.60–62), is not only an insufferably patronizing English hibernophile but also an emphatically undesirable houseguest. Finding this incur-sion intolerable, Stephen tells Mulligan "if he stays on here, I am off" (1.62–63), an arrangement that Mulligan tacitly accepts and formal-izes later in the episode when he asks for the key to the tower (1.721). The "stately" Mulligan (1.1), like the most brazen comprador operator, is coolly setting up house with the colonizer on whose wealth and

power his future prospects depend while passing the bill for this dubious guest's upkeep on to his dispossessed compatriot. Joyce emphasizes Haines and Mulligan's impending ascent into a new archipelagic
elite destined to usurp the figurative throne once controlled by the
Irish poets when Mulligan demands that Stephen (who has already
paid the rent) contribute "four omnipotent sovereigns" to buy the
drinks in celebration of Mulligan's and Haines's anticipated "corona-
tion day" (1.297–305).[20]

As Valente notes, Joyce's references to Oxbridge Hellenism enable
him to elaborate on the significant influence of class, educational, and
national background for both sexual and artistic freedom across the
British archipelago.[21] Oxford's glamour seems to ennoble the charm-
less sponger Haines in the eyes of both Mulligan and the milkwoman,
and it is by recourse to Oxbridge Hellenism that Mulligan repeatedly
justifies his actions and motives toward Stephen. Through the competition over Wilde between Mulligan and Stephen, Joyce assesses the
artistic and political implications of Oxonian cultural elitism. In a
war of wits employing Wilde's own words, images, and ideas, Mulligan claims Wilde as an exemplar of the Oxonian Hellenism he shares
with Haines, while Stephen situates Wilde in opposition to the hegemonic authority to which Mulligan lays claim. As we will see on closer
examination, Stephen redefines Wilde as having been martyred by
morally and aesthetically complacent English audiences enthralled,
like Haines, by the uncontestable superiority of their own cultural
values and conventions.

Amidst Mulligan's nearly incessant positioning of Stephen and
himself relative to Oxford in the novel's opening episode is a bit of stage
business that recalls the allegorical tableau with which Joyce ends his
Triestene essay on Wilde: English scandal journalists gambling and
gamboling over the last effects of the crucified Wilde. Although this
figurative indictment of scandal journalism is also recalled in later
episodes in *Ulysses*, Joyce's comparison of Wilde to Jesus as the victim of a theft at once shockingly petty, opportunistic, and sacrilegious
first appears in *Ulysses* in "Telemachus," when Mulligan proudly displays a personal effect stolen from a servant: the fractured mirror of
his aunt's skivvy, Ursula (1.38–40). That *this* is the cracked looking

glass that Mulligan, with his unerring New Journalist instincts, uses to "transmit" his scandalous syphilis charges against Stephen across the Irish Sea is sadly appropriate.

When Mulligan holds up this cracked mirror he has stolen, apparently to revenge the unattractive maid's lack of potential for sexual exploitation (1.139), he proves that he is another of those men whose stance toward working-class women is what *Dubliners'* Lily refers to as "all palaver and what they can get out of" them. In so doing, Mulligan reveals the sort of gallantry with which he will treat Stephen throughout *Ulysses*. Having engaged Stephen's interest in his own reflection in Ursula's cracked mirror, Mulligan snatches it away, describing Stephen's startled response as "the rage of Caliban at not seeing his face in a mirror. . . . If Wilde were only alive to see you!" (1.143–44). Enacting the paradigmatic work of scandal, Mulligan crudely decontextualizes some of Wilde's words from the preface of *The Picture of Dorian Gray* to humiliate and devalue Stephen. Like the *Punch* cartoon, "The Irish Tempest," Mulligan reductively equates Stephen's Irish poverty with monstrosity, coded, via Wilde, as philistinism. This misapplication of Wilde's words from the preface maliciously distorts Wilde's meaning, literally and figuratively ignoring the fact that it is the damaged mirror, not Stephen's face, that renders Stephen's image monstrous. Wilde had used Caliban to figure the spiritual deformity of British middle-class audiences who rejected both naturalism and modernism because both styles failed to deliver the narcissistic validation they so craved. Within the representational framework Wilde critiques in *Dorian Gray*, the Irish serve as flattering foils to the falsely, impossibly normative English: the same distortions that render the English middle class beautiful render the mere Irish monstrous.[22] In his essay "Oscar Wilde: The Poet of *Salomé*," Joyce figures Wilde's attempts to redress these distortions as lying at the root of his martyrdom, asserting that Wilde was fated "to break the lance of his paradoxical eloquence against the ranks of useful conventions" (148). Wilde himself, then, was broken by his repeated assaults on the same distorting conventions that Mulligan is now marshaling against Stephen.

By putting Stephen in the place of the philistine classes Wilde derides in the preface to *The Picture of Dorian Gray*, Mulligan emphasizes

Stephen's inferior class and educational background and suggests that Wilde, were he still alive, would find Stephen contemptible. According to Wilde, Mulligan implies, Stephen needs to upgrade his disreputable class and national affiliations if he is to command decent compensation and respect as an artist. Stephen, however, picking up the lance of Wilde's paradoxical eloquence, parries Mulligan's thrust with a play on another Wildean aphorism involving mirrors and art. Pointing at the broken mirror, Stephen retorts in a tone reminiscent of Lily's bitter denunciation of sexual exploitation that "it is a symbol of Irish art. The cracked lookingglass of a servant" (1.146). Stephen's language here recalls that of the Triestene essays, which claimed "the figure of this bewildered old man," Myles Joyce, "is a symbol of the Irish nation" ("Ireland at the Bar," 146) and that Wilde is a figure for Ireland whose "name symbolizes him" ("Oscar Wilde," 148).

The Wildean image to which Stephen's retort refers appears in Wilde's essay "The Decay of Lying," in which Vivian, a Wildean alter ego, refutes Hamlet's "unfortunate aphorism about Art holding the mirror up to Nature," pointing out that, in popular understanding, the implications of this line have been virtually reversed, just as Mulligan has reversed the implications of Wilde's aphorisms: the line is, in fact, "deliberately said by Hamlet in order to convince the bystanders of his absolute insanity in all art-matters" ("The Decay of Lying," 28). Cyril, Vivian's earnest interlocutor, endorses Wilde's critique of art as nature's mirror when he observes, "I can quite understand your objection to art being treated as a mirror. You think it would reduce genius to the position of a cracked looking-glass" (30). Through his allusion to this Wilde essay, Stephen is therefore accusing Mulligan of reducing him to the position of a cracked looking glass, a counterscandalous accusation that allows the cracked mirror to embody simultaneously the original distortions of British print capitalism, the Irish artist discredited by those distortions, and what Ellmann refers to as the "extravagant excursions into forbidden territories" necessary to remediate centuries of representational distortion.[23] When Stephen points at the cracked mirror and retorts, "It is a symbol of Irish art," he aligns his distorted image in the broken mirror with the figures of Myles Joyce and of Wilde himself, all three of whom symbolize

Ireland's discredited position in the "cracked looking-glass" of British print culture.

The grotesque reflection of Stephen that Mulligan creates through his stolen mirror and palaver is underwritten by his use of Wilde to reaffirm the hegemonic Oxonian worldview within which Mulligan, a middle-class medical man with Oxford connections, will always outrank Stephen, a poor Irish Catholic artist. Mulligan's approach to Wilde effaces the effects of the Wilde scandal itself, keeping Wilde's cultural capital while casually shucking off the injuries that scandal inflicted on Wilde personally and leaving unchallenged the ongoing toxic effects of the scandal on men of his own generation. Stephen's parry, on the other hand, defines Ursula's mirror not only by its function, or rather its dysfunction, but also by its moral and cultural provenance. By reasserting its identity as an article stolen from an Irish servant, Stephen makes the theft of and damage to her mirror symbolic of his own predicament as an Irish artist. The only artistic tools Stephen has at his disposal are damaged, and his subject matter is discredited from the start. Stephen thus identifies with both Wilde and a working-class Irish woman whom Mulligan has callously exploited, one of the many instances in *Ulysses* in which Joyce points out common interests uniting multiple marginalized groups with respect to scandal.[24]

Stephen, rather than simply restoring Wilde to an imagined position of class-based cultural authority, instead holds "a mirror up to culture," in Seamus Deane's words, calling attention to the historical crack in the cultural mirror that ultimately made the insistent visibility of Wilde's ambitious, resistant cultural productions disastrously unsustainable.[25] Stephen reconfigures the hierarchy asserted by Mulligan's joke by refiguring the broken mirror's specificity within the context of Ireland's subservient position relative to England. As an artist seeking to "rectify matters a little" by making Ireland more visible and comprehensible to both the Irish and the world, Joyce/Stephen is himself, in an admirable sense, "a server of a servant" (1.312). Already, in the novel's opening pages, Stephen's earnest desire to serve rather than simply to get on in the world renders him especially vulnerable to insults and exploitation.

As Mulligan suggests, Stephen, with his "real Oxford manner," could (and in Mulligan's view, should) pass himself off as one of the cultural elect, adopting Oxbridge Hellenism to obscure his discreditable origins. Mulligan, wielding the servant's broken mirror, aligns himself and Wilde as arbiters of class-inflected taste, seeking to correct Stephen's disabling marks of cultural inferiority. Stephen, however, asserts his and Wilde's vulnerability to British audiences' snobbish contempt by identifying the servant, Ursula, as the mirror's rightful owner. Stephen implies that Mulligan's cynical plundering of both Ursula's and Stephen's effects constitutes the same opportunism that led simoniacal journalists to pick through Wilde's private life for scandal fragments to distort in the broken mirror of British print capitalism. As Irish artists, Oscar Wilde and Stephen Dedalus (and through them, the young Joyce himself) are united in a shared cultural marginalization that makes their private lives and persons—like Ursula's, like Lily's—vulnerable to wanton intrusion. Joyce, through Stephen, wittily reappropriates Wilde as a martyred outsider and a rightful ally of the intellectually dissenting and socially vulnerable, claiming the right to represent themselves for Ireland's women, Ireland's poor, and Ireland's artists.

Both Mulligan and Stephen recognize this subtle victory, Mulligan most decisively toward the end of the episode when he tells Haines "we have grown out of Wilde and paradoxes" (1.554), implying that Joyce's strategies for interweaving the factual and the fictional have not only built on but surpassed those that had failed Wilde.[26] Although Mulligan initially treats Stephen as a lackey, he soon improves his offer. He promotes Stephen from underling to junior partner when he famously reenacts Satan's temptation of Jesus. Standing on high at Stephen's side, Mulligan tempts Stephen by offering to restore to him the awe-inspiring, culturally defining powers of the precolonial Irish poet, provided he agrees to define Irish culture along the lines specified by English cultural arbiters like Matthew Arnold. He urges Stephen to work with him to "do something for the island. Hellenize it" (1.157–58). As a budding statesman, Mulligan is in effect offering Stephen an entry-level position in the emergent Irish Catholic power structure that will run the island after independence. Here and throughout *Ulysses*, Mulligan and others, including Myles Crawford in "Aeolus" and Bloom in "Eumaeus," insist that Stephen should sell "the lancet of his art" to this incipient ruling class. As their private remarks about Haines make clear, both men understand that any new state relying for its ideas and capital on dullards like Haines, "bursting with money and indigestion," is going to need all the rhetorical window dressing it can get (1.52–53). By the episode's end, however, Stephen will choose to surrender his key to this imperial outpost to Mulligan, through this act symbolically rejecting Mulligan's invitation to join the new archipelagic ruling class on any terms.

"ONE ... WHO WANTS ME FOR ODD JOBS"

In "Telemachus," scandal is figured as a weapon that can be used both to "menace," "disar[m]," and "wors[t]" dissenters and to parry the "lances and . . . shields" wielded by the "embattled angels of the church" (1.663). Yet scandal's function as a weapon is conflated with scandal as a medium for theft and also, at least potentially, as a mechanism for restitution. Ursula's round, shiny mirror visually recalls, for instance, both the coin from "Two Gallants" and the clumsy recompense that Gabriel in "The Dead" attempts with the gold coin that he presses into the hand of the obscurely damaged house servant, Lily. But while Gabriel's restitution to Eliza Armstrong's alternate fictional counterpart, "Lily the caretaker's daughter," is botched because it so crudely economizes the theft it purports to redress, Stephen, by calling attention to Mulligan's theft of Ursula's hand mirror and to the balance the three men owe to the milkwoman, reasserts the extramonetary value of what others have reduced to loose change. As a server of a servant, Stephen's first odd jobs aim, literally and figuratively, to recompense female victims of Mulligan's and Haines's pishoguery: the milkwoman and the maid Ursula. In this, Stephen's scandal work figuratively descends from and improves on that of W. T. Stead and Gabriel, "pennyboys" who strove too precipitously to redress complex symbolic thefts.

Mulligan and Stephen's breakup in "Telemachus," negotiated under the sign of Oscar Wilde, is formalized through the transfer of a key—a fragment that is both uniquely personal and domestic and emblematic of the portal between the realm of the personal and the larger public realm—to a building that is simultaneously a private dwelling and a military outpost. Throughout *Ulysses*, as in the opening episode's interpenetration of the Wilde scandal and the subtle rituals negotiating the terms of proximity and access within Mulligan and Stephen's relationship, Joyce relentlessly counters the disintegratory, sensationalizing logic of the sex scandal. Some of these reclaimed scandal fragments unquestionably belong to Joyce and some to Oliver St. John Gogarty, but easily verified biographical details—such as the fact that it was Gogarty, not Joyce, who paid the rent on the Martello tower—should warn us that even the most seemingly straightforward moments in *Ulysses* have often been booby-trapped through inversion or other forms of obfuscation.

Like Wilde, Joyce is clearly using art to render the dangerously personal public.[27] Such work is *odd* in the sense that it is queer, counter to commonsense expectations and imperatives. As in the best scholarly explications of pishoguery, especially in Angela Bourke's *The Burning of Bridget Cleary*, a close analysis of Joyce's proceedings feels a little dirty.[28] He is enacting what amounts to self-pishoguery, exhibiting embarrassing, taboo personal details to generate a mode of affective social power in a paradoxically protective circle of self-incrimination. He mimics Wilde by "putting himself before the world," but also acts on his wish, expressed to Stanislaus after reading *Dorian Gray*, that Wilde would have made his book better if he had chosen to "develop the allusions." In "Telemachus" and throughout *Ulysses*, Joyce makes the obscurely personal crimes, transgressions, and queer tics he exposes far more explicit than had Wilde, while making their relationship to specific private lives—his own or others'—always tantalizingly probable though never claimed outright, a universalizing ambiguity to correct the isolating certainties of the New Journalist sex scandal.

CHAPTER 5

The Protracted Labor of the New Journalist Sex Scandal

"Lodged in the Room of Infinite Possibilities"

How a poet is to earn an honest living is a problem to which there is no entirely satisfactory solution.

        —W. H. Auden, obituary for Louis MacNeice

In the episodes that follow "Telemachus," Stephen labors to create an artistic path that neither hides his own dissenting, deviant private life behind a wall of placating, conformist writing nor lays it open to the scandal machinery that was tearing apart so many others who sought to do battle with middle-class morality. Though Joyce opens *Ulysses* by identifying Stephen, and thus his own younger self, with Oscar Wilde, in the "Nestor" episode Stephen explicitly resolves against following in Wilde's professional footsteps.

Joyce develops his critique of scandal as a treacherous cultural weapon throughout "Nestor," with particular emphasis on its use within the imperial system to control, debase, and corrupt colonized artists. Here Stephen is charged with the delivery of a ridiculously pompous letter by his employer, the headmaster Garrett Deasy, to the editors of the *Evening Telegraph* and the *Irish Homestead*, thereby initiating between Stephen and Deasy a race to capture an Irish audience that is so thoroughly rigged as to virtually guarantee Stephen's defeat. Later, in "Aeolus," Stephen is given a different charge by those directly implicated in Irish scandal journalism, one that he will eventually embrace in a way quite unanticipated by the members of the Irish "pressgang" who offer it. As we shall see, in both this episode and in "Aeolus," Stephen finds himself being swept back into the role of "imperial jester" that he firmly abjures, caught in a cultural riptide against which he will continue to struggle over the course of the narrative.

As "Nestor" opens, Stephen finds himself once again unable to reach an Irish audience, in this case a classroom of privileged and indifferent students. In this context, Stephen is, like the witticism he makes regarding the Kingston pier, "a disappointed bridge," unable to span an imperial breach (2.39). His students are the sons of Irish burghers, men who, like Mulligan and Deasy, admire and court English lords while despising the likes of Stephen, whose shabbiness reflects Ireland's political, economic, and representational dispossession. Stephen, like Ireland, is discredited in the eyes of this Irish middle-class audience by his "lack of rule" and economic dependency on "the fees their papas pay" (2.29). Stephen's mind, wandering from his hapless efforts to engage his students' interest, revisits Mulligan's suggestion that he cultivate Haines and court an English audience instead, and he envisions himself "tonight deftly amid wild drink and talk . . . pierce[ing] the polished mail of [Haines's] mind" (2.42–43).

With this imagery, which recalls Joyce's association of knives and assassination with Tim Healy in "Et Tu, Healy" and in the later "Eumaeus" with "the O'Brienite scribes" (16.1503), Joyce figures an adept Irish writer's encounter with British print capitalism as a medieval parlay between an Irish warrior and an English knight or lord in terms that subtly recall the methods of both Parnell and Wilde and the limits of their effectiveness:

Tonight deftly amid wild drink and talk, to pierce the polished mail of his mind. What then? A jester at the court of his master, indulged and disesteemed, winning a clement master's praise. Why had they chosen all that part? Not wholly for the smooth caress. For them too history was a tale like any other too often heard, their land a pawnshop.

Had Pyrrhus not fallen by a beldam's hand in Argos or Julius Caesar not been knifed to death. They are not to be thought away. Time has branded them and fettered they are lodged in the room of the infinite possibilities they have ousted. (2.42–51)

Having briefly envisioned a triumph over Haines, Stephen quickly recognizes that his prize would likely be only to become "a jester at the court of his master, indulged and disesteemed, winning a clement master's praise" (2.44–45). Already he seems aware that such a Pyrrhic victory is all but inevitable within an imperial status quo in which Irish artistic or intellectual victories lead only to more insidious forms of subjugation, as illustrated by the figure of the court jester.[1]

The wording of this inner debate recalls the moment in "Poet of Salomé" when Joyce describes Wilde—like other Irish playwrights, from "Sheridan and Goldsmith to Bernard Shaw" (149)—as a jester. This comparison carries an implied connection between the stock figure of the jester and that of the stage Irishman, a sine qua non for an Irish play's success with English audiences throughout the long nineteenth century. Wilde differed from his predecessors, Joyce implies, only by writing stage Englishmen and making himself rather than his Irish characters the derisory object of the English gaze.[2] When Stephen considers piercing Haines's polished mail—when he envisions himself, like Wilde, making a conquest of an English lord—he quickly recognizes that the likeliest outcome would be to end up like Wilde, with the double implication that he would become an "indulged and disesteemed" captive, subject to the whims of English audiences and perpetually dependent on their praise, and that he too might wind up tried in an English court. And just as he did in "Poet of Salomé," Joyce expands the image of the jester to implicitly include not just Wilde but all talented Irish writers who have cultivated English audiences. Wondering "why had they chosen all that part?" Stephen concludes it was "not wholly for the smooth caress." Rather, he recognizes, those artists struggled with the same dilemma he now faces: "For them too history was a tale like any other too often heard, their land a pawnshop," the entire island, its resources and labor, effectively in hock to England, the Irish themselves rendered mere pawns.

Stephen's thoughts then turn to those sorts of violent disruptions that leave contested histories and blighted economies in their wake, implicating not only political leaders but Irish writers who have sold their pens to England as having left an indelible, silencing mark on a futurity that is not to be thought away. As Stephen considers the fate of Pyrrhus, "fallen by a beldam's hand" (a photonegative metaphor for the consequences for Irish writers like Wilde of "winning the palm" of the English press), and Julius Caesar, "knifed to death" by an ally (a well-established reference to Parnell), he concludes each is "branded," "fettered," and "lodged in the room of the infinite possibilities they have ousted." Stephen's thoughts thus link the foreclosed possibilities of the Irish, including Irish writers like himself, to the New Journalism's *moral* assassinations—many committed by Irish writers and leaders working in England—during the Home Rule scandal wars. Irish artists, intellectuals, and leaders such as Wilde and Shaw, Parnell and Healy, went to London, the imperial court of their master, seeking escape from their country's labyrinthine history and tawdry odd jobs. Like Mulligan in the previous episode and Deasy later in this one, they aimed to advance their own careers on the battleground of English print culture while simultaneously advancing the most personally convenient version of Ireland's collective interests along the way. Ultimately, these figures wound up imperial captives, forced by the demands and expectations of English audiences to produce only that which their adversaries wished to consume or to become dependent on the fickle loyalties of literal imperial masters, as Parnell had been on Gladstone. In this germinal passage, Joyce conflates careerism, martyrdom, and the foreclosure of artistic and political possibilities under the sign of Oscar Wilde, preeminent emblem of the New Journalist sex scandal.

Stephen's dilemma as an artist, therefore, is how to refuse the position of either scandalmonger or scandal victim so as to avoid becoming what in the next episode, "Proteus," he calls the "master of others or their slave," which amount to the same thing (3.295–96). Whether another sort of life might be conceived, whether lost futures can be retrieved from the historical crypt to which moral and political assassinations have banished them, Stephen is at this point not quite sure, asking himself, "But can those have been possible seeing they never were? Or was that only possible which came to pass? Weave, weaver of the wind" (2.51–53).

"THOSE BIG WORDS, WHICH MAKE US SO UNHAPPY"

Having resolved to steer clear of English masters, Stephen emerges from his classroom only to be summoned by the headmaster, Deasy, to an airless chamber in which Irish history and Stephen's personal agency both hang suspended. As Stephen enters Deasy's stale, smoky study, he notes its changeless quality, thinking "as it was in the beginning, is now" (2.200–201). The "Stuart coins" Deasy displays suggest a little dragon's hoard of stolen loot, the "base treasure of a bog" (2.201–2), which through their affiliation with other coins in Joyce's work refigure the decisive defeat of the Stuarts at the hands of the Hanoverians at the Battle of the Boyne as an enduring act of magical appropriation. Deasy's coins, like coins seen earlier in the hands of Corley, Gabriel, and Mulligan, mark a moment of rupture when one future eradicated alternate futurities, leaving the English masters, like cruel deities, permanently in power, "world without end" (2.203–4). This theme of malignant perpetual stasis saturates the rest of the episode, as Deasy pointedly enacts scandal's capacity to hold its audiences and its potential targets captive. By using a series of scandal gambits, Deasy seeks both to command the unwilling Stephen's attention and to masterfully credit specific groups and ideologies while discrediting others.

Joyce clearly represents Deasy as another English master, whose unionist loyalties grant him power to unilaterally assign social and moral value. In this, he is a pointed parallel to Haines, "the seas' ruler," who steals the cream from his Irish neighbors.[3] Deasy, a singularly unreliable interlocutor on a broad range of topics, obliges the cornered Stephen to listen to a lengthy monologue in which he repeatedly deprecates specific scandal figures and whole scandalized constituencies. Unlike Mulligan's plan to "Hellenize" Ireland, which aims to blur cultural distinctions and obscure class and national loyalties, Deasy's entire epistemology turns on making absolute binary distinctions. In the opposite of E. M. Forster's famous dictum, "Only connect," the emotional and analytical imperative for Deasy is to disconnect. Defining himself in opposition to an array of Irish constituencies whom he discredits with scandal fragments, his emphasis throughout his interaction with Stephen is on his own mutable but always creditable distinctiveness, which he codes first as English, only then as Irish, and finally as Ulsterite.[4]

Bolstering his dubious encomiums to England, Ulster, and empire with a series of inapt scandal claims, Deasy glories in his imagined legacy as an Englishman, an Orangeman, and an heir to a long-defunct strain of anti-Catholic Irish nationalism, thus crediting himself and a broadly constituted unionist/Protestant front with the contributions of a full range of ethnic and religious groups to Irish history from which he imaginatively excludes Stephen and his ancestors. This, we have learned, is the third time Stephen has had to undergo this ritual discreditation: "The same room and hour, the same wisdom" (2.233–34). Deasy's pocketbook with its sinister leather thong has thus three times set a noose around him (2.334). Trapped by his material status in this imperial court, Stephen is a captive audience who can parry Deasy's "lance" only with ripostes too subtle to register (2.425). Certainly, for instance, the pompous Deasy would never suppose that it is, both figuratively and literally, his own garbled, self-serving account of history as a series of scandals that Stephen describes as "a nightmare from which I am trying to awake" (2.377).

Like a caricature of the New Journalism, with its drive to evaluate the world by means of scandal, Deasy rushes headlong from one historical scapegoat to another with little logic save the need to portray some other—*any* other   as the villain. The Anglophilic Deasy even trots out nationalist traditions that represent English rule in Ireland as a curse brought on and perpetuated by sexually deviant women, thus embodying scandal's uncanny power to forge affective unity among otherwise divided constituencies. In his garbled, heavily moralizing account of Irish history, Deasy alludes not only to the twin pillars of Western misogyny, Eve and Helen of Troy, but to specifically Irish targets Devorgilla and Katharine O'Shea: "A woman brought sin into the world. For a woman who was no better than she should be, Helen, the runaway wife of Menelaus, ten years the Greeks made war on Troy. A faithless wife first brought the strangers to our shore here, MacMurrough's wife and her leman, O'Rourke prince of Breffini. A woman too brought Parnell low" (2.390–94).[5] To rationalize his outrage concerning the sex lives of Devorgilla and O'Shea, however, Deasy must now recast himself as an Irish nationalist. Given his passionate identification with the English, Deasy's outrage against Devorgilla, who brought "the strangers to our shore here," and toward O'Shea, who "brought Parnell low," rings absurdly hollow. Yet his imperious drive to express righteous outrage against scandalous women unites him here with Joycean figures from *Portrait*'s Dante to the citizen in "Cyclops" and Skin the Goat in "Eumaeus," all of whom share a hatred of Katharine O'Shea so deep-seated as to temporarily suppress any otherwise cherished political distinctions whenever her name is invoked.

During his extended soliloquy, Deasy, like Haines earlier, also seeks to legitimate his own political and moral rectitude by discrediting another perennial scandal target: the Jews.[6] Just as Haines feared that Jews were England's most pressing "national problem" (1.678), Deasy is sure that Jews are killing England, if indeed it is not already "dead by now" (2.354). Casting himself as Stephen's Irish compatriot, he reflects, "*We* have committed many errors and many sins . . . but not the one sin," presumably that of having put Christ (and England) to death (2.394–95). Here Deasy issues a charge at once legible to those familiar with its usual meaning and evocative of any number of unspeakable sins. As Joyce was certainly aware, in early 1904 certain

Irish priests had made shameful use of anti-Semitism's new currency by instigating the Limerick pogroms, in which nearly every member of Limerick's small Jewish community was driven out of the city in a series of riots and boycotts.[7] Haines's and Deasy's opportunistic anti-Semitism calls Joyce's readers' attention to Ireland's participation in the emergence across early-twentieth-century Europe of a scandalized Jewish identity about which virtually any claim could permissibly be made. Mulligan, too, will reenact this maneuver with a twist at the end of "Scylla and Charybdis," seeking to patch things up with Stephen by accusing Bloom, "the wandering jew," of sexual stalking (2.361). These uses of anti-Semitism to assert a spurious Irish unity foreshadow Leopold Bloom's role as an all-purpose scandal figure whose representational/spectral Jewishness will accrue, across the text, a range of scandalized sexual identities.

In "Nestor," Deasy charges the Jews as a group with a paradigmatically Joycean scandal act, claiming that "they sinned against the light" (2.361). Like the smugging scandal at Clongowes and the mysterious sin against the Holy Ghost that preoccupies Stephen later in *Portrait* (142), Deasy's charge against the Jews is simultaneously hyperbolic and unspecified, shrieked and unspoken.[8] But Stephen suavely disarms the scandal charges through which the unionist, imperialist headmaster proposes to his Irish Catholic underling an updated "act of union" among archipelagic Christians united against the Jews. When Deasy accuses the Jews of "sinning against the light," Stephen fails to respond with the scandalized repudiation of the other that Deasy is soliciting. Instead he renders harmless the unnamable, unspeakably repugnant "one sin" with which Deasy charges the Jews by casually accepting it, whatever it is, as just another part of the shared human condition, asking Deasy indifferently, "Who has not?" (2.373). In declaring Ireland's complete freedom from the unspecified "one sin"—a murky combination of the Jews' alleged "sin against the light" and the period's more conventional unspeakable crime, homosexuality—Deasy is, like Healy and the anti-Parnellites, rhetorically cleansing Ireland of the taint of scandal by projecting scandal elsewhere.[9] Yet just as when he implies that Ireland's sex scandals have all been heterosexual and the fault of the women involved, he is in obvious error when he claims that Ireland never admitted the Jews (2.438–42) and when he laughably insists that the English pay for all they take (2.264).

"CROPPIES LIE DOWN"

In the "Nestor" episode, Deasy's incapacity to argue rationally renders him a cartoonish personification of scandal itself, supporting his sweeping moral claims with evidence that is mischaracterized, misattributed, or simply wrong and, in any case, always irrelevant. Yet this does not keep him from also enacting the hegemonic power of scandalous accusations, however trivial, speculative, or wrong, to reinforce historical power differentials and suppress captive futurities like those about which Stephen has been thinking. Not only does Deasy, like scandal itself, compel his audience's attention and powerfully delimit its operative definitions of morality, identity, and agency, but, even more definitively and ominously, he also directs its actions. While Stephen has no trouble verbally outmaneuvering Deasy in ways that Joyce's readers can appreciate (even if Deasy himself cannot), his verbal and intellectual acuity ultimately binds him to, rather than frees him from, Deasy's purse strings. That Stephen's wits are materially subordinated to Deasy's imperial power is most significantly demonstrated by Deasy's casual directive to Stephen to get a letter filled with his own ill-informed views placed before the nationalist newspaper-reading public.

Over the course of their interview, Deasy has, through a series of scandal claims, figuratively reduced Stephen to a landless woodkerne (2.273–75), a croppy (2.276), and a fenian (2.272), in the process elevating himself to a "princely presence" (2.299). When Deasy instructs Stephen to deliver two copies of a fatuous, cliché-ridden letter to "the press" (2.290), he relegates Stephen to the role of a royal messenger directed by the princely Deasy to use his contacts to place Deasy's pronouncements before the public. In the context of Stephen's preoccupation with the difficulty of placing his own writing, Deasy's imperious directive effectively lowers the starting flag on a shockingly

asymmetrical competition between Deasy's already composed letter and the as-yet-unwritten poetry fragment Stephen will compose
on a piece torn from that letter in the following episode, "Proteus"
(3.406–7). As we shall see, Joyce's juxtaposition of these two pieces of
writing in *Ulysses*'s opening episodes serves to emphasize dynamics
endemic to British print capitalism, including Irish nationalist print
culture, that seamlessly exclude minority viewpoints.

As Deasy copies out his absurd letter, Stephen sits silently as directed, surrounded by framed "images of vanished horses," which
likewise stand silently "in homage," powerful creatures that, like
Stephen, are branded and fettered, reduced to the "meek" playthings
of princes (2.294–304). As Joyce demonstrates Deasy's power to ca-
priciously dictate the terms and pace of public discourse when he
cries out, "Full stop," and then calls for the "prompt ventilation of
this allimportant question" (2.305–6), Stephen envisions a horse race
in progress, recalling details gleaned during a day at the racetrack
with Cranly, including the excited cry, "Fair Rebel, Fair Rebel" (2.309).
This name, invoking aesthetics, dissent, and a commitment to social
justice, uses details recalled from a day spent in the homoerotically
charged company of Cranly to figure the involuntarily detained Stephen as in a race against the onrushing Deasy. In "Aeolus," we will see
Deasy win this figurative race at a canter, his letter assured of publication in the *Evening Telegraph* (7.520–86), while Stephen finishes out
of the money. In "Scylla and Charybdis," Stephen again finishes last
when he delivers Deasy's letter to poet and newspaper editor George
Russell (A.E.) and simultaneously learns that he has not even been
informed of, much less invited to, a gathering to honor Ireland's most
promising "younger poets" (9.289–319).

Deasy's banal letter on foot-and-mouth disease also references
post-1904 developments in the north of Ireland that he sums up in
the tautological and partly prophetic slogan, "Ulster will fight, and
Ulster will be right" (2.397–98). Deasy's letter exemplifies in microcosm the Northern Irish unionists' use of newspapers to exacerbate
the already existing representational crack discrediting Irish nationalists, allowing Joyce to implicitly connect the prosecutorial role of
arch-Ulster loyalist Edward Carson in the 1885 Wilde scandal to the

ongoing scandalization of Irish nationalism and Catholicism in early-twentieth-century Irish and British newspapers. As Brian G. Caraher has pointed out, in 1912 Joyce wrote his own letter to the editor of the *Freeman's Journal* in which he linked the arguments in Deasy's letter to Carson's 1912 Ulster Covenant pledging armed resistance to Home Rule, condemning attempts to ban the export of Irish cattle as part of a larger Tory/Unionist effort to undermine Ireland's economic growth by means of arbitrary boundary restrictions.[10] Stephen's subordination to an Ulster loyalist who submits an apparently laughable rant about foot-and-mouth disease to two Dublin newspapers thus renders in miniature the means by which a xenophobic and defensive loyalist subculture in Belfast and Derry was injecting a constant stream of scandal talk, or "agro," pathologizing and containing Irish nationalists in particular and Irish Catholics in general into newspapers around the British Isles.

Stephen, though charged by Deasy as a Fenian, is nonetheless forced into the service of Ulster loyalism, using his contacts among his father's circle of sentimental Parnellites to extend early loyalism's influence into the two most influential organs of mainstream nationalism. While the ultimate literalization of the crack in the mirror of the British press— the partition of Ireland—would not occur until the year of *Ulysses*'s publication, Joyce not only foresees this likelihood in his Triestene writing but in *Ulysses* assigns to Stephen the odd job of "bullock befriending bard" (2.431)—an educator and writer involuntarily obliged to befriend John Bull so as to advance Ulster loyalism's divisive ends.

As Stephen's reading conveys, Deasy's letter merely recycles trite newspaper phrases emphasizing and reinforcing prefabricated moral metaphors of space and distance. Thematically, Deasy embellishes his inscrutable position on cattle husbandry with unmotivated, cliched references to economic theories, current events, and scandalous classical women. All of these serve as vacuous but high-status signs of erudition that claim an imagined bond with readers who share Deasy's purported cultural and moral superiority, demonstrating scandal talk's serviceability as an emulsion in which unrelated political agendas are dissolved for easy public consumption. Through the letter's peroration, Joyce also calls our attention to newspaper pages as private property and to newspapers as commodities; even letters to the editor must earn their keep if they are to "trespass" on this "valuable space" (2.324). The "doctrine of laissez faire" referred to in the letter continues its leitmotif of capitalist exchange while also recalling the Great Famine, another traumatic breach or moral assassination created when the British state, in response to the potato blight, temporarily withdrew its customary hands-on management of the Irish economy. In Dublin at this time, the term "laissez-faire" would still have invoked the policy of Famine-era British MPs, early disaster capitalists who framed mass starvation as a structural adjustment necessary to redress purported bad planning on the part of people who did not own their land and could not run their economy.[11]

As the "Nestor" episode comes to a close, Stephen broods on his self-described role as a "server of a servant," "bowing to [Deasy's] bent back" and mentally agreeing, however reluctantly, to "help him in his fight" (2.426–30). In accepting this odd job (and serving, as Gabriel realizes of himself at the end of "The Dead," as a "pennyboy"), he becomes a bullockbefriending "jester at the court of his master" after all, serving the ends of empire because his dependent position makes it impossible for him to refuse. To add to his difficulties, as this episode and "Proteus" make clear, Stephen's writing, unlike Deasy's, exists outside of economic and institutional networks. Like the "job" on Sandymount Strand, presumably urination, that in "Proteus" Stephen must "get . . . over quick" to avoid the eyes of the public, the job he undertakes of working out and then drafting lines of poetry is symbolically cordoned away from the public discourse for which it is inherently unsuited (3.399–438). The sensual images Stephen conveys in just those few lines—"bloodying the sea," "mouth to her mouth's kiss"—make the unspeakable real by challenging accustomed categories and meanings. In contrast, Deasy's words, as exemplars of journalistic writing, are a pastiche of popular clichés so widely trafficked in that they are virtually devoid of meaning. Deasy's language belongs to the process of reification through which print capitalism—which requires readily recognizable and consumable signs in order to circulate its wares—drains language of semantic and aesthetic content.

Thus, in a ratio inversely proportional to originality and semantic weight, Deasy's writing is effortlessly conveyed into print, whereas Stephen's fragmentary stanza is in every sense a scrap, lacking the instant cultural legibility that would enable it to circulate as a commodity and thus to find a readership.

In a theme that Joyce will drive home in "Oxen of the Sun" and in "Circe," Stephen is, like his bit of writing, an artistic orphan. His writing, devoid of Deasy's stock moral caricatures, lacks the instant recognizability prerequisite to print capitalism's smooth conversion of words into commodities. More ominously yet, by refusing Mulligan, Haines, and eventually Deasy—and the masters they serve—Stephen has run out of potential patrons. Thus Stephen, like the Irish in their figurative "race" against the English, remains bound by the purse strings that have fettered him from the outset.

"PUT US ALL INTO IT"

In the "Aeolus" episode, which itself parodies the format of tabloid journalism by breaking the narrative into bits each topped by a blaring all-caps headline, an embarrassed Stephen fulfills his charge by submitting Deasy's letter to the combined offices of two of Dublin's major nationalist newspapers, the *Evening Telegraph* and the *Freeman's Journal and National Press*. Stephen enters the newspaper offices close on the heels of O'Madden Burke (the *Freeman's Journal* reporter who in "A Mother" destroyed Kathleen Kearney's career by declaring her mother's "performance" a scandal), who introduces Stephen to the other men gathered there with a Wilde-like aphorism, referring to him as "Youth led by Experience visit[ing] Notoriety" (7.508–9).

Within moments, Stephen is subjected to some good-natured discrediting by the most powerful man in the room, editor and gatekeeper Myles Crawford, whose name combines those of two of the Home Rule era's great scandal figures, Myles Joyce, the Maamtrasna martyr, and Mrs. Crawford, whose scandalous allegations put a stop to Charles Dilke's efforts on Home Rule's behalf. Like nearly everyone in Joyce's Dublin, Myles Crawford holds a retrospective, sentimental

form of Parnellism, the powerful but politically neutralizing structure of feeling that Joyce had mapped out in "Ivy Day in the Committee Room," and in that spirit he cordially greets Stephen, the son of a
particularly loyal one-time Parnellite activist, Simon Dedalus, who
had just recently departed the room. When Stephen wordlessly hands
over "the typed sheets, pointing to the title and signature," Crawford,
noting the torn page, asks, "Who tore it? Was he short taken?" jocu-
larly implying that "someone," presumably Stephen, has torn a strip
from Deasy's letter to wipe himself after defecating, leaving behind
incriminating evidence of the act (7.521).

Crawford's humorous accusation, however innocuous it might
appear, is actually one of Joyce's most masterful bits of scandal work:
Crawford's jocular interrogation of Stephen constitutes one of several references in *Ulysses* to the iconic trial evidence of Oscar Wilde's
shit-smeared sheets. Here the Wilde trials' most incriminating scandal fragment crops up in close proximity to the small-time scandal
journalist O'Madden Burke's Wildean quip so as to encode honest,
noncommercial writing as a high-risk activity. By having Crawford
refigure the scrap of paper on which Stephen wrote his poem as a shit-
marked sheet, Joyce subtly compares his own writing to Wilde's with
particular emphasis on how Wilde's writing was used against him as
criminal evidence. These broad indications that both Joyce and Stephen are vulnerable to genuinely dangerous scandal charges also call
attention to an extended scandalous countercharge that Joyce brings
against newspapers several times in this episode: that the condition of
their sheets constitutes clear evidence of dirty, secret arrangements.

As if to underscore the power relations that underlie these arrangements, Joyce follows Stephen's delivery of Deasy's letter with
a discussion between the newspapermen of the thankless nature of
service to princes (7.546–58) and of Ireland's tradition of serving history's victors while identifying sentimentally with the vanquished.[12]
And it is with these men that Joyce depicts Stephen making his own
dirty, secret arrangements as he negotiates with them the terms of the
alternative odd job he will undertake on Ireland's behalf. Beginning
in the segment headlined "YOU CAN DO IT!" Joyce himself, in the
person of Stephen, receives his instructions to produce his subsequent

work from Parnell's erstwhile followers, in the persons of the novel's own characters. Though Stephen's poetic revisions here offer a lyrical depiction of the British Empire's seductive misappropriation of Irish words, the "pale vampire" that feeds on the words of Irish writers "mouth to my mouth" (7.524–25), *Ulysses* itself offers the blueprint for a unique reappropriation.

In a moment of ironic literary self-insemination, Myles Crawford, an avatar of the "pale vampire" of print capitalism, lays a hand on Stephen and tells him "I want you to write something for me. . . . Something with a bite in it" (7.616).[13] Crawford in effect exhorts Stephen to commit the ultimate act of anticolonial pishoguery, culturally reappropriating Dublin lock, stock, and barrel by creating a literary corpus out of not just bits of people and experiences but the whole of the city. Crawford, a latter-day O'Brienite scribe, commands Stephen to "put us all into it, damn its soul, Father, Son and Holy Ghost and Jakes McCarthy" (7.621–22). O'Madden Burke concurs, assuring Stephen on behalf of all Dubliners that "we can all supply mental pabulum" (7.623). As Stephen's thoughts and comments in the later pages of the episode continually remind us, Joyce/Stephen's preliminary work on this commission, which he will ultimately fulfill in the pages of *Ulysses*, will commence with the first drafts of *Dubliners'* earliest stories.

Yet Joyce also depicts Stephen as secretly misinterpreting those instructions, getting them wrong to get them right. Stephen's willful misconstrual of Crawford's intended meaning is made particularly explicit through his responses to Crawford's celebration of conventional Home Rule–era scandalmongering as the key to professional success. Beginning with the item titled "THE GREAT GALLAHER," Joyce examines in detail the role of nationalist newspapers and journalists in launching and fueling the Home Rule scandal wars around the time of Joyce/Stephen's birth. Sensing potential greatness in Stephen, Crawford is inspired to recount decisive moments in the period that was, for him, the golden age of Irish nationalist newspaper reporting: the immediate aftermath of the Phoenix Park Murders. Crawford recalls that the daily *Freeman's Journal*, or "the Old Woman of Prince's Street," was there first, a comment that implicitly notes the

inability of the Land League's weekly, the *United Ireland*, to respond
to the murders until days after the *Freeman's Journal* had broadly accepted the (false) premise that the murders reflected violent extrem-
ism inherent within mainstream nationalism (7.684–85).[14] Again
representing the New Journalism in terms of rupture or separation,
Crawford figures the crack or tear created by the sensational coverage
of the Phoenix Park murders in biblical terms, comparing the nationalist newspapers scooped by the *Freeman's Journal* to those souls God
casts out of heaven, from whom there will be "weeping and gnashing
of teeth" (7.685). Yet the tone set by the *Freeman's Journal*'s actual coverage of the Phoenix Park murders precipitated weeping and gnashing of teeth in other respects as well, catalyzing a sort of widespread
self-incriminating horror and setting off a chorus of mea culpas that
largely paralyzed the whole of the Irish nationalist movement.

Fittingly, for Crawford the heroic embodiment of Irish journalism's achievements in the wake of Phoenix Park is "A Little Cloud's"
London-based journalist, Ignatius Gallaher, whose characteristic
boast was, "We'll paralyse Europe!" (7.628). Gallaher first "made his
mark" at the time of the Phoenix Park murders through what Crawford describes as "the smartest piece of journalism ever known": using
telegrams and a simple code to cable the Invincibles' escape route to
the *New York World* after the murders in Phoenix Park (7.631–69).
Gallaher, whose preening, bullying behavior in "A Little Cloud"
marks him as an imperial jester sadly lacking in Wilde's, Mulligan's,
or even Lenehan's charm, is nonetheless credited with a distinctly
Joycean strategy: encoding scandal fragments that can only be deci-
phered through the application of an external key. But because Gallaher's priority is to protect the commercial value of his "tit-bits" rather
than their communicative autonomy, his scandal work is the obverse
of Joyce's own. Crawford crows that Gallaher "gave it to them on a
hot plate"—that is, "the whole bloody history," describing Gallaher's
scandal fragments as food that he cleverly kept secret so as to serve
them "hot" to the comparatively militant Fenians on the other side
of the Atlantic (7.676–77). In the long run, Gallaher's smuggling of
"fresh" and "bloody" details to New York City, where they would have
fed North American nationalists' belief that political negotiations

were futile while armed struggle was inevitable and desirable, would have accentuated the tensions that eventually destroyed the Home Rule movement. Gallaher's scandalmongering "coup" thus is really just one more Pyrrhic victory, invoking in miniature the actual problems posed to Parnell and the Land League by the Phoenix Park assassinations and their coverage by nationalist as well as unionist and London-based newspapers, as described earlier.[15]

Gallaher's careerist coup thus recalls the "whole bloody history" of the Phoenix Park murders, which through the imperial circuitry of international newspaper networks gave birth to "a nightmare from which [Ireland] will never awake" (7.678). Moreover, Gallaher's reputed ambition to paralyze Europe with his sensational scoops pointedly recalls the paralysis that Joyce first anatomized in *Dubliners* with this echo of what is arguably that work's best-known trope, suggesting that the "hemipelagia of the will," which Joyce diagnosed in *Dubliners*, is closely related to the "deadly work" that stymied and ultimately assassinated the Home Rule movement.[16] Crawford himself seems unconcerned that the scandal work he praises would have substantially furthered the Invincibles' presumable aims: to scuttle promising Home Rule negotiations so as to force an armed confrontation between Ireland and the British state.[17] Thus Crawford's celebratory description of Gallaher's scandal work, with its sentimental Parnellite flavor, and Stephen's interpolated reactions to it dialogically comment on the horrible and lasting effects of the newspaper industry's relentless pursuit of scandal fragments and further define Stephen's abstentionist position relative to print capitalism's scandal economy.

Crawford goes on to admiringly recount the meteoric ascent up the New Journalist ladder made possible by Gallaher's coup at the *Freeman's Journal* (7.686–89). Gallaher had gotten his initial "leg up" from Gregor Grey, a draftsman at the *Weekly Freeman* who created the advertisement through which he transmitted his coded map of the Invincibles' escape route. He was then helped by one Paddy Hooper who, Crawford recalls, "worked Tay Pay"—that is, T. P. O'Connor, the powerful Irish-born, London-based newspaper editor—who offered him the job in London of which Little Chandler in "A Little Cloud" is so envious. "Now," Crawford crows, "he's got in with Blumenfeld," the

expatriate American editor of London's *Daily Express*. As Crawford's
account unwittingly reveals, Gallaher's climb up the ladder is not so
much a matter of "talent" as of being well-connected within a transnational homosocial network in which personal loyalties and ambition
vastly overdetermine the content of newspaper copy. "That's press,"
Crawford declares. "Pyatt! He was all their daddies!" (7.688–89).

Critics have commonly assumed that the "he" who "was all their
daddies" in this genealogy of the New Journalism refers to Pyatt,
whom Gifford identifies as Felix Pyatt, a revolutionary and journalist
who worked in London (1810–1889). Yet Joyce immediately follows this
reference with "the father of scare journalism, Lenehan confirmed,
and the brother-in-law of Chris Callinan" (7.690–91). Since the fictional Gallaher seems much more likely than the little-known Pyatt
to have had a brother-in-law named Callinan, given the context of
Crawford's adoring account of Gallaher's prowess and Lenehan's role
throughout Joyce's work as an interlocutor of scandal, this line is more
credibly read as nominating Gallaher as *Ulysses*'s mythical originator
of the modern newspaper scandal that blew "the O'Brienite scribes"
off course. The revolutionary Felix Pyatt seems, indeed, to momentarily surface from Crawford's historical unconscious as an almost
entirely forgotten one-time antithesis to capitalist scandal journalism's now overwhelmingly triumphant thesis. Thus, in the dialogic,
multivalent mythology that Joyce delivers through the twitching
mouth of the possibly syphilitic Crawford—a distinctly Irish "pale
vampire"—it was ambitious Irish nationalist journalists who opened
the bag of winds of scandal, fathering "scare journalism," "paralyzing
Europe," and rendering history itself an increasingly unfamiliar, mili-
tarized nightmare from which modernity cannot awake.

"THE WHOLE AFTERCOURSE OF BOTH OUR LIVES"

In the following section, however, Joyce anticipates David Lloyd in
proposing that, while one might be unable to wake from the nightmare of history, alternate possibilities remain suspended within that
nightmare, fragmentary and incoherent tangents of purportedly

impossiblized trajectories.[18] Here Joyce fuses moments of violent historical rupture from ancient myth and history with modern scandal fragments to create an alternative mythic telos. When Professor MacHugh mentions "hawkers [who have just been] taken up before the recorder" for selling a commemoration postcard of one of the Invincibles to the wife of the current lord lieutenant "right outside the viceregal lodge" (7.704), images of the Phoenix Park scandal converge with those of the Oscar Wilde scandal: Joyce's characters discuss a case in which postcards commemorating the Phoenix Park murders prompted a trial, just as the Marquess of Queensberry's offensive postcard prompted Oscar Wilde's original libel case. In this fictional treatment of a minor historical episode, which was in fact reported by the *Freeman's Journal* on June 9, 1904, past scandal trajectories seem to converge in the present moment.

So as to underscore this convergence, as J. J. O'Molloy (who shares Joyce's initials and is now called "Messenger") pauses in his account of these proceedings to strike a match, an unidentified first-person narrator, in a completely uncharacteristic high realist apostrophe, solemnly announces that "I have often thought since on looking back over that strange time that it was that small act, trivial in itself, that striking of that match, that determined the whole aftercourse of both our lives" (7.763–65). Given Joyce's longstanding hostility to the "prison-house of realism," it is impossible to deny the satirical element of this pointedly Dickensian interpolation. Yet it is just as undeniable that Joyce's stylistic shift backward into the speech of his nineteenth-century precursors also creates a strikingly defamiliarizing effect and a heightened, even uncanny sense of direct address that marks the moment at which the stories of Stephen Dedalus and James Joyce converge. In response to the historical and conventional trajectories mapped by the episode, it is at this moment that Stephen becomes the writer who will one day write *Ulysses* in an epiphany that will determine "the whole aftercourse of both [their] lives."

This reading places Joyce's decision to undertake an odd job on Ireland's behalf squarely within the scandal sequence that started with the emergence of Parnellite nationalism and the Home Rule debates and situates Joyce's own project as an intervention in this trajectory.

Joyce/Stephen's epiphanic sense of mission in response to a Messenger's flame identifies him both with Moses and with Parnell, the Irish Moses, whose failure to reach the Promised Land of Home Rule is registered indexically throughout Crawford's account of Gallaher's rise.[19] Having received Myles Crawford's unwittingly cautionary account of how Irish nationalism was blown off course by the storm its own scandalmongering unleashed, Stephen, in the remaining portion of the episode, will set a new course through the continuing gale, navigating dialogically between the fictional and the nonfictional, the popular and the high modernist, the sentimental and the scandalous.

Beginning in "A MAN OF HIGH MORALE," Professor MacHugh purports to recite from memory John Taylor's 1901 speech making the case for Irish cultural nationalism. Taylor's speech, as recalled by MacHugh, turns on a specific rhetorical conceit: Taylor simply reiterates the arguments that his opponent, Gerald Fitzgibbon, has just made against the emerging Gaelic League, recasting them as they could have been used to persuade the young Moses to accept the Hebrew people's continuing enslavement in Egypt. MacHugh describes the gaunt, bearded Taylor, who had risen from his sick bed to make the speech, as Parnell's ghostly double and aligns Gerald Fitzgibbon with Parnell's symbolic Brutus, Tim Healy (7.800).[20] MacHugh's reenactment of Taylor's speech constitutes a trial scene with Stephen positioned as "the youth of Ireland," a young Moses momentously weighing the arguments of both sides with a particular question in mind: "Could you try your hand at it yourself?" (7.828–40).[21] MacHugh's recalled précis of the speech ends triumphantly; Taylor demolishes Fitzgibbon with the claim that if the youthful Moses had been swayed to the view that the Jews were worthy only to be slaves, the Jews would never have become God's chosen people and the Ten Commandments would never have been conveyed to the world.

In response to this stirring call, Stephen receives a vision confirming his own prophetic role. His thoughts go from the ancient Hebrews, who, unlike the written Ten Commandments, are "gone with the wind," to Daniel O'Connell's enormous rallies and how his words and the aspirations of the people who had "sheltered within his voice" had over time also "scattered to the four winds" (7.880–82). The phrase "a people sheltered within his voice" also summons an image of Stephen himself giving symbolic shelter to his own contemporaries by capturing their voices so that, even once dead, they will still speak. He foresees that his work will be a record of "all that ever anywhere wherever was," thereby transcending both his individual life and his time, when he himself is "me no more" (7.883). As if reading and responding to Stephen's thoughts (and inscribing a bitter joke at Joyce's own expense concerning his interminable difficulties getting his work into print), J. J. O'Molloy wishes Stephen well, saying "I hope you will live to see it published" (7.907).

Figuratively, Stephen here takes up the visionary, nation-building movement that Parnell once led and that Healy had impossiblized. In the following section, "LET US HOPE," Joyce/Stephen famously chooses his lifelong theme: "Dublin" (7.915). The emphasis placed by Taylor's imagined high Egyptian priest on cities, which the Egyptians and English had and which the Hebrews and Irish allegedly did not, emphasizes the political significance of Stephen's choice: to bridge the imagined abyss that separates the colonizer from the colonized and into which cultural producers from the periphery and the larger aspirations they embody repeatedly fall. Following in the steps of O'Connell, Parnell, and Wilde, Stephen, like Joyce, will seek and eventually find new modes of Irish linguistic/artistic sovereignty while simultaneously surpassing his political and artistic forerunners by avoiding the abyss.

In "Aeolus," Stephen thus takes on the vast project of "realizing" a representationally impossiblized city and its people. As he and the other men walk the streets of Dublin from the newspaper offices to a pub, Stephen responds to MacHugh's account of Taylor's stirring speech by telling him, "I have a vision too." When the professor both authorizes Stephen's envisioned work and bids him to elaborate by answering yes, Stephen shares with him the name of his vision— "Dubliners" (7.922)—and begins the first telling of his story of two Dubliners. This story, titled "A Pisgah Sight of Palestine, or The Parable of the Plums," is set at Nelson's Pillar in the center of Dublin. Lord Nelson, the English "one-handled adulterer," famously had an open affair over which, for political expediency, the English chose not to be scandalized. Invoked as it is in the midst of "Aeolus," this column, an imperial tribute to Nelson that occupies the center of Dublin's contemporary social order, stands in clear opposition to the columns the press dedicated to Parnell's affair.

"The Parable of the Plums" is, by implication, the first of what will become a series of vignettes from the lives of Dubliners. That Stephen has begun his commission on behalf of all Dubliners, whose spokesperson, Myles Crawford, has asked Stephen to "write something for me" and to "put us all into it," is confirmed by Professor MacHugh, who tells J. J. O'Molloy, "Moses and the promised land. We gave him that idea" (7.1061–62). Following the parable's characteristically abrupt closure (Myles Crawford checks to see if it is really over, asking "Finished?" [7.1031]), MacHugh introduces *The Odyssey* into the conversation by invoking Penelope, famed for the heroic lengths to which she went to abstain from a scandalous transgression of her "bedvows." Likening Stephen to the Greek Cynic philosopher Antisthenes, MacHugh recalls that it was Antisthenes who "took away the palm of beauty from Argive Helen and handed it to poor Penelope" (7.1038–39), thus hinting that Stephen, as a modern-day Antisthenes, should replace the current tragic vision of Ireland as irretrievably conquered with a comic, local, domestic vision.[22] Stephen responds by thinking of Penelope Rich, a historical scandal figure who negotiated a way between the poles of Penelope's private self-sacrifice and Helen of Troy's scandalous, divinely compelled self-immolation.

In the late sixteenth century, Lady Penelope Rich, married unhappily and probably involuntarily to Robert Lord Rich, publicly asserted her own sexual desires with extraordinary courage and thereby secured a destiny of her own choosing. Lady Rich appeared publicly, if in coded form, as Sir Philip Sidney's muse, Stella, before living openly with Lord Mountjoy and bearing several children, marrying him after obtaining a divorce from Robert Rich in 1605.[23] In one tendril of the nineteenth century's many speculations about Shakespeare, Penelope Rich was also proposed as the "dark lady" of the sonnets, who turns up in "Scylla and Charybdis" as one of Buck Mulligan's literary counterparts. Although both "Argive Helen" and Penelope Rich were "women who did" openly violate sexual prohibitions, Lady Rich, unlike the divinely compelled Helen, consciously made the choice to sow the wind and did so without reaping the whirlwind.

The figure of Penelope Rich thus evokes the equilibrium that Joyce repeatedly attains in *Ulysses* by balancing scandalous disclosures about himself against scandalous disclosures concerning others. That Joyce/Stephen will refrain from handing "the palm" to either Penelope while honoring the Odyssean wit and persistence of both is indicated in the ambivalence of the chiasmatic oxymoron "Poor Penelope. Penelope Rich" (7.1040). This artistic policy is echoed in Professor MacHugh's remark that Stephen reminds him of Antisthenes, of whom it was said "none could tell if he were bitterer against others or against himself," and in the dilemma of the "two old Dublin women on the top of Nelson's pillar" in Stephen's story, who cannot bear to look either up or down and who therefore hunker down, up the pole though they be, to eat their bag of plums (7.1023–27). These three concluding, imbricated images of precarious balance also relate to figures that are associated with sex scandal throughout *Ulysses*. In the trinity of Helen/Penelope/Penelope Rich evoked in this segment, Helen's story recalls the vast political and historical powers that sex scandal can unleash; Penelope's story encodes the heroic levels of effort and self-sacrifice required to evade the powerful social and intrapsychic forces that impel us toward booby-trapped transgressions; and Penelope Rich's nearly anomalous success in the face of the forces of scandal make her a dark horse who beat the field against incalculable odds.

Antisthenes's ambivalent hostilities, distributed equally between himself and others, similarly figure a balancing act between sadistic scandalmongering and masochistic sentimentalism that is pragmatically achieved through the even-handed condemnation of self and others. And the two elderly Dubliners are "up a plumtree," entrapped between the military/imperial heights and scandalous personal depths embodied by the "one-handled adulterer," Lord Nelson. Thus Joyce/Stephen, trapped between untenable extremes, has committed himself to a middle course between the spectacular aspirations, self-exposure, and martyrdom of Julius Caesar, Charles Stewart Parnell, and Oscar Wilde and "poor Penelope's" closeted, labor-intensive self-erasure. Joyce/Stephen attains this middle path through a hybrid prose form in which historical and personal facts, both plausible and fantastic, promiscuously intermingle with lies and fictional people, places, and details.

As Sean Latham argues, the hybrid of fact and fiction characteristic of the Joycean middle course has contributed a great deal to *Ulysses*'s notorious interpretive difficulties. Given the ever-increasing distance between turn-of-the-century Dublin and Joyce's readers, much of what Latham describes as Joyce's "essentially unprecedented campaign of libel" has either remained or become "relatively illegible."[24] Yet while *Ulysses*'s vast web of factual, semifactual, and pseudofactual fragments did, as Latham argues, break down "the tenuous legal distinction between novels and news," Joyce's strategies for doing so were multivalent, commingling fact and fiction in a manner that libeled both himself and others while at the same time generating a seemingly ineradicable aura of uncertainty in regard to each potentially scandalous detail. As we shall see, through this inclusion of both public and private lived experience, some self-incriminating, some incriminating of others, and some fictional, Joyce retained aspects of the discourses of both scandal and sentimentalism without falling prey to either the self-devouring psychic cannibalism unleashed by the former or the dangerous political masochism instilled by the latter.

In a moment of parodic self-portraiture in *Finnegans Wake*, Joyce would aptly describe the complexly self-implicating scandal work that Stephen is here first developing. Describing his alter ego, Shem the Penman, Joyce writes, "A few toughnecks are still getatable who pretend that aboriginally he was of respectable stemming . . . but every honest to goodness man in the land of the space of today knows that his back life will not stand being written about in black and white. Putting truth and untruth together a shot may be made at what this hybrid actually was like to look at" (169). Much of the power of this passage turns on the ambiguity of the pronouns "he" and "his," which irreconcilably muddle the distinction between Shem the Penman as unique, unlike others, or as an everyman, who "knows that his back life will not stand being written about." This passage both is and is not about Joyce, and thus both does and does not comment on the excessiveness of Joyce's particular personal transgressions. In this artistic manifesto, as elsewhere, Joyce acknowledges the presence of personal scandal throughout his oeuvre while meticulously neglecting to validate any particular scandal fragment, thereby short-circuiting the grinding, tearing scandal machines by which we are all "getatable" if our lives should ever be written about in the black and white moral palette of scandal. As Stephen is just beginning to understand, by combining truth (scandal) and untruth (sentiment), an artist can take a shot at describing what his own back life, and the history that produced it, is actually like.

CHAPTER 6

James Joyce's Self-Protective Self-Exposure

Confessing in a Foreign Language

To be understood is to be found out.

—Oscar Wilde

In Part II of *Ulysses*, Joyce continues to both portray and deploy ambiguous self-exposure as a strategy for flying by scandal's nets. Whereas in the Telemachiad Joyce had incriminated his younger self by proxy in the person of Stephen, in the following episodes he introduces a second alter ego, Leopold Bloom, a modern Odysseus who both shares some of Joyce's known or presumed private vulnerabilities and enacts several of Joyce's defensive scandal tactics. Through Bloom, Joyce seriocomically asserts that it is only through adroit scandal work, undertaken at the interstices of the fictional and the factual, that an irreparably deviant Irishman such as Bloom (or Joyce himself) might evade the entrapping, double-binding realist conventions that have turned language, in Wilde's terms, into a "prison-house."[1] Like

Joyce in authoring the novel, in *Ulysses* Bloom is both shamefully exposed and, in the intricate maneuvers through which he labors to evade scandal, ostentatiously self-protective. In this, he represents an embodied answer to Stephen's seemingly insoluble problem of how to evade the snares of scandal and the distortions imposed by the cracked mirror of British print capitalism by redefining the ethical parameters of the human and the terms of artistic success.

JOYCE'S MASTERSTROKE

As we have seen in the previous chapter, in "Aeolus" Joyce compares Stephen to Wilde when Crawford cross-examines him about the scandalous use to which he has supposedly subjected Deasy's written sheets. In Bloom's famous visit to the jakes in the final scene of the opening episode of Part II, "Calypso," Bloom is similarly linked to both Wilde and Joyce through a pointed reference to shit-marked sheets. In the jakes, Bloom defecates with the aid of a "tabloid," a term through which Joyce conflates newspapers and quack medicines as made up of worthless filler: "All breadcrumbs they are. About six hundred percent profit" (6.61–62). While Bloom is himself superlatively exposed to the novel's readers in the jakes, his own reading likewise exposes and discredits Philip Beaufoy's prizewinning short story, "Matcham's Masterstroke," in the highly commercial "light weekly" *Tit-Bits*, which Bloom peruses and then uses as toilet paper. Through Bloom, Joyce charges his fictionalized Beaufoy with having converted his own risqué personal details into the "prize titbit" that won him "three pounds thirteen and six" (4.505). Bloom's quick scan of the story uncovers a series of suggestive although not explicitly improper phrases that, strung together, hint at a scandalous sexual transaction hidden in a seemingly wholesome story on the pages of a New Journalist weekly—as scandal fragments ambiguously fictionalized in the pages of a factual newspaper that is itself represented in a fictional/factual novel. "Matcham's Masterstroke" thus serves as an involuted figure that both symbolizes and enacts the coded public circulation of private improprieties.

"Matcham's Masterstroke's" status as a textual container for scandalously publicized private details is, of course, further emphasized in its textual position within the conventionally private space of the outhouse and the subsequent highly personal use to which Bloom puts it. Yet the story emerges as a very different and more specific figure for shameful personal details when we recall that as a fifteen-year-old, Joyce himself had submitted the story to which "Matcham's Masterstroke" corresponds to *Tit-Bits*, which rejected it in favor of "For Vera's Sake," a similar story written by a commercial writer named Philip J. Beaufoy.[2] The print industry thus "handed the palm" (7.1038) to Beaufoy just as Myles Crawford and A.E., in "Aeolus" and "Scylla and Charybdis," will hand the palm of publication to Deasy.[3] Critics have frequently observed that Bloom's performance in the jakes constitutes what Brandon Kershner calls a kind of literary criticism,[4] and have also noted the story's inherent ambiguity in that it is Joyce's own youthful work that is, in one important sense, subjected to Bloom's scatological critique. Yet the full significance of "Matcham's Masterstroke" for an understanding of Joyce's scandal work becomes clear only by recognizing that by including it in *Ulysses*, Joyce simultaneously exposed and protected an even more vulnerable and precious personal detail. Through the specific coded scandal fragments that attract Bloom's attention, Joyce most explicitly exposes details of his first sexual communion with Nora Barnacle, which, in a famous letter, he referred to as a "sacrament" that filled him with "amazed joy."[5]

Joyce's incorporation of "Matcham's Masterstroke" into *Ulysses* thus exemplifies the turn toward self-exposure that Stanislaus Joyce noted in James Joyce's prose style as far back as 1904, when the Revivalist intelligentsia had rejected Joyce's "narrative essay"—the earliest chapter draft of what would eventually become *Portrait of the Artist*—because of its sexual content.[6] In his journal, however, Stanislaus astutely observed that Joyce's style was not, despite the reactions of many readers from that time to this, an exercise in unmitigated explicitness; rather, as he noted, "Jim is thought to be very frank about himself but his style is such that it might be contended that he confesses in a foreign language."[7] Bloom's reading of Joyce/Beaufoy's story represents an elaborate instance of just such an encoded Joycean confession. The

particular phrases Bloom registers are all booby-trapped double en-
tendres along the lines of *Chamber Music*, the decorous title of Joyce's
first poetry collection and a cheeky scatological reference.[8] As in that
instance, the suggestive phrases in "Matcham's Masterstroke" could
easily pass the closest inspection of editors, readers, and the purity
movement, since to notice their possible but indefinite impropriety
would discredit the one who noticed rather than the author, just as
Joyce had claimed about Wilde's writing.[9]

The story describes a literary protagonist, "Matcham," who "always remembers" the "masterstroke" with which he won the hand
of a laughing witch. "Winning" is frequently associated with sex in
Ulysses: in conventional male exchanges such as those between Mulligan and his mates at the Forty Foot about their friends' new con-
quests, but also in far more elaborate representations of sex as a
competition in later episodes.[10] Elsewhere in *Ulysses*, Joyce eroticizes
laughing women, making laughter a cognate for orgasm.[11] The term
"witch" prefigures the significance of the *Odyssey*'s Circe as a sign for
sexual desire's capacity to transform a man, stripping him of his civilized defenses or, as Joyce described Barnacle's power, allowing him
"to leave aside [his] contemptuous, suspicious nature."[12] The name
"Matcham" recalls the proverb invoked elsewhere in *Ulysses* that "as
God made them, he matched them," a bit of folk wisdom explaining
the magically transformative experience of love at first sight (13.976).
In both sound and meaning, the term "masterstroke" recalls the act of
manual and probably mutual masturbation shared by Nora Barnacle
and James Joyce on their famous first walk.[13] Joyce certainly won Nora
Barnacle's hand on that occasion; indeed, in the transaction that Joyce
implicitly but never explicitly dated to Bloomsday, they may have
handed each other the palm.[14] The term "masterstroke" also recalls
Joyce's troping of scandal as a lightning bolt or thunderclap, acknowledging the power of all these coded details to destroy both Barnacle
and himself if they were to be exposed in a juridical, journalistic, or
clerical context rather than in the coded way in which they appear
through Bloom's reading of Beaufoy's story.[15] Joyce is here doing what
Bloom thinks Beaufoy has done: sanitizing the story's details by rendering them "quick and neat" in an authorized generic frame that

"begins and ends morally," an observation quite suggestive of moral impropriety throughout the rest of the story (4.511–15).[16]

While reading this pedestrian story, which "did not move or touch him," Bloom reflects that in the slow, "silly" summer season, the newspapers will carry anything, a discrediting charge against the press that Joyce, in a final masterstroke, dramatically echoes by having Bloom tear "away half the prize story sharply" and wipe himself with it (4.511–37). Through the political sex scandal, as discussed earlier, the New Journalism had repeatedly publicized tasteless, shameful details from the private lives of dissenting Irish politicians and artists while assigning the shame of these disclosures to their victims and their constituencies. In this scene, Joyce turns the tables, exposing the disreputable private activities of a supposedly upright newspaper author and projecting the shame of this exposure onto the New Journalist press as a whole. As Bloom's culminating act in the jakes makes clear, New Journalist tabloids will indeed include *anything* on their pages.

Thus Beaufoy's ambiguous self-exposure parallels Joyce's strategy throughout *Ulysses* of exposing what are, or seem to be, potentially compromising personal details. By rendering his own juvenile writing and the commercial writing of the New Journalists equally the object of shameful exposure, however, Joyce employs the scandalous energies he invokes to consolidate rather than polarize. This slippery codistribution of shameful details between Joyce and his various adversaries is one significant way in which Joyce, as Kershner contends, actively positions readers as coauthors.[17] Readers are constantly pressured to choose between ascribing specific embarrassing details to Joyce, a choice that leads us to read them and the characters they implicate naturalistically and sympathetically, or to other people, which leads us to read them as metaphoric and censorious. Yet Joyce disrupts this very binary, which replicates the moralizing structure of scandal itself, by repeatedly complicating the terms in which he presents his real or seeming scandal fragments so as to undermine the careful reader's attempts to choose.

Like Joyce/Beaufoy's coded celebration of a public, nonprocreative, masturbatory, extramarital sex act, Bloom's help-wanted ad in the following episode, "Lotus Eaters," represents yet another improved version of Oscar Wilde's homeopathic or defensive self-exposures. As we learn in this episode, Bloom, using the pseudonym of Henry Flower, has published scandalous personal details in the pages of the *Irish Times* while carefully managing their routes and visibility in the public sphere so as to deflect any risk. This style has "grown out of"—in the sense of having grown or started from, developed from, or being indebted to—Wilde and paradoxes because it is simultaneously more explicit, more specialized, and, above all, more participatory on the part of its readers. Through an apparent obedience to conventions that allows for their flagrant public violation, Bloom, like Joyce, ensures that he will be understood by none but voluntary conspirators in the cocreation of meanings that are unspeakable within the conventions of public discourse. Joyce/Beaufoy/Bloom's self-publicized transgressions cannot be "found out" and recirculated by hostile scandalmongers because they are perceptible only to libidinally literate readers. Bloom can decode Joyce/Beaufoy's story because he can conceive of a whirlwind courtship joyously consummated in a sacred, back-alley hand job. Among most *Tit-Bits* readers, however, Beaufoy's secret is safe, and those few who read it as Bloom does can be relied on to keep their deviant interpretations to themselves. The same is true of respondents to Bloom's help-wanted ad: only a very particular job applicant would have responded to whatever letter Bloom sent back to initial applicants.

Martha Clifford, Bloom's correspondent, is herself a Joycean scandal fragment, as she shares her given name and her distinctive status as erotic pen pal with the Swiss Marthe Fleischmann, with whom Joyce carried on a largely epistolary affair in 1918–1919.[18] In her most recent letter to Bloom, Martha is clearly a willing, informed participant in an adulterous, sadomasochistic epistolary affair. To have arrived at this stage in their correspondence, she must at some earlier point have responded both favorably and conversantly to an ostentatiously dodgy "job offer" couched in provocatively sadomasochistic language.[19] As with two individuals engaged in any consensual anonymous sexual exchange, chances that either Flower/Bloom or Martha could have wound up in this interaction without first having both

supplied and responded to a series of specialized ("Masonic") signs
or passwords are infinitesimal. Joyce is thus depicting underground
communications that are routed, in code, through the mainstream
communications infrastructure. Even should a collaborative reader/
participant within such a subterranean counterpublic attempt to
bring charges after the fact, as Bloom fears Martha might, she would
have no means to publicize the author's transgressions without exposing her own. The case is the same for Bloom as Beaufoy's reader, for
Martha as Flowers's reader, or for ourselves as Joyce's readers.[20] Belat-
edly conscience-stricken readers would, like Martha, remain compromised by their own complicity, unable to complain to the authorities
without risking self-incrimination and explaining why they had accepted or even understood such a solicitation in the first place.[21]

"BREAKDOWN. HEART."

In "Hades" references to private effects hidden in public envelopes
proliferate in representations of death, burial, and death's aftereffects. One well-known such figure is the Plumtree's Potted Meat advertisement, which is unfortunately placed on the obituary page by
the *Freeman's Journal*, inadvertently calling attention to both the ad
and the product as containers in which sex, death, and food scandalously commingle.[22] This trope of a secret sexual meaning housed
in a publicly circulating container recurs in the funeral carriage en
route to Glasnevin Cemetery, in which Simon Dedalus and Martin
Cunningham notice crumbs—and something else they do not describe out loud, presumably semen stains—on the seats (6.100–108).
The two men silently and rather happily regard evidence of some
prior unspeakable activity that structurally parallels the evidence of
the speakable if uncouth act of messy public eating. Eyeing the unmentionable stains to which Cunningham has directed his attention,
Dedalus observes complacently, "It's the most natural thing in the
world" (6.108). In these among other representations of publicly conveyed sexual secrets, Joyce repeatedly demonstrates that when a scandal fragment remains in some way unofficial, circulating publicly as

tacitly shared or implicit knowledge, it, like Mr. Power's barmaid, can be accepted with broadminded generosity (6.244–45).

If secret transgressions contingently contained recur throughout "Hades," so too do the "falls" that result when the fragile balance that containment necessitates is lost. In this episode, Bloom's thoughts and conversations with fellow mourners demonstrate the vigorous, autonomous afterlife in the Dublin "underworld" of the New Journalist sex scandal that brought about the cataclysmic fall of Parnell. During its course, Bloom envisions Glasnevin Cemetery as a network of parasitic insects and rats feeding on the dead, recalling the transnational networks of scandal transmission Joyce complained of in his Triestene journalism, as well as the images of Parnell being hounded and set upon by clergy like rats in a sewer in the Christmas dinner scene in *Portrait* (38–46). Throughout the episode, the burial of bodies, described in terms of falls, descents, and lowerings, is couched in language consistent with the operations of the newspaper scandal.

The funeral Bloom attends in "Hades" is for the alcoholic Dignam, who through the manner and timing of his death is associated with Odysseus's man Elpenor. Elpenor, recently killed by a drunken fall in Circe's hall, is the first shade Odysseus meets in the underworld. The parallel with Elpenor and the claim that Dignam died of a heart ailment call attention to Dignam's status as the broken-hearted victim of a self-inflicted fall, a grotesque caricature of Parnell. Joyce reinforces the parallel between Dignam and Parnell later in the novel, when Alf Bergan claims to have seen Dignam walking around Dublin after his death and when, in a comic communication from the afterlife, Dignam/Parnell reveals that he is "still submitted to trial at the hands of certain bloodthirsty entities on the lower astral levels" (12.346–47). Here and elsewhere, Joyce calls attention to the afterlife of scandal by invoking the serious belief in Parnell's survival that circulated well into the twentieth century among certain Irish nationalists.[23] This emphasis on the uncertain boundary between life and death recalls the figure of the room of infinite possibilities in "Nestor" and the ongoing aftereffects of political assassinations that are "not to be thought away" (2.49).

Victims of moral assassination also number among the unquiet dead; they do not rest, but rather exhibit an ongoing, supernatural vitality. In the course of these meditations on the uncanny afterlife of scandal, Joyce again invokes the malign magic of pishoguery, the folk ritual whereby misappropriated personal effects may unleash destructive forces. Bloom thinks briefly of pishoguery when he envisions the neighbor women who traditionally help with the laying out of the dead as potentially secreting hair and fingernail clippings in an envelope and momentarily wonders whether his son, Rudy, was the victim of such a malicious, secret expropriation.[24] Like the hair of a corpse that, as Bloom reflects, "grows all the same after," the "unclean job" of both Irish and English scandalmongering during the Home Rule scandal wars continues to cast a pall over the Irish social order (6.20).

In the details that Bloom notes along the route of the funeral procession, Joyce develops the analogy between the newly absent Dignam and the fallen Parnell, as when Bloom registers that they are passing the literally and symbolically empty "foundation stone for Parnell" and recalls both men's cause of death: "Breakdown. Heart" (6.320). Once at the graveyard, the Caesar/Parnell parallel that Joyce first established in "Et Tu, Healy" again casts Dignam as Parnell. As the gathered mourners "split" when Dignam's coffin is moved into position at the grave site, Bloom muses, "Burying him. We come to bury Caesar" (6.803). If Dignam's burial reenacts Parnell's falling into a hole created by his followers when they split, Bloom notes that in another sense we all dig our own graves. Reflecting on the case of an individual stranded on an uninhabited island, Bloom thinks that such a castaway wouldn't have anyone "to sod him after he died" (6.808–9). This obscene pun conflating sodomy and necrophilia serves, like the British journalists' picking through Oscar Wilde's clothes in Joyce's "Poet of *Salomé*," the Clongowes smugging episode in *Portrait*, and Deasy's references to "the one sin" and the "sin against the light," to emphasize homosexuality's status as scandal's most paradigmatic and long-lasting charge. But although an isolated individual outside of any social network has no one to sod (or scandalously stigmatize) him even in death, such a castaway is still free, like the victim of scandal, to "dig his own grave."

Noting the risk of self-incrimination that is an unavoidable feature of modern scandal culture, Bloom sadly decides, "We all do" (6.809). All citizens under print capitalism's imperial sway are doomed in the course of their private lives to "dig holes" into which, owing to the ever-expanding vocabulary of scandal in which newspaper readers participate, they themselves may fall. When they do fall, Bloom thinks, the insects and rats "make short work" of them, "pick[ing] the bones clean no matter who" they are (6.980–81). By wondering whether "the news go[es] about whenever a fresh one is let down" through "underground communication," Bloom explicitly connects the collective feeding of graveyard scavengers to scandal when he notes with uncharacteristic acerbity that the citizens of modernity have learned from scavengers how to feed on the dead: "we learned that from them" (6.990–91).

The wind imagery that Joyce uses in "Aeolus" to parody the bluster, bombast, and moral inconstancy of the press first appears in a darker mode in "Hades" when Bloom envisions scandal's reduction of bodies to fragments (such as Parnell's "broken heart") as generating a noxious gas poisoning Glasnevin, Dublin's microcosmic "city of the dead."[25] Bloom's most extreme and revolting vision of relations between the living and the dead is also the episode's most horrific metaphorization of the New Journalist sex scandal and its afterlife, in which Bloom recalls a case he read of in a newspaper in which necrophiles had disinterred "fresh buried females or even putrefied [ones] with running gravesores" (6.998–99). This imagery connects the role of the journalist as undiscriminating scavenger, defiling corpses and reveling in the grotesque, to the technique that Joyce specified for the episode in the Gilbert schema: "incubism," or the practice of both haunting and feeding on the unconscious. Joyce thus defined his own writing in "Hades" as both exposing and enacting the worst excesses of scandal journalism. Like the sinister "pale vampire" that recurs in the "Proteus" and "Aeolus" episodes that bookend "Hades," Joyce's own writing both participates in and parodies the New Journalism's unsavory practices by feeding indiscriminately on the living and the dead. In doing so, Joyce mobilizes what he viewed as the New Journalism's sacrilegious practices—grave robbing, simony, and pishoguery—which he himself employs homeopathically throughout the novel to guard against some of the New Journalism's most damaging effects.

"THERE'S A HURRICANE BLOWING"

Throughout *Ulysses*, Bloom exhibits a distinct affinity for newspapers as readily available natural resources that he uses to an array of ends, from subversive self-entertainment to personal hygiene to initiating an anonymous affair. As an advertising agent, placing items in newspapers is also as essential to his livelihood as it is to would-be Irish authors like Stephen. This shared connection to newspapers and the sensationalism of the New Journalism is made obvious in the "Aeolus" episode, where, as discussed in the previous chapter, Stephen rejoins the narrative, narrowly missing Bloom in the combined offices of two of Dublin's major nationalist newspapers, the *Freeman's Journal* and the *Evening Telegraph,* and which itself mimics the format of tabloid journalism.

If Hades's Glasnevin Cemetery, as Brandon Lamson argues, is a microcosmic representation of Dublin as a partly disinterred corpse, in "Aeolus," Dublin is resurrected as a monstrous living machine. While lungs and air are the ruling metaphors of this episode named for the Greek god of the wind, Joyce carries the heart imagery of "Hades" into its early segments. The episode's central trope, Dublin's city center as an imagined bellows—disseminating citizens, mail, commodities, and news across the archipelago—is first presented as a pump. Trams and mail are pumped in and out from "THE HEART OF THE HIBERNIAN METROPOLIS" (7.1–2) like blood. This early imagery figures the "GENTLEMEN OF THE PRESS" (7.21), who enliven the episode as cells in the city's bloodstream. In the episode's first dialogue, Bloom and newspaperman Red Murray exchange literal pieces of news, like corpuscles meant to transport nutrients around the body. Murray gives Bloom a copy of the House of Keyes advertisement currently running in the paper and offers Keyes, Bloom's prospective client, a "par," or an advertisement masquerading as a news item (7.34–35). Murray's offer to run an ostensible news item on the wine, tea, and spirit merchant Keyes to sweeten his demand for a three-month contract parallels other pointed examples of the "bread-crumbs," or empty calories, that are invisibly malnourishing Dublin's civic body.

The episode's early imagery comparing newspaper items to empty calories entering the political bloodstream soon ramifies into a series of images emphasizing the mechanical (i.e., mindless, amoral) character of newspaper production and print capitalism's tendency to reduce writing to junk. As we see here and throughout *Ulysses*, the "news" in newspapers results less from public-minded investigative journalism than from an array of gentlemen's agreements and back-room deals. Among the examples of worthless filler in the episode are Hynes's unsubstantiated insertion of McCoy into the list of mourn-ers at Dignam's funeral (cynically brokered by Bloom at McCoy's request), the verbatim reporting of Dan Dawson's vapid speech, and virtually all of the verbiage that Bloom watches pouring forth from the giant presses. (The coverage of speeches and sermons in full dur-ing this period was one way in which the newspapers filled column inches with little reportorial effort and inserted highly partisan views, particularly those of the church hierarchy, as "news" rather than com-mentary). Prior to Myles Crawford's unwittingly damning account of Ignatius Gallaher's greatest scoop later in the episode, discussed in the previous chapter, Joyce's most noteworthy examples of the poli-tics of newspaper composition are the letters submitted by the arch-bishop of Dublin and by Deasy. Under the headline "THE CROZIER AND THE PEN" (7.61), which signals the church's wholesale capture of mainstream nationalist journalism in the wake of Parnell's fall, Bloom learns that the archbishop of Dublin, "His grace," has "phoned down twice this morning" to ensure that a letter of his will run in the two preeminent nationalist newspapers (7.62). Thus the archbishop, like Deasy, is able to place one letter in two newspapers without any editorial vetting and without any legwork, while Bloom, in contrast, must engage in extensive legwork to publish a paid advertisement and still fails to do so.

As discussed in chapter 5, the aftereffects of the Home Rule scandal wars resound throughout "Aeolus." Indeed, Joyce's figurative allusion to the "bag of winds" loosed by Aeolus can be read as pointedly referring to the sequence of newspaper scandals that drove Home Rule nationalism so disastrously off course. Just as the destructive forces unleashed in the Home Rule scandal wars were shown in "Hades" to live on "forever practically" (6.781), in "Aeolus" they are the "hurricane [still] blowing" through the Irish press (7.399–400). Following the ambiguous question, "but will he save the circulation?" which might allude to the press's owner, to the archbishop, or to a telegraph boy (recalling the role of telegraph boys in the lucrative Cleveland Street and Wilde scandals), Joyce describes the presses as beating like a heart: "Thumping. Thumping" (7.71–72). Parnell's heart, broken by the Irish press, has been supplanted by a mechanical, self-perpetuating machine, fueled by and itself constituting a monstrous form of social reproduction (98). These "machines," Bloom thinks, could "smash a man to atoms if they got him caught" (7.80–81).

In an allusion to W. T. Stead's aspiration to government by journalism, Bloom reflects that these dangerous machines "rule the world today" (7.81) and then makes the global personal by reflecting on the impact of scandal politics on his own domestic security. Figuring Molly Bloom's incipient affair with her manager, Blazes Boylan, as a domestic scandal, Bloom's thoughts turn to Boylan's "machineries" that are "pegging away too" because they, quite literally, "got out of hand" (7.81–83). This figure of speech cleverly describes private effects moving outside of Bloom's control and symbolically figures the loss of the palm or the hand of the laughing witch won in "Matcham's Masterstroke." This particular incipient scandal—Molly's imminent infidelity—is setting in motion local scandal machinery that is "working away, tearing away," again alluding to the particular use to which newspapers put the ostensibly private, shameful details torn from the private context in which they have been hidden as creating a crack or tear and as constituting work. Bloom feels surrounded by scandal machinery that is, like "that old grey rat" in "Hades," tearing to get into the envelope that contingently protects his vulnerable private life (7.82–83).

Bloom leaves the *Freeman's Journal*'s offices seeking, like Parnell, to broker a "union of hearts"—a contemporary newspaper term for the Parnell/Gladstone alliance[26]—between his client, Keyes, and the *Evening Telegraph* editor, Myles Crawford. Yet his extensive and knowledgeable efforts to get even "an innuendo of home rule" (in the form of an image of crossed keys as part of the Keyes advertisement) into a nationalist newspaper fail when the nationalist press—personified by Crawford—turns on him as it did on Parnell (7.150). Bloom's failure to broker a deal signifying Irish home rule also reflects his continuing inability to protect his own home against expropriation. Bloom's position within his own domestic sphere is obviously uncertain, and his failure to secure compensation for his day's labor makes that position only more precarious. Like the insecure tenant farmers whose mass evictions launched the Land Wars, Bloom is inhabiting his home and his marriage on an "at will" basis, in no small part because Molly's earning capacity is greater than his. He is currently at risk of being symbolically or literally evicted by Blazes Boylan, as Stephen has been shoved out by Haines. Rumor has it that Boylan's father, like Haines's, made a fortune through a colonial swindle, so Bloom is handicapped relative to Blazes as Stephen is to Haines and Deasy; indeed, all three of these men—Boylan, Haines, and Deasy—are Irish and British faces of the new archipelagic oligarchy, bankrolled by colonial loot (12.998–99). As with Stephen, an economic reliance on the print industry has subordinated Bloom to dispossessing forces hostile to his own interests, rendering him complicit in his own exploitation. Crucially, however, Bloom's refusal to function in his own sex scandal along conventional lines by, for instance, dragging Molly into court and naming Boylan as her codefendant in a divorce suit, calls attention to the obstructive practices and strategies through which Stephen's future self, the mature Joyce, will elude and disrupt the prevailing, scandal-based representational economy.

Whereas this study's focus in *Ulysses* is principally on Stephen's struggles, read as Joyce's account of his own youthful attempts to "fly by" the nets of scandal, Leopold Bloom relates to Joyce/Stephen's trajectory dialectically as the harbinger of a future Joyce who will, in writing *Ulysses*, find "another way" out of the imperial labyrinth

(*Portrait*, 182). Throughout *Ulysses*, Stephen repeatedly loses the contests by which a writer's commercial viability and artistic talent are gauged. Like Joyce in his Dublin apprenticeship, Stephen is beaten into print by unworthy adversaries, snubbed and ridiculed by the Celtic Revivalists, and bluntly reminded that his "capful of light odes" do not, as yet, support his lofty pretensions (14.1119). Crucially, however, from "Calypso" on, Joyce, through Bloom, redefines the terms of artistic success through an alter ego who is at once ingeniously self-protective and shamefully exposed. As Joyce's object demonstration that the problems with which Stephen is grappling will be resolved in the alternate futurity that both Stephen's artistic discoveries and the novel's events make possible, Bloom influences Stephen mimetically but also subtextually, through what, according to David Cotter, "might only be described as magic." Acting as Stephen's "subversive father," Bloom "teaches him not how to fly, but how to fall, how to return."[27]

Bloom's very generic status as a character is unascertainable: Is he a hapless clown of modernity like Estragon, Vladimir, or Chaplin's Little Tramp, or is he a mythic, heroic underdog along the lines of Odysseus, Moses, or Jesus? In relation to all the most foundational generic conventions, including fiction and nonfiction, tragedy and comedy, popular and high culture, sentimental evocations of compassion and scandalous condemnation, Bloom navigates the labyrinth of commercially and legally enforced literary convention by means of radical syncretism. Rather than defying all laws, he submits to a matrix or "table of the law" (7.868–69), simultaneously conforming to multiple conventions within multiple genres. Through Bloom's elaborate scandal exposures and evasions, Joyce advocates "winning" by means of a radical and promiscuous surrender, modeling an abject submission that allows for control over one's meaning "without being found out."[28]

Following Bloom's appearance in the text, Stephen grows more decisive—both internally and in his interactions with others. Whereas across the Telemachiad Stephen repeatedly fails to find an audience, in "Aeolus," as we have seen, he inwardly clarifies his artistic aspirations while outwardly attracting an Irish audience whose members he induces to collaboratively contribute to his enigmatic performances. Having "tried his hand" at this new mode of scandal work at the end of "Aeolus" by presenting "The Parable of the Plums" to the tattered remnants of the Parnellite movement, in "Scylla and Charybdis" Stephen, buoyed by Bloom's textual proximity, will undertake a far more ambitious and risky performance before a more skeptical Irish audience.

CHAPTER 7

(Re)Fusing Sentimentalism and Scandal

"Poor Penelope. Penelope Rich"

My opinion is that if I put down a bucket into my own soul's well, sexual department, I draw up Griffith's and Ibsen's and Skeffington's and Bernard Vaughn's and St. Aloysius' and Shelley's and Renan's water along with my own. I am going to do that in my novel (inter alia) and plank the bucket down before the shades and substances above mentioned to see how they like it.

—James Joyce to Stanislaus Joyce, November 13, 1906

He found in the world without as actual what was in his world within as possible. . . . Every life is many days, day after day. We walk through ourselves, meeting robbers, ghosts, giants, old men, young men, wives, widows, brothers-in-love, but always meeting ourselves.

—James Joyce, *Ulysses*

In "Scylla and Charybdis" and several of the following episodes of *Ulysses,* Joyce continues to employ the artistic strategy Stephen has just discovered: using ambiguous self-exposure to chart his own path through a literary landscape whose borders have been redrawn by the conventions of the New Journalism. In this episode, Stephen must navigate between the ravaging monster of commercial odd jobs and the all-consuming whirlpool of Celtic revivalism; his refusal to entertain either of these options is made clear both by his final rejection of the route represented by Mulligan and Haines and by his verbal jousting about Shakespeare with several leading members of the Irish Literary Revival in the National Library. Joyce thereby positions Stephen not only in opposition to the "hard words" of Parnellite obstructionism and scandalmongering but to the sentimental "soft words" through which the divided and traumatized post-Parnellite nationalists transformed an earlier tradition of nationalist romantic allegory into a sentimentalized cultural nationalism agreeable to both British and Irish cultural producers.

THE IMMENSE DEBTORSHIP OF A THING DONE

Sentimentalism figures prominently in this episode, Stephen's next attempt to sever ties with Mulligan and British print capitalism. In "Scylla and Charybdis," we learn that Stephen has sent Mulligan a telegram indirectly declining an imposition posed as an opportunity to win Haines's patronizing patronage. Refusing to buy the "pints apiece" that he has left Mulligan and Haines fruitlessly awaiting (9.561–62), Stephen, quoting a maxim from George Meredith's *The Ordeal of Richard Feverel*, describes sentimentalism as the emotional equivalent of "barsponging": "*The sentimentalist is he who would enjoy without incurring the immense debtorship of a thing done.* Signed: Dedalus" (9.550–51).[1] When he declines this chance to subsidize Mulligan's enjoyment at his own economic expense, Stephen is also declining to sentimentalize their relationship, refusing to softly play on Haines's sentimental love of things Irish so as to gain approval or financial reward from this colonial representative. This new and more explicit attempt on Stephen's part to break off relations with Mulligan also identifies sentimentalism itself as serving, like scandal,

to invisibly credit "the sentimentalist"—in this case, the English imperial audience—at the expense of the sentimentalized Irish.

Nor does Stephen seek to conquer Haines through the hard
words that he, in his persona as the Aristotelian philosopher Kinch,
could wield so as to compel Haines's respect through a show of intellectual superiority. The figurative conflation of scandal words with
physical violence through images of and puns on jousting, parrying,
lancets, and mail in Part I of the novel continues in Part II through
a complex trajectory of hard words, violent acts, and their afterlife in
the soft words of the sentimentalist. Beginning with Stephen's earlier delivery of Deasy's letter to the editor (or "English mail"), this
trajectory extends to his self-mocking role as "bullock befriending
bard" first to Myles Crawford in "Aeolus" and then to the influential
Celtic Revivalist poet and editor A.E. (George Russell) in "Scylla and
Charybdis."[2] As we shall see, in this episode Joyce/Stephen reposi-
tions himself relative to the dominant nationalist discourses of sentimentalism and scandal, crafting an alternate discourse that borrows
from both scandal discourse and sentimentalism without being subordinated to either.

"ALL OR NOT AT ALL"

The figure of a "middle path" between perilous extremes is, as one
would expect, writ large in "Scylla and Charybdis," in which Stephen's adroit rhetorical negotiations famously invoke the incommensurability of the Platonic, transcendentalist beliefs of leading Celtic
Revivalists such as A.E. and Yeats with Joyce/Stephen's own Aristo-
telianism. With considerably more immediate political and artistic
implications, however, the episode also pairs sentimentalism and
scandal invective as the opposed threats between which Stephen—
adapting Parnell's, Stead's, and Wilde's strategies of hyperbolic self-
exposure—must navigate. Having sent Mulligan a telegram in which
he effectively rejects sentimentalism in writing and in life, in the
course of the episode, Stephen will extend his rejection of sentimental
attachments even to his mythic progenitor, Parnell.

In "Scylla and Charybdis," Stephen reenacts Odysseus's perilous passage by speaking publicly of private sexual experiences without his craft's breaking into the decontextualized fragments of the sex scandal or disappearing in the swirling excesses of sentimental melodrama that Joyce reviled as "lying drivel about pure men and pure women and spiritual love and love for ever: blatant lying in the face of the truth."[3] He flagrantly reenacts Wilde's account of a scandalous "forgery" made to assert a historic truth in an argument that is more obviously evocative of Wilde's desires than Shakespeare's. In Wilde's "The Portrait of Mr. W.H.," discussed by the National Library conversants as they probe, both fearfully and eagerly, into Shakespeare's sexual secrets, Wilde pries open Shakespeare's private life to "prove" the historical existence of homosexual desire through an obviously fabricated first-person, anecdotal vignette in which another young man who, like Stephen, had a strange theory about a certain work of art (in Stephen's case, *Hamlet*), committed a forgery so as to produce, as Mullen has it, "a literary theory to die for" (37). In this episode, Stephen adapts Wilde's strategy for fending off the hostile misappropriation of personal disclosures by telling a story that is self-evidently, if not entirely, his own as though it were another's. This strategy makes his "loss . . . his gain," as he claims Shakespeare also did (9.476), by converting his own shameful sexual secrets into art.[4] Through Stephen's insistently biographical reading of Shakespeare's *Hamlet* as a roman à clef that both conceals and reveals a real-life sex scandal, Joyce calls attention to the significance of biographical intertexts for his own account of a dispossessed son. By telling a true story in which he professes to disbelieve those very elements that his audience knows are autobiographical, Joyce/Stephen hides his dirty secrets in plain sight and turns his readers/listeners into his "accomplices" (9.158).

John Nash describes "Scylla and Charybdis" as staging a shift in Stephen's primary audiences from the intimate "whetstones" represented by his brother Stanislaus, Cranly, and Mulligan to the public figures of the Celtic Revival, which in turn registers a movement from one kind of representation to another.[5] While it is true that "Scylla and Charybdis" negotiates a significant shift in both Stephen's and Joyce's modes of representation, the episode also presents a suturing of intimate discourse to public speech, an operation that transforms the kind of talk usually considered suitable only for exchanges between family, friends, and lovers into an erudite discussion regarding public figures that is both brilliant and clearly fictionalized. This process prepares the way for a thoroughgoing critique of both scandal and sentiment as commercial, representational strategies for enjoying "a thing done" while charging its expense to others. By intermingling elements of his own experience with aspects of Shakespeare's biography, Joyce shows Stephen treating Shakespeare as Joyce himself treats many other nonfictional figures in the novel.[6]

Joyce's notorious inclusion of historical individuals is at its most pronounced in the "Scylla and Charybdis" episode, in which every character except Bloom has a readily identifiable historical counterpart. Thus it is in this episode, with its particular claims to historicity, that Joyce, through Stephen, unveils a new stage in his scandal work. Joyce/Stephen, one could say, blatantly lies in the face of truth so as to truthfully reintegrate the contents of the "soul's well, sexual department" that have been either scandalized or sentimentalized into lying drivel. Rather than either sentimentalizing or scandalizing the writer whose idealized greatness even the Irish nationalists in attendance see as evidence of English superiority, Stephen artistically merges with him, ascribing to Shakespeare sexual wounds that are simultaneously fictional and historic, simultaneously Shakespeare's, Stephen's, Joyce's, and those of many members of his audience. Through his readings of Shakespeare's work, Joyce, as Stephen, thus both stages and artistically claims his own sexual vulnerabilities without sentimentalizing them or making others pay for them. He secures his own "follies" against malignant scandalmongering by publicizing them himself, thereby threading a way through the impossibly narrow shoals that separate scandal from sentiment in public conversations about sex.

Stephen's readings of *Hamlet* and of many of the other plays in Shakespeare's oeuvre construe art as the byproduct of a subtle but pervasive form of erotic entrapment, the psychic progeny of sexual trauma. Stephen traces Shakespeare's interweaving of personal pain and literary imagination to a traumatic wound originating in Shakespeare's untimely sexual initiation by Anne Hathaway and the masochistic entanglements—with his brothers, a "scandalous girl," and an English lord—that followed (9.453). By drawing on this wound, Stephen suggests, Shakespeare became his own scandal victim or pishogue, continually tormenting himself by publicly exposing his own shameful transgressions: "His unremitting intellect is the hornmad Iago ceaselessly willing that the moor in him shall suffer" (9.1023–24). According to Stephen, Shakespeare's continual "licking [of] an old sore" enabled the writer to "pas[s] on towards eternity an undiminished personality, untaught by the wisdom he has written or by the laws he has revealed" (9.475–78). Stephen, a young bard who has just undertaken to write the Irish national epic that those literary figures gathered in the National Library agree is as yet unwritten (9.309), is clearly both competing and identifying himself with Shakespeare. His reading of the corpus of England's national bard thus also supplies what Latham calls "an encoded and satirical set of instructions from the author himself about how we might go about reading *Ulysses*," the Irish national epic that Stephen, as Joyce, will subsequently produce.[7] Stephen's performance constitutes *Ulysses* itself not only as a roman à clef, as Latham argues, but as a vast artistic edifice erected on a scandalous sexual secret that it hides in plain sight by elaborating it beyond all recognition.[8] For Stephen's Shakespeare, as for Joyce himself, the lived, felt shame of private transgression that flooded an unprepared psyche with the trauma and ecstasy of *jouissance* is thus both publicized and hidden through a creative process that it defines, motivates, and thoroughly imbues.

The elaborate pattern of remembering and forgetting that Stephen ascribes to Shakespeare's writing in one respect resembles the daily weavings that the fictional "poor Penelope" nightly undid. Like Penelope, the Shakespeare described by Stephen wove an intricate sequence of temporizing escapes that could never decisively release him from the psychic and material conditions in which he was entrapped. In this respect, Shakespeare's creative labors as described by Stephen served a purpose similar to Penelope's in that both use complex creative tactics to hold in place marital relations in dynamic, ongoing crisis.[9] Yet whereas Penelope protected her marital bond by repeatedly annihilating her own creative productions, Stephen's

Shakespeare attempted to symbolically undo his marriage with each creative iteration, holding the sexual shame to which his relationship with Anne Hathaway bound him in incremental abeyance. While Penelope's creative output was sacrificed to the defense of her marriage, Stephen claims that Shakespeare's art was enlivened by his imaginative unravelings. Although the work of both represents a dalliance between what Stephen calls "conjugial [sic] love and its chaste delights and scortatory love and its foul pleasures" (9.631–32), Penelope makes and unmakes her art in order to save her imperiled marriage; whereas Shakespeare's art, in Stephen's analysis, makes and unmakes his marriage in order to salve his wounded heart. In Penelope's case, the task of avoiding scandal renders the artist "poor" and exacts a horrific toll: the systematic and uncompromising destruction of her art. In the case of Shakespeare, however—"an old dog licking an old sore"—it is the art that benefits and the artist himself who is undone (9.475–76). "Overborne" by a dominant older woman in a time and place not of his choosing, Stephen argues, Shakespeare was traumatically shamed in his own eyes, "stricken mortally," and found that "no later undoing will undo the first undoing" (9.456–59). In both cases, energetic artistic creation sustains a protected, mediating position between the "heartscalding" disappointments of marriage and the frequently ruinous dangers posed by a life lived outside of normative family obligations and protections. In both, however, safe passage between the two poles is attained only at high personal cost.

Stephen's account of Shakespeare's dis/empowering initiation in the arms of a sexually experienced older woman corresponds recognizably to Stephen's own traumatic yet artistically galvanizing sexual initiation as described in *Portrait*. As Mulligan later quips concerning his own bawdy "national immorality in three orgasms," Joyce/Stephen's disguise is thin, but it is crucial. By calling attention to his many thin though never absent disguises in the course of *Ulysses*, Joyce invites us to read Stephen's sensational decoding of Shakespeare's sexual trauma as an extended commentary on the narrative strategies that both he and the New Journalism employ, strategies that allow the author and the reader to simultaneously "light[ly] touch" and disavow their own trauma (9.530) so as to "hide himself from himself" (9.475).

The fundamental difference between the New Journalism's scandal work and Joyce's is that whereas the former, like a nineteenth-century melodrama, projects the blame for secret violations onto villains who are emphatically distinct both from the author and the audience, Joyce's intricate and incessant self-implication makes it impossible to disentangle the author from his various fictional and nonfictional villains/victims. Moreover, by making the argument that Shakespeare's sexual sufferings led to an inescapable unconscious drive to both expose and deny, Joyce offers readers not a thrilling respite from the anxieties of modern subjectivity that Freud and the sexologists were just bringing into the open, but rather an inescapable exploration of their own investments in them.

To understand the full significance of Stephen's performance in "Scylla and Charybdis," we must review his earlier struggles with what has, throughout *Portrait*'s and *Ulysses*'s early chapters, constituted his most shameful and deeply suppressed sexual secret. As Joyceans reading *Portrait* through a queer theoretical lens have shown, the homosexual panic the child Stephen evinces in response to the Clongowes smugging scandal recurs in the adult Stephen's snubbing of Cranly's romantic overture, a break that precipitates *Portrait*'s late, heady plunge from third-person into first-person narration. In "Telemachus," in "Proteus," and once again in "Scylla and Charybdis," Stephen repeatedly takes note of sedimentary memories that Mulligan has stirred up: the residue of his youthful, libidinally charged dependence on Cranly as his "whetstone."[10] For Stephen, Cranly's figure resembles that of Sally Seton in *Mrs. Dalloway*, the phantom of a choice not only not made but, within the contemporary social imaginary, undreamt of, whose haunting significance Stephen has, over the course of *Ulysses*, been gradually decoding.

In these episodes Cranly appears to Stephen repeatedly, always in the context of a triangular relationship between Stephen, Cranly, and Mulligan and framed by references to Oscar Wilde. Stephen's recollection of Cranly's touch first occurs in "Telemachus," elicited by Mulligan's possessive grasping of Stephen's arm, and recurs in a strikingly sensuous passage in "Proteus" that has important implications for a reading of homoeroticism in "Scylla and Charybdis." In this frequently cited passage, Stephen surrenders to transgressive sensual pleasures associated with Mulligan, feet, cross-dressing, Cranly, and "the love that dare not speak its name":

> His gaze brooded on his broadtoed boot, a buck's castoffs, ne-benienander. He counted the creases of rucked leather wherein another's foot had nested warm. The foot that beat the ground in tripudium, foot I dislove. But you were delighted when Esther Osvalt's shoe went on you: girl I knew in Paris. *Tiens, quel petit pied!* Stanch friend, a brother soul: Wilde's love that dare not speak its name. His arm: Cranly's arm. He now will leave me. And the blame? As I am. As I am. All or not at all. (3.446–52)

Stephen's meditations on a series of sensual pleasures in this passage—associatively linked because all are considered potentially symptomatic of sexological perversions—are followed by a secretive act that could, at a glance, be mistaken for masturbation. Languidly pissing "long lassoes from the Cock lake" that "rise and chafe against the low rocks, swirling [and] passing," Stephen's thoughts, at odds with his body's mood of receptive surrender, curtly order his body to "get this job over quick" (3.453–56). He thus attempts to call to order the cock whose allegiances—in the course of Stephen's extended thought experiment of attending exclusively to sensory input—appear alarmingly heterogeneous.

In the same passage, Stephen uses a similar process of intellectual suppression to assuage the stirrings that the imprint of Mulligan's foot in the shoe he now wears has aroused with the thought "all or not at all." Like so many phrases in Joyce's oeuvre, "all or not at all," lifted from Ibsen, can be read in a range of ways. The reading that makes the most sense within the context of this scene, with its atmosphere of luscious eroticism mingled with surrender, regret, and defensiveness, is that Stephen uses this phrase to calm an episode of sexual arousal accompanied by homosexual panic. With this phrase, he reasserts the mastery of mind over body by endorsing the phallogocentric principle that love and touch between men short of full penetrative sexual intercourse—surrendering and giving "all"—is "not at all" sexologically significant.[11]

Stephen's panicky conviction in "Proteus" that he is not an unspeakable deviant because he has not given "all" either to Cranly or to Mulligan is significantly reformulated in "Scylla and Charybdis," where "all or not at all" reflects Joyce's artistic and moral determination to describe his—and presumably everyone's—sexuality without the reductions conventionally imposed by the moralizing and normalizing filters of sentiment and scandal. In particular, Joyce indicates that Stephen, in the course of his newly articulated rejection of sentimentality, is acknowledging that his feelings are not simply "spiritual love" for "pure men" but also contain a measure of sexual desire. Stephen, watching Mulligan's glance "touc[h Best's and Eglinton's] faces lightly as he smiled," thinks that Mulligan is "a blond ephebe. . . . Tame essence of Wilde" (9.531–32), thereby (as in his later thought, "catamite") insulting Mulligan by imagining him as the junior and presumably commercially motivated sexual partner, and then nonetheless admits to himself, "You're darned witty . . . [but] you would give your five wits for youth's proud livery he pranks in" (9.537–38). This admission acknowledges not only Stephen's envy of Mulligan's easy, boyish demeanor, but that for him, as well as for Best and Eglinton, the sexually undiscriminating *buonaroba* Mulligan embodies the "lineaments of gratified desire" (9.538).[12] Though Stephen has had little trouble declining Mulligan's economic and artistic enticements (poor Haines never did get his promised pint), he cannot so easily dismiss the "sunny smile" of his "loose" friend (9.509).

"LAPWING. ICARUS. PATER."

Through his reading of Shakespeare in "Scylla and Charybdis," Stephen is able to both publicly and privately take possession of his own complex sexual history and capacities, thereby limiting the ability of others to steal and recirculate them for their own profit. By accepting homosexual desire as a literal component of his and others' makeup,

Stephen abandons the self-protective eroticized continuentalization of the fallen Parnell that has supplied a fundamental, unifying structure of feeling for himself and for the Irish nationalists among whom he came of age. Only by abandoning faith in such sentimental homosocial bonds as the antidote to the harsh betrayal of scandal has Joyce/Stephen become ready to commit what is, in the context of his childhood experiences and family values, the final heresy.[13] At last enabled to explicitly and fully abandon his youthful wish to emulate the aquiline Parnell, Stephen takes up the swan of Avon as a means to remythologize himself. Instead of using Shakespeare's well-known sexual ambiguities and excesses according to the rules of scandal, discrediting Shakespeare as he bolsters his own credibility, Joyce, as Stephen, "cuts the bread even" (9.940), distributing sexual deviance equally among Shakespeare, himself, and his auditors. As an emblem of this artistic reorientation, Stephen, the "wandering Aengus of the birds" (9.1093), then repopulates the imperial aviary with the Athenian/Odyssean lapwing.

In a brief play script that appears in the episode (prefiguring the format of "Circe," discussed in the next chapter) and in the following interchange between Stephen and the attendant Celtic Revivalists, Stephen describes the signs and portents that distinguished Shakespeare's birth and claims his name, hat, and walking stick as his own distinguishing birthrights: "*Stephanos*, my crown. My sword" (9.947). With a sense of having come into manhood through this imagined initiation, he instructs himself to "wait to be wooed and won" (9.938)—that is, to hold out for both a lover and a publisher who will desire him for himself, not as a means to an end. Stephen's repeated references to a sexual initiation that has yet to occur—as well as to an odd job that has yet to be undertaken—clearly signal that the transformative initiation into manhood that Joyce experienced with Nora Barnacle and the artistic awakening that it ritualized is still to come. In the meantime, Stephen decides that Mulligan's boots are "spoiling the shape of my feet" and plans to buy a pair of his own (9.947–48). In this context, Stephen's thought in "Proteus" that he was "delighted" to slip his foot into a girl's shoe—an insertion he found to be a comfortable fit—is especially provocative (3.449).[14]

These thoughts are immediately followed by an interchange in which Stephen explicitly recontextualizes his last name. When John Eglinton comments on Stephen's strange name, which he supposes must explain Stephen's "fantastical humor," Stephen responds by inwardly revising his vision at the end of *Portrait* in light of intervening events: "Fabulous artificer. The hawklike man. You flew. Whereto? Newhaven-Dieppe, Steerage passenger. Paris and back. Lapwing. Icarus. Pater, ait. Seabedabled, fallen, weltering. Lapwing you are. Lapwing be" (9.949–54). In Ovid's *Metamorphoses*, the lapwing is identified as the bird into which Athena, "who favors the quick-witted," transformed Icarus's inventive cousin, who had been flung from the Acropolis by the jealous Daedalus.[15] In *Portrait* and thus far in *Ulysses*, Stephen has been identified with the inventor/father, Daedalus, whose name he bears, and the fallen son, Icarus. Now to this Janus-faced figure for scandal culture's characteristic rise and fall Joyce adds the gifted cousin on whom the grief-stricken Daedalus vented his anguish as well as the "lovely mummer" Athena, the transformative, all-powerful deus ex machina whose bolt of divine transformation partially rectified an otherwise hopeless situation (1.97). In this new figuration, therefore, Joyce/Stephen's fall is both self-inflicted and self-redeemed.

In Gifford's translation of Ovid, the lapwing "does not lift her body in flight . . . but she flutters along near the ground and lays her eggs in hedgerows; and remembering that old fall, she is ever fearful of lofty places."[16] In Stephen's new literary coat of arms–"Lapwing you are. Lapwing be"—Joyce refigures *Portrait*'s concluding image, invoking a new scandal trinity in the phrase "Lapwing. Icarus. Pater." While "Pater" is easily read as the Latin "father," this mythic trinity is even more meaningful if we read its third term as a reference to Oxford Don Walter Pater, who had sent a frisson of homosexual panic/exhilaration through late Victorian society when, in the famous conclusion of his study *The Renaissance*, he (like Wilde's fictional Dorian Gray) celebrated aesthetic pleasure as its own reward. As a result, Pater was publicly charged with encouraging unrestrained erotic expression, most especially homoerotic expression,[17] charges that were professionally and personally costly to Pater, as was Oscar Wilde's later insistent claiming of Pater as his mentor, a claim that Pater did his best to refute. Pater's response to this early brush with homosexual scandal resembled the response of poor Penelope to the sexual danger that surrounded her: he sought to unmake his own self-inflicted public persona through the miserable work of apparently unrelenting celibacy.[18] Joyce/Stephen, however, means to do as he had earlier claimed Shakespeare did: to dally in his work between the chaste and the profane (9.631–32), using lapwing-like bursts to fly without falling. In other words, Stephen (like Joyce) will emulate not the aquiline Parnell but the erratic lapwing, continually forestalling by repeatedly staging his own scandalous "fall." This "fall" alludes both to Joyce/Stephen's privately scarring and publicly compromising "youthful follies" and to the spectacular public falls of other gifted Irishmen whose actual or supposed private follies had become public through scandals. Like Shakespeare, Joyce/Stephen will also steer clear of disaster by repeatedly incorporating an "old fall" into his writing; unlike Shakespeare, however, he will do so consciously, shamelessly, "ever remembering," rather than as a form of unconscious, self-administered torment.

"AN ANDROGYNOUS ANGEL, BEING A WIFE UNTO HIMSELF"

By creating a psychologically and factually tenable account of Shakespeare's inner world and then declaring it to be a fiction, Joyce, through the character of Stephen, theorizes his own middle course with respect to scandal, navigating between the two modalities of life and art through the repeated invocation of truth and lies, of castigation and self-indictment, of the scabrous and the sentimental. Joyce/Stephen thus commits himself to an inclusive balance in his own writing between scandalized sexual improprieties and the equally appalling, if more socially acceptable, lie of sentimentalized conjugal love. No poor Penelope he, Stephen means to "eat [his] cake and have it" too (9.738–39), like Penelope Rich, who openly left an unsatisfactory marriage to live and bear children with a man of her choosing.

In thus becoming his own evasive, erratic scandalmonger, Stephen has symbolically put his hands into his own pockets, recalling a recurring trope in *Portrait* and *Ulysses* in which a person's placing a hand into another's pocket suggests both sexual seduction and theft. By here putting his hands in his own pocket, Stephen conjoins the ideas of self-pishoguery, self-exposure, and self-abuse (masturbation). This altered stance, as we shall see, palpably transforms Stephen's view of Mulligan, his would-be pishoguerist and potential Lord Alfred Douglas/Anne Hathaway. Just as Shakespeare "drew Shylock out of his own long pocket" (9.741–42), Stephen is laying representational claim to the embarrassing personal truths that make for great art. By admitting to himself his actual desires as well as his most shameful acts, Joyce/Stephen is freed both to work with them artistically and to steel himself against making a tempting but disastrous mistake. His relationship with Mulligan and the British press, thus transformed, becomes "no mistak[e]," but a consciously chosen error affording an artistic "porta[l] of discovery" (9.228–29).[19]

Joyce elaborates on the "strange theory" that informs his and Stephen's representational bid to have and tell it all in a debate that Mulligan, joining the discussion in the library, stirs up over the question of Shakespeare's homosexuality. Mulligan piques the company's interest by announcing abruptly, "I must tell you what Dowden said!" (9.727). When "Besteglinton" collectively take the bait, showing themselves eager to hear the thoughts of the sexually suspect aesthete Edward Dowden, Trinity University's historical counterpart to Walter Pater, Mulligan "suspire[s] amorously": "I asked him what he thought of the charge of pederasty brought against the bard. He lifted his hands and said: *All we can say is that life ran very high in those days.* Lovely!" (9.731–33). Stephen immediately thinks "catamite," by which he must be referring to Mulligan, as Mulligan is exposing neither Shakespeare nor Dowden as a catamite but rather implying that they might be pederasts, or adult men of the sort who would desire catamites (9.734). Mulligan, on the other hand, is a "douce youngling, minion of pleasure" (9.1138–39) who is, at this moment, teasingly soliciting the sexual interest of two older men, John Eglinton and Richard Best.[20]

For Stephen's entertainment and as a form of flirtation, Mulligan is doing what Queensberry accused Wilde of—posing as a sodomite— by introducing the subject of pederasty with a breathy, amorous familiarity. Both Eglinton and Best react with horror, insisting that deviant desire must be excised from art, even at the expense of truth and beauty. Best argues against artistic license, following those who condemned Pater's original conclusion to *The Renaissance* as immoral when he cautions, "The sense of beauty leads us astray" (9.735). For his part, Eglinton attempts to restore literature to the position of empirical and imperial immunity—the belief that the artistic works of those anointed as Great Authors reflect only the authors' imaginations and not evidence of their actual deeds—that Carson's prosecution of Wilde officially foreclosed. He declares angrily that literature must be kept free of any references to life's impure realities, saying that if we need to know, "the doctor can tell us what those words mean. You cannot eat your cake and have it" (9.738–39). Stephen, determined to relinquish neither beauty nor truth, rejects both of these strategies for evading scandal. Rebutting the folk wisdom with which Eglinton sums up his rejection of art as a mirror of life—that you cannot show life both beautifully and honestly—Stephen dismissively thinks, "Sayest thou so?" (9.740). Having committed himself to art that will simultaneously have a political/cultural use value and an aesthetic exchange value, Stephen inwardly resolves not to cede "the palm of beauty" that "they [seek to] wrest from us, from me" (9.740).[21]

By the end of "Scylla and Charybdis," Joyce depicts Stephen as breaking out of the imperial room of ousted possibilities by holding to a middle course between the narrative pressures of epic tragedy overdetermined by the great man's rise and fall and a safe but fundamentally dishonest focus on domesticity's private vicissitudes, between the scandalously scortatory and the sentimentally chaste. As we have seen earlier in the novel, Stephen's aim to create Akasic records unleashing present but unheard voices corresponds to his determination to escape his own appointed role within British print capitalism as a colonial jester whose work, however clever or ambitious, will "serve" only imperial interests. That Stephen, like Joyce, has heard and will ultimately give voice to his silenced Dublin youth is prefigured toward the end of the episode when he follows Mulligan, a "lubber jester" destined to remain landlocked in an Irish state he will help to found, "out of the vaulted cell" of the National Library "into a shattering daylight of no thought" and pauses to inventory his gleanings, musing, "What have I learned? Of them? Of me?" (9.1111–13).

"THE DISGUISE IS THIN"

Stephen's most definitive break with Mulligan occurs as they leave the library together at the end of "Scylla and Charybdis." Over the course of the public disclosure of his own "secret history" thinly disguised as Shakespeare's, Stephen has confessed publicly and to himself his one-time desire for Cranly and his still operative desire for Mulligan and has consciously chosen to take possession of his most shameful secrets as a defense against scandal's devastating distortions. The decisive shift that has occurred between Stephen and Mulligan is registered economically when Stephen coolly tells Mulligan that for a guinea he can publish "this interview," his now concluded performance (9.1085). Mulligan, who despite his many efforts was unable to interrupt or reframe the speech for which Stephen now purports to charge him, has irrevocably lost his erstwhile proprietary control over Stephen and his work. Nonetheless, Mulligan makes one last attempt to reinstate himself as Stephen's advisor, chiding him for endangering the "job on the paper" that Lady Gregory had gotten him by writing a scathing review of Gregory's latest folklore collection, "slat[ing] her drivel to Jaysus" (9.1158–60). Once again he tries to steer Stephen into an accommodating relationship with the print industry, advising him to "do the Yeats touch," which he mimics with cruel accuracy: "The most beautiful book that has come out of our country in my time. One thinks of Homer" (9.1161–65).

When Stephen doesn't answer, Mulligan resorts to lighthearted blackmail, subtly reminding Stephen that he knows secrets that could destroy him. He reads aloud from his "tablet" his own national epic, a "national immorality in three orgasms," in which the cast of "thinly disguised" characters includes two medical students, Medical Dick and Medical Davy, "two birds with one stone," who presumably rollick as one with their counterparts, Fresh Nelly and Rosalie the coalquay whore (9.1172–90). Here and elsewhere in *Ulysses*, Joyce hints that both men either know of— or perhaps, heavy drinkers that they are, merely suspect that they have shared—wild episodes in which their homosocial whoring crossed the line into direct homosexual expression. Mulligan's thinly disguised triangular account of two birds with only one stone (or shot) between is certainly recalled in "Oxen of the Sun," in Stephen's famous dictum that there can be no greater love than "that a man lay down his wife for his friend" (14.358–62).[22] This echo of Mulligan's subtly menacing tomfoolery is particularly noteworthy, since to lay down a woman could imply, in addition to hospitably offering her up, as Bloom will consider doing for Stephen, or engaging in three-way coitus, as in the case of Beaumont and Fletcher, who, as Stephen uncertainly recalls, "had but the one doxy between them," could equally plausibly connote setting her down or pushing her aside in favor of one's friend.[23] Most certainly, in this instance, whatever else Mulligan is hinting at, he has certainly impugned Stephen's sexual behavior by facetiously claiming to have found him "in the company of" these two specific "gonorrheal ladies" (9.1090–91) and, by conceiving a public performance that includes references to Stephen's purported private peccadilloes, issues a thinly veiled threat to turn scandal's shaming and silencing gaze upon him.

As Stephen continues to walk silently behind Mulligan, Mulligan seems at last to drop his own "thin disguise" and engages in his ugliest act of pishoguery, which at this point can only serve to remind Stephen that Mulligan can and will do Stephen more harm as an avowed enemy than as a fair-weather friend. Citing an event from Joyce's own life, Mulligan, figured as one of Odysseus's men conversing with the dead during Odysseus's voyage to Hades, "told the shadows, souls of men" about "the night in Camden hall when the daughters of Erin had to lift their skirts to step over you as you lay in your mulberrycoloured, multicoloured, multitudinous vomit!" (9.1191–94). This spectacular, Technicolor image of Joyce/Stephen passed out in a pool of mulberry-colored puke with young ladies obliged to step over him on their way out of a national theatre performance is one of the rare scandal charges against Stephen in *Ulysses* for which we have direct autobiographical corroboration.[24] In describing it, Mulligan—addressing the souls of the living and the dead—reinscribes as national allegory what can only have been a deeply humiliating experience for the young Joyce and refigures Joyce (and by extension, his art) as a revolting, abject object from which a national audience, the daughters of Erin, will inevitably recoil but cannot evade.

Although they will later drink at the same table in "Oxen of the Sun," narratively this is the moment of Mulligan and Stephen's final parting. Mimetically, Mulligan's description of Stephen's humiliating fall is his cruel parting shot, an implicit notification that he is abandoning whatever restraint he has hitherto exercised when speaking of Stephen. Understanding this, Stephen reflects, "Part. The moment is now" (9.1199). When Bloom, also leaving the library, ritualizes the breach as he "passed out between them" (9.1203), both Stephen and Mulligan perceive in Bloom a portent of Stephen's immediate sexual future. Mulligan continues to insist that Bloom is stalking Stephen and warns Stephen "with clown's [i.e., jester's] awe" of an imminent "peril" that can only be understood as full anal penetration by Bloom, a reading made glaringly obvious by Mulligan's histrionic entreaty to "get thee a breechpad" (9.1209–12). Stephen, however, is impervious to Mulligan's gibes now; his mental shrug in response recalls Epictetus's detached observation, in the story told to Stephen by the dean of studies in *Portrait*, that it is in the nature of a thief to steal (*Portrait*, 164). Well aware that it is in the nature of people like Mulligan—those with the "manner of Oxenford"—to start spewing scandalous accusations any time their prerogatives are threatened, Stephen indifferently thinks, "Offend me still. Speak on" (9.1217).

In this exchange, Mulligan, in the manner of his privileged class, seizes on Bloom as a convenient scandal monster who, he implies, will soon have Stephen chloroformed and sold in one of the Monto's more specialized brothels. Stephen, however, perceives in Bloom the portent of artistic and sexual fulfillment from which scandal's many perils, real and imagined, internal and external, can no longer keep him. He recalls a dream in which he "flew. Easily flew" as men wondered, followed by a "street of harlots after" (9.1207–8), a dream that prophesizes both Stephen's mythic, mid-fall metamorphosis prefigured in the trial flight he has just completed among the Irish intelligentsia and the coming consensual union for which Stephen has been yearning since preadolescence. Stephen, again imagined as "Aengus of the birds" that "go" out so that they might "come," suddenly remembers that in his dream Bloom held out to him a "creamfruit melon," an emblem of luscious, complete sexual fullness, of breasts and buttocks, and reassured him, "In. You will see" (9.1206–8).

In the episodes that follow, Stephen disappears from the narrative for several hours, leaving a glaring but indecipherable gap similar to the queer old josser's suggestive but never definitive activities beyond our field of vision in "An Encounter." In that story, Joyce used a textual lacunae to invoke but not depict public masturbation within the view of boys, with the result that what the queer old josser is doing in that story is pretty well "known" to most minimally attentive readers, although this conviction is the product not only of Joyce's depiction but of our own complicit construals. In *Ulysses*, a far larger textual gap similarly invokes, by seeming to occlude, Joyce's first sexual communion with Nora Barnacle. As with Mahony's cry in "An Encounter"— "I say. . . . Look! . . . He's a queer old josser"—*Ulysses* supplies only one textual tip beyond the gap itself when, in "Oxen of the Sun," that connoisseur of scandal, Lenehan, announces to the roistering medical students that Stephen has "besmirched the lily virtue of a confiding virgin." Stephen responds to this scandalous accusation with a complacency rivaling that with which W. T. Stead reacted to public complaints concerning his widely self-publicized nonpenetrative encounter with a virgin named Lily, declaring himself, in direct contradiction to the stringent sexual norms the sex scandal both exploited and upheld, to be quintessentially innocent, "ever-virgin." Thus, as Stephen's dream foretells, at the end of "Scylla and Charybdis" Joyce, as Stephen, is poised on the brink of the "onanistic conspiracy" that would transform his life and his work.[25]

CHAPTER 8

Dublin's Tabloid Unconscious

"A Hairshirt of Purely Irish Manufacture"

Let us not desert one another; we are an injured body.

—Jane Austen, *Northanger Abbey*, on the necessity of solidarity
among fictional protagonists and their authors

You're soaking in it.

—Allison Bechdel, *Fun Home*

In "Circe," *Ulysses*'s famous one-hundred-and-fifty-page tour de force, Joyce transposes Odysseus's quest to rescue his men, whom the temptress Circe has drugged and turned into swine, into Leopold Bloom's epic journey through Dublin's Nighttown, where he will ultimately rescue Stephen Dedalus from the perils of scandal itself. As most Joyce scholars would agree, this disorienting episode, presented in dramatic form and making no distinction between actual events and imagined, increasingly hallucinatory scenarios, spectacularly exposes Bloom's most private thoughts. Focusing on the central, defining position of the newspaper sex scandal within the episode offers new insights into Joyce's dramatization of Bloom's and, by extension, Dublin's, unconscious. Indeed, "Nighttown" is Dublin slang for the newspaper night shift, implying that the terrain that Bloom must navigate in Joyce's most wildly expressive rendering of 1904 Dublin's collective psyche is virtually coterminous with and best apprehended through the stuff of tabloids.[1]

In particular, the New Journalism's keynote sex scandal, "The Maiden Tribute of Modern Babylon," flagrantly informs Bloom's surreal descent into Dublin's brothel district. The Maiden Tribute's defining role in "Circe" illustrates the pervasive influence of Fleet Street and the New Journalism on Dublin's economic and social order, as well as its citizens' individual and collective subjectivity.[2] In a reenactment of W. T. Stead's ambiguous rescue/abduction of Eliza Armstrong, Bloom comes to Circe's Island/Nighttown in pursuit of an imperiled "virgin"—as Stephen has proclaimed himself in "Oxen"—who arouses in him an honest compassion that is inextricably entangled with an array of selfish economic, social, and sexual motivations.[3] And, like Stead, Bloom will wind up on trial for, among other things, a scandalous transaction that was elaborately structured so as to avoid sexual harm to another virgin, Gerty MacDowell. Although Bloom's familiarity with Stead's famous newspaper series will be confirmed in "Eumaeus," where he thinks of traveling to London to see "our modern Babylon" (16.514), the scandal's pervasive impact on Bloom's unconscious colors the whole of "Circe": he grapples incessantly with the fear that his "unnatural" lust has, like Stead's horrible London Minotaur, transformed shoals of innocent maidens into prostitutes.[4] The episode repeatedly recalls Stead's mythopoeic representation of a sex industry run by monstrous men who ceaselessly turn virgins into whores and human beings into beasts or objects, the quintessential subjects and products of the same malignant magic that imbues the New Journalism's "black and sinister arts."[5] In this nightmare world of sex scandal, as we shall see, every detail of Bloom's private life, from the innocuous to the plausibly incriminating, is susceptible to recontextualization as evidence of the most sensational, extreme, and shameful of sexual crimes.

Bloom's sequential rises and falls in the course of "Circe" recall not only the Maiden Tribute scandal but also several other of the New Journalism's scandals, including its other two great turn-of-the-century engagements with the archipelagic sexual imaginary, the Parnell and Wilde scandals.[6] Like the leading men in all three of these scandals, Bloom is both an author and a victim of Nighttown's scandal transformations. Over the course of the episode, he repeatedly and comically enacts the process by which the Parnellites, subjected to the "father and mother of a bating" at the hands of the London press, attempted to use sex scandal to promote an anticolonial, redistributive nationalist agenda, only (as the figure of Aeolus earlier recalls) to be blown backward into increasingly vulnerable positions by the very energies they had unleashed. In response to the torrent of accusations hurled at him throughout the episode, Bloom maneuvers to protect himself first by directing scandal charges elsewhere and then by affiliating himself with imperial politics, ideologies, and subject positions that confer scandal immunity. In doing so, Bloom operates as a human scandal barometer, registering the forces that shaped and reshaped the newspaper scandal as a genre from the Land Wars through the Wilde trials.

Bloom's exposed, stigmatized position in Dublin society parallels that of the disenfranchised Irish nationalists whom the British press placed under constant, hostile scrutiny. Throughout "Circe," the genuinely empathetic Bloom attempts to wield scandal in pursuit of socially just aims that he cannot openly declare. When his presence in Nighttown is challenged, for example, Bloom cannot admit that he is hunting through Dublin's brothels in pursuit of an inebriated medical-school dropout, since earlier incidents in the novel clearly indicate that he is already in danger of being ostracized (or worse) for supposed sexual deviancy. In "Cyclops," Bloom has been slandered as a cuckold, as queer, and as impotent and effeminate. Just after Lenehan wrongly announces in Barney Kiernan's pub that Bloom has won on a horse race but stingily failed to buy them all drinks, Martin Cunningham, perhaps stirred up by Lenehan's anti-Semitic stereotypes, opens Bloom's sex life to public scrutiny by describing his lapsed

Judaism with the ambiguous phrase "perverted Jew."[7] In "Oxen,"
Mulligan has insultingly offered Bloom his "services," implying that
Bloom is a john seeking a rent boy. Most ominously, in "Scylla and
Charybdis," Mulligan has accused Bloom of stalking Stephen with a
view to sexual abduction, a scandal charge of which Bloom's subse-
quent actions do nothing to exonerate him.

Bloom's position of enforced dissembling parallels that of Parnell
and the Land League, who had to distance themselves from any association with armed struggle or aspiration to self-defense owing to the
British media's ongoing, distorting characterization of Irish nationalism as irrationally violent. Thus Bloom's efforts in "Circe" to look
after the genuinely imperiled "youth of Ireland" without succumbing
to scandal's destructive thunderbolts reenact the New Journalism's
rapid, panicky reorientation from social justice to moral bombast.
Out of this unfair fight, reflected in Bloom's increasingly desperate
responses to scandal attacks, emerged the profit-motivated scandal
discourse that Laurel Brake terms the New Journalism's second wave.[8]
Tracking Bloom's movements through "Circe," we see that Joyce understood both the origins of the New Journalist sex scandal and its
trajectory. Through the various, sequenced defensive strategies Bloom
employs—sometimes successfully, often disastrously—we see Joyce
developing, through trial and error, his own self-protective scandal
work.

"DISFIGURED BY THE HALLMARK OF THE BEAST"

An early paranoid fantasy of Bloom's involving a run-in with old
flame Josie Breen serves as a model in miniature of scandal's slippery
aims. Bloom claims to be in Nighttown rescuing fallen women for
the Magdalene Asylum, a disingenuous but logically coherent and
rhetorically self-serving cover story that reflects the emphasis on the
rescue and protection of the weak associated with the New Journalism's first wave. But when Josie Breen dismisses Bloom's claim that
he is in Nighttown to rehabilitate prostitutes, he changes tack and
instead denounces his wife's purportedly low and unnatural sexual

tastes. Having entered the brothel district, like W. T. Stead, on a secret mission to find and protect an obscurely threatened virgin, Bloom first pursues his kindly but compromising aims by substituting fallen women for Stephen as his object of solicitude. When this appeal to Josie's compassion fails, Bloom next seeks to silence Josie's threats to expose him by stirring her to self-righteous outrage with the claim that he has been wronged by his sexually depraved wife. Here, as at other moments in "Circe," Bloom can protect himself only when he uses the tactics of second-wave scandalmongering, calculated to outrage or intimidate.

This early brush with potential exposure soon escalates into Bloom's imagined arrest and trial for a series of accusations that variously enact the narrowly scripted roles assigned to scandal figures. As Bloom attempts to explain away the dangerous scandal evidence of the false name "Flower" on his business card to the RIC officers who stop him, Martha Clifford appears as the wronged innocent, one of the scandal girl's various types, brandishing the *Irish Times* and begging Bloom to "clear [her] name" (15.752–54). Bloom retaliates with a torrent of counterscandal whose terms showcase the new pressures the archipelagic sex scandal was exerting on Irish women, on whose sexual purity Irish nationalism was defensively insisting with ever-greater fervor.[9] Bloom first discredits Martha, saying she is drunk, and then claims the status of righteous scandal author, crediting himself with a character "without a stain" (15.777). He attempts to further insulate himself by identifying himself as a "staunch Britisher" who "fought . . . in the absentminded war under general Gough in the park" and did "all a white man could" through his affiliations with "the British and Irish press" (15.794–805). Fittingly, Bloom's attempt to forge British credentials is undone from the start by his confusion of the Gough who fought in the Boer War with the General Gough whose statue stood in Phoenix Park, a site where, for scandalous reasons made clear in this study's earlier chapters, an Irish man's aggression would not have been at all welcomed by British forces. Revealing a Little Chandler–like aspiration to the position of imperial jester, Bloom also claims to "follow a literary occupation" (15.801) and presents himself as the author of Philip Beaufoy's story, "Matcham's

Masterstroke," precipitating a slapstick reenactment of the Stead and Wilde trials in a courtroom quarrel over a "prize titbit" that turns out to be a submerged scandal fragment.

In this portion of the trial, it is Beaufoy, defending his authorship of "Matcham's Masterstroke" (and standing in for Joyce, the actual author of a piece with that title), who, like Stead and Wilde, imprudently introduces the moral status of his own writing into courtroom deliberations and calls attention to its scandalous subtext (surely introduced or exaggerated in Joyce's later revision of this failed 1896 *Tit-Bits* submission as a burlesque).[10] Beaufoy's unwarranted defensiveness, coupled with Bloom's shy admission that the "bit about the laughing witch hand in hand" might be objectionable (15.829–30), recalls both the earlier phrase "masterstroke by which he won the laughing witch" (4.513–14) and Joyce's first sexual encounter with Nora Barnacle, which included mutually orgasmic manual masterstrokes and produced a "titbit" that Joyce "prized," both in the sense of honoring it in his writing and of guarding and protecting it. With Beaufoy's assertion that his writing is "beneath suspicion" (15.825), Joyce explicitly places a shard of his own subtly interpolated text under review. This slyly inverted phrase is itself a particularly apt characterization of Joyce's writing in "Matcham's Masterstroke," an assertion that his work is *beneath* his readers' suspicion, obliging them to interpret it innocently since the unspeakably sordid alternate interpretations it solicits would only prove the "moral rottenness" of anyone who dared make them (15.842).

Indeed, Beaufoy uses this very tactic to thwart Bloom's attempts to read beneath the surface of his sentimental narrative, shouting, "It's a damnably foul lie, showing the moral rottenness of the man! . . . We have here damning evidence, the *corpus delicti*, my lord, a specimen of my maturer work disfigured by the hallmark of the beast" (15.842–45). This reference to Bloom's earlier shit-marked newspaper sheet—personal evidence retrieved from his session in the jakes—corresponds to the most sensational evidence to have been brought against Oscar Wilde, in which a hotel chambermaid testified that, in supposed evidence of sexual perversion, he had soiled his hotel bed linens with excrement. The public exposure of the shit on Oscar Wilde's sheets was indeed shocking and offensive, though it could only, at most, have proven that various messy mishaps involving feces, while publicly unmentionable and unpleasant to contemplate, nonetheless do occur. Having sensationally demonstrated precisely that point as regards Bloom, Beaufoy repeatedly calls the court's attention to the private life to which his scandal fragment affords access, spewing out a string of meaningless scandal charges: "Why, look at the man's private life! Leading a quadruple existence! Street angel and house devil. Not fit to be mentioned in mixed society! The archconspirator of the age!" (15.853–55). Beaufoy thus uses Bloom's soiled newspaper sheet as a moral synecdoche for Bloom's private life that can be used both to destroy him personally and to discredit his politics—which, as it happens, are socialist. Through this public exposure of a fragment from Bloom's private life, Beaufoy thus reenacts the tautology built into modern scandal logic through libel law's definitive loophole: since only those private details that constitute a public danger are publishable, all published scandal-worthy private details must be evidence of what are now constituted, however irrationally, as essentially political crimes.

The silencing, reifying effects of sex scandal culminate in a malevolent transformation that enfolds references to several of the New Journalism's biggest scandals. Bloom is reduced to a "grotesque" figure whose purported physical deformities serve as metaphors for his abominable moral irregularities (15.898–961), a fate Wilde also suffered over the course of his trials at the hands of a hostile, scandal-hungry press.[11] Beginning with his "long unintelligible speech" while holding "a full blown waterlily" (15.898), Bloom's dissolution into a fantastic amalgam of classed and racial stereotypes (black sheep, erring father, poor foreign immigrant, stowaway, aberration of heredity, atavistic throwback, Mongol, fawning oriental) also calls to mind Maamtrasna martyr Myles Joyce and his fruitless attempts to defend himself on the stand, as well as, of course, Mulligan's transformation of Stephen into the Irish Caliban. Like Myles Joyce, Bloom's testimony is discredited from the outset, in this case by the court official who calls him to the stand by solemnly announcing, "the accused will now make a bogus statement" (15.897), and fragmented by reporters who urge him to "get it out in bits" that they can fit easily into a scandal narrative (15.928). Bloom's desperate, comically bathetic speech from the dock also pointedly recalls Wilde's famous speech from the dock in defense of the pederastic tradition, which Bloom has already reenacted in the heroic register in an impassioned defense of Judaism in "Cyclops" and here as farce as he delivers gibberish while holding a flower emblematizing both Wilde's floral ostentation and the Maiden Tribute scandal's central protagonist, W. T. Stead's Lily.

"ANOTHER GIRL'S PLAIT CUT"

Joyce is concerned less with the guilt, innocence, or credibility of particular scandal victims than with the reliability of scandal itself. Earlier in "Circe," Joyce introduces the New Journalism's signature scandal charge, the deflowering of a sexually immature female virgin, when in response to the Bawd's offer of a "maidenhead" for ten shillings, Bloom's guilty conscience conjures a vision of Gerty Mac-Dowell limping forward, holding out decisive evidence of her own violation: her bloodied clout, or underwear (15.359–73). Gerty exposes her stained undergarment as material evidence of an act that readers, having observed Gerty's sexually charged but strictly visual encounter with Bloom in "Nausicaa," know did not occur. It is the scandal fragment, not Gerty, that indicts Bloom, and it is the scandal fragment's status as morally infallible evidence, rather than either Gerty or Bloom, that Joyce tries and condemns in this passage. The capacity of scandalous attacks to generate further scandal is illustrated by Bloom's panicky lie in response to Gerty's accusation, claiming that he "never saw" her (15.378). Bloom himself is thus instantaneously transformed from an "innocent" into a guilty liar by the seeming irrefutability of conventionally incriminating scandal evidence, a quality that provokes those accused to make rebuttals based not on truth but on whatever claims will place them furthest outside the scandal fragment's scope.

The credence given various scandal accusations is, of course, highly dependent on the class of the accuser and the accused. The

Bawd, like the various sex industry insiders who helped Stead to buy
a virgin in the name of social reform, quickly jumps in on the side of
"the gentleman," Bloom, charging Gerty with an array of false scandal
claims—of writing Bloom false letters, streetwalking, and soliciting—
and threatens to return her to her mother so she can "take the strap to
you at the bedpost" (15.381–82). Gerty, discredited by her lameness and
subjected to this scandalous counterassault by the same "bawd" who
just marketed her as a virgin, makes her own false countercharges,
recasting the mutual pleasure that she and Bloom enjoyed in "Nau-
sicca" as an act of unsolicited domestic intrusion like Buck Mulligan's
pilfering of Ursula's hand mirror, claiming that he had seen "all the
secrets of [her] bottom drawer" (15.384). Gerty's accusations against
Bloom are but one of several ethically murkier circumstances in this
and other episodes of the novel in which Bloom could be seen as col-
luding, in various ways and often inadvertently, in the institutionalized exploitation of socially vulnerable women.[12] Significantly, Gerty's
and Martha's recourse to the resources of civilization that sex scandal
had made available to the wronged innocent leaves them both, like the
Land League, the worse for the attempt.

Bloom, for his part, having become a scandal figure, continues
to accrue additional scandal charges. When his status as a cuckold
is published in the Saint Patrick's Day supplement of the *Evening
Telegraph* (15.1125–27), Bloom is exposed, through the scandalous
headline "another girl's plait cut," as the Dublin Minotaur, a serial
deflowerer of virgins with overtones of Jack the Ripper (15.1153). Joyce
here invokes "The Rape of the Lock," Alexander Pope's satire of a
minor scandal among the eighteenth-century gentry, to figure early-
twentieth-century sex scandals through the misappropriation of hair,
a theft suggestive of pishoguery. This reference to cutting invokes both
the Invincibles, whose clandestine cutting changed the course of Irish
decolonization, and the New Journalism's "moral assassins," who, like
the well-heeled "carvers" or nationalist benefactors Bloom reflects on
in "Lestrygonians," claim to take a laudable interest in the welfare of
the young while quietly sacrificing the lives and reputations of available maidens for their own political gain (8.471).[13] As the result of these
background machinations, Bloom, like the Parnellites and their allies,

is cast as hyperviolent and sexually monstrous. In a series of scandal charges with particular relevance to the serial Parnell scandals, Bloom is featured as a scandalous "dynamitard," forger, bigamist, bawd, cuckold, public nuisance, and again, as the Minotaur, the "odious pest" at the heart of Dublin's "white slave traffic" (15.1158–60).[14]

In the incredible evolutions that follow, Bloom rises to spectacular heights of power both because of and in spite of scandal's transformative powers. Like Wilde, he temporarily benefits from what Joyce earlier termed "the fantastic myth of the apostle of beauty [that] form[s] itself around him" ("Oscar Wilde," 149). His ascent is ritualized by his putting on of a ruby ring before "ascend[ing] and stand[ing] on the stone of destiny," suggesting that for a time Bloom, like Parnell, Stead, and Wilde, directs the forces of scandal to serve his own ends (15.1490–91). Parnell's brother, John Howard Parnell, designates Bloom as the "successor to my brother" (15.1513–14) shortly before Bloom, like Parnell, is accused of having a double life as a crypto-terrorist (15.1561–62). Like Parnell, Bloom initially recovers from scandal's threats, only to be toppled precisely at the moment he seeks land reform and an end to economic exploitation (15.1685–93).

Here Joyce calls attention to the opportunism as well as the efficacy of political scandalmongering by having the Irish newspapers and clergy erupt into hostile objections to Bloom's personal morality when he threatens to establish a "free lay church in a free lay state," or a church, and thus a future state, in which the laity would have a voice and enjoy "free" or decommodified and institutionally unregulated sex (15.1693). His voiced support of "mixed races and mixed marriage" offers members of the nationalist power structure an angle of attack that does not acknowledge their own self-interest and that reconstitutes Bloom as a threat not to them but to the very people he is trying to help (15.1699). The concomitance of Bloom's attempted economic and social improvements and his sexual/racial/religious discreditation reflects the inseparability, in sex scandal, of personal morality and political agenda through which a leader's actual or even supposed private predilections can be used to scuttle otherwise popular reforms. Thus when Bloom redistributes land and threatens to dislodge "dropsical imposters and barspongers" from their accustomed positions of leadership within the nationalist movement (15.1692), he is personally attacked first by a nationalist scandalmonger in the pay of the *Freeman's Journal*, O'Madden Burke, and then by a Father Farley, who blasts him as an "Episcopalian, an agnostic, an anythingerian, selling our holy faith" (15.1712–13). The efficacy of such charges is aptly illustrated by Mrs. (Dante) Riordan's cry to Bloom, "I'm disappointed in you! You bad man!" (15.1715), echoing her rebuke of the scandalized Parnell in *Portrait*.

In a charge that exemplifies the moral and empirical ambiguity that Joyce ascribes to all scandalous sexual charges, the embattled Bloom is next accused of using "a mechanical device to frustrate the ends of nature," a crime of which Joyce empirically shows Bloom to be both innocent and guilty (15.1741–42). While Bloom is indeed carrying a condom or "French letter" in his pocketbook, we have seen in his interactions with Martha Clifford and Gerty MacDowell the extreme lengths to which he has gone not to use it, obtaining sexual release through nonpenetrative prophylaxis. His possession of the condom is itself proof that he has not used it, a point emphasized in "Penelope" when Molly thinks that she will check to make sure he still has it. Though unsubstantiated, the scandal charge that Bloom practices birth control (and is thus non-Catholic and non-Irish) relegates Bloom's proposed redistribution of wealth and power to the room of ousted possibilities.

With Bloom thus reduced to a figure with all the nuance of a *Punch* caricature—again, the Irish Caliban—his once adoring compatriots call for his lynching or burning on the grounds that he is "as bad as Parnell," hurling at him the Healy scandal shard, "Mr. Fox" (15.1762). His fantasized career as Ireland's savior foundering, Bloom/Parnell momentarily attempts to shift blame onto his "double," his brother "Henry" (John Henry Parnell), but quickly abandons this strategy as unworkable (15.1769–70). The dynamics at play here are those Valente observes in the Parnell split, in which "the destruction of Parnell's manly stature . . . redoun[ded] upon his party and his people" in the form "of petulant and intemperate recriminations on both sides of the power struggle."[15] As scandal's infantilizing bluster is fully unleashed, Bloom's Irish audience barrages him with a range of "objects of little or no commercial value," including condensed milk tins (15.1764–65). These tins poignantly recall not only the Plumtree's Potted Meat advertisement that appears on the obituary page of the *Freeman's Journal* and the biscuit tin the citizen hurls at Bloom at the end of "Cyclops," but also a 1901 scandal concerning the stripping of fats and nutritious solids out of condensed milk that caused the spread of malnutrition among Ireland's poorest children.[16] The condensed milk tins also explicitly unite scandal and pishoguery, processes of destructive theft accomplished at a distance and against which there is no defense. Bloom, his masculinity publicly demolished and his life threatened with an item that specifically figures poor children's vulnerability to covert or hypocritical exploitation, is himself now transformed into the New Journalism's emblematic vulnerable scandal child.

Lapsing briefly into bad Irish, the beleaguered Bloom then turns to *Ulysses*'s preeminent figure of Irish middle-class opportunism, Buck Mulligan, for salvation. In this passage, Mulligan's various specializations as scandalmonger, pishoguerist, catamite, attempted pimp, and medical practitioner confer on him the title of "sex specialist" (15.1772), in which capacity he subjects Bloom to a public version of the medical inspection suffered by the New Journalism's paradigmatic innocent child, Eliza Armstrong/Lily. Thus over the course of "Circe," Bloom is, in effect, unmanned so that he may be spectacularly unmaided. Yet Bloom, like *Ulysses*'s central scandal icons and Odysseus in a range of tight spots, means to go down fighting. He briefly restores his popularity through a campaign of vigorous identification with a range of figures associated in scandal discourse with innocence and purity. Although the medical examinations to which Bloom submits are invasive and shaming, Mulligan's sensational finding that Bloom is, like Eliza Armstrong, "*virgo intacta*" does indeed temporarily forestall Bloom's definitive personal downfall (15.1785–86). Scientifically certified as sexually pure following the humiliating actual or symbolic misappropriation of his body hairs, his genitalia, and his bodily odor, Bloom is subsequently proven to be a good Catholic nationalist, wearing "a hairshirt of pure Irish manufacture" (15.1805–6). Bloom's "purely" Irish hairshirt constitutes a comic restitution of the "anal, axillary, pectoral and pubic hairs" that Mulligan has misappropriated, offering a witty visual redressal of the castration for which pishoguery is a symbolic correlative. In the course of Bloom's ritualized exposure, the discovery of the hairshirt empirically demonstrates his exorbitant guilt and thus his underlying conformity to the most repressive, Jansenist Catholic attitudes, thereby buying him a temporary respite at exorbitant cost.

In the rituals of public exposure to which Bloom submits at the hands of Buck Mulligan and his team, the procedures of medical examination and scandalous exposé converge. Through an ambitious public relations campaign actuated through these rituals of masochistic self-exposure, Bloom refashions himself as a comically overdetermined amalgamation of all those values the nationalist sex scandal purports to protect: childhood, virginity, Irishness, Catholicism, and motherhood. Calling into question Mulligan's competence at determining virginity, Bloom gives birth to octuplets, transforming from scandal figure to celebrity. In an apparent parody of Irish American nationalists' enthusiasm for Irish Catholic purity, Americans in particular pour forth support for Bloom's truly singular act of reproductive piety. "A wealthy American makes a street collection for Bloom," and a wide range of personal valuables pour in, many familiar in Joyce's oeuvre as objects of pishoguery: "Gold and silver coins, blank checques, banknotes, jewels, treasury bonds, maturing bills of exchange, I.O.U's, wedding rings, watchchains, lockets, necklaces and bracelets are rapidly collected" (15.1811–15).[17]

Embodying the argument early in "Oxen" that childbirth is central to the production of wealth and of political and military power (14.13), Bloom's "eight male yellow and white children . . . appear on a redcarpeted staircase adorned with expensive plants." The coin-like octuplets are "handsome, with valuable metallic faces, well-made, respectably dressed and wellconducted, speaking five modern languages fluently and interested in various arts and sciences. Each has his name printed in legible letters on his shirtfront." Furthermore, these offspring are "immediately appointed to positions of high public trust in several different countries as managing directors of banks, traffic managers of railways, chairmen of limited liability companies, vicechairmen of hotel syndicates" (15.1821–32).[18] As with Bloom's earlier reflexive lie in the face of Gerty's outrageous sexual accusations, this scandal defense is deceptively ineffective. Although Bloom appears to have surmounted the scandal forces menacing him, the results ultimately strengthen imperial economic and communications networks rather than Bloom or his discredited political aims. The teratogenic pressures of sex scandal engender an unnatural, octopoid birth, the strangely inhuman, hybrid product of which resembles capital imperfectly represented as human. Bloom's metallic, multilingual offspring span out like the tentacles of that industrial octopus William Martin Murphy, who used the *Irish Independent*—originally founded by Parnell in a bid to save himself—to align mainstream nationalism with the values of an emerging archipelagic capitalist elite. Bloom's hallucinatory birthing of valuable, fungible offspring therefore recalls that Parnell's final attempts to salvage his career further empowered the very resources of civilization that had destroyed him and his movement.[19]

Although he earlier ascended to the height of not just international but interstellar prominence, Bloom's final descent is emphatically local. In a parodic reenactment of the North American lynching touted in the "Cyclops" headline, "Black Beast Burned," Bloom is routinely processed in a civil auto-da-fé, with Lieutenant Meyers of the Dublin Fire Brigade setting him on fire "by general request" (15.1930). Surviving the ordeal, "stand[ing] upright amid phoenix flames" (15.1935), Bloom exhibits his burns to Dublin reporters, a secular ritual that registers newspapers' appropriation of the ecclesiastical role of moral verification, with reporters standing in for priests and scandal fragments as sacral objects or relics. Following the media's confirmation of his bona fides, Bloom undergoes a brief resurrection as a parodic Irish Catholic/Ulyssean deity, breaking into fluent Syngean Celticism—"Let me be going now, woman of the house, for by all the goats in Connemara I'm after having the father and mother of a bating"—and lying down to die (15.1962–68). The "bating" he has received from a hostile press, as this sequence implies, leaves him no option for self-expression outside the cod Celticism that British print capitalism demands of the public Irishman.

Bloom's meteoric ascent and cataclysmic fall herald the Irish end times, a cultural apocalypse that is, of course, reported in the newspapers. As newsboys proclaim the "safe arrival of antichrist" (15.2141), Joyce conjoins the themes of newspapers, scandal, and monstrosity while satirizing the New Journalism's morally stupefying effects. With the advent of the apocalypse, the two-headed Anglo-Scots octopus that A.E. associates in "Lestrygonians" with newspapers, empire, and apocalypse, reappears as Elijah's Master of Ceremonies.[20] In a wildly hyperbolic reinvention of Stead's reform-oriented visits to "Circe's Island," Elijah speaks from a rostrum draped with "the banner of old glory" in the voice of an American evangelical huckster, calling on a pointedly political God—"Mr. President"—to save the three whores, Kitty, Zoe, and Florry, who dutifully recite the stories of their respective sexual "falls." This vision of apocalypse is a multilayered portrait of the New Journalist sex scandal's micro and macro effects, showcasing the loss of standing that scandal imposes on individuals and groups and foreshadowing the British Empire's own impending loss of control over its octopoid "resources of civilization," as the center of imperial economics and communications migrates westward to the United States (15.2184–222).

"IN HERE ... I MUST KILL THE PRIEST AND THE KING"

In its later scenes, "Circe" reunites Bloom and Stephen and returns to the question of Stephen's professional and personal future, a question both men answer, in part, with counterscandal work. Wildly inebriated and menaced by a phantom of the dead mother he scandalously refused to pray for, Stephen, calling on the magical sword *Nothung*, smashes the chandelier above him (15.4242–44).[21] Throughout *Ulysses*, swords and knives are associated with scandal's capacity to disrupt not only individual lives but historical trajectories, imposing lasting, blighting changes on affect, norms, and group identity. But through his mock-heroic reenactment of the climactic scene in the second opera of Wagner's Ring Cycle, in which Siegmund attempts to defend himself with the sword but fails, shattering it and dying in his attempt,

Stephen effectively turns the preferred weapon of the scandalmonger against itself by turning it on himself, at once taking possession of and destroying scandal, the lancet of his art, in a blow that simultaneously obliterates and liberates him.[22]

In the eyes of his observers, who see simply a drunk hitting a lamp with his walking stick, this potently disruptive action exposes Stephen himself to a kind of death: the social death reserved not just for the scandalous transgressor but for the criminally insane. By publicly engaging in a violent outburst that is, crucially, far more alarming and incomprehensible because it targets property rather than a sentient being, Stephen, like Joyce in producing *Ulysses* itself, exposes himself in a way that others find completely unintelligible, so as to surmount the scandalous double binds that hold public speech within impossibly narrow and falsely moralizing strictures. Following this cataclysmic thrust, both invoking and radically revising the knifing of Caesar that has figured the violent historical truncations of scandal in Joyce's work since the age of nine, Stephen becomes the focal point of everyone's urgent and predictable efforts to restore the status quo. Lynch "seizes Stephen's hand" and orders him not to "run amok," construing Stephen as a native whose violent disruption of the colonial order springs from atavistic irrationality (15.4251–52). Bella reenacts the role of colonial overseer/entrepreneur that she had earlier embodied in Bloom's fantasies, calling for the police and angrily demanding exorbitant reparations from the Irish clients she sees as a captive market ripe for exploitation.

In what could be viewed as the novel's climax, it is Bloom who will wield scandal fragments so as to protect Joyce/Stephen from moral martyrdom and lead him safely out of the Circean labyrinth. Bloom rescues Stephen both from scandal—the prison house of discourse—and from literal imprisonment with a single reference to irate brothel-owner Bella Cohen's private life. As a paradigmatic owner of capital, Cohen is accustomed to unilaterally defining which acts constitute scandal-worthy transgressions and how any such transgressions will be redressed. While Stephen's damage to the chandelier is minimal, Cohen tries to claim the remains of his monthly pay—ten shillings, or one sovereign—in compensation (15.4275–76).[23] At this moment, Stephen is staggering on the threshold of the room of infinite futurity. If Cohen takes the rest of his pay, he will have to return, perforce, either to his father or to Mulligan and Haines. At best he will be obliged to keep his job at Deasy's school, his one slim link to funds and respectability. In any case, pressure to earn quick money to subsidize Simon's or Mulligan's drinking habits would rapidly overwhelm Stephen's ethical and artistic resolutions, and, like his sister Dilly, he would drown (10.874–75). If he is arrested, as Bella threatens, he knows no one with both the means and the will to post bail or to see to his defense. Bloom is thus addressing the essential danger the situation poses to Stephen when he tries to persuade Bella Cohen that she does not "want a scandal" (15.4299–300).

But Cohen, of course, does want a scandal, as long as it is one she can direct; Bloom only eggs her on when he credits Stephen with the fabricated social status of Trinity student and nephew of the vice chancellor (15.4297–300). Cohen, seeing Bloom's attempts to intervene on Stephen's behalf as a challenge to her absolute authority, grows more explicitly vindictive, asserting that she will charge Stephen and disgrace him (15.4303–4). Like a newspaper or a confessional, Cohen's brothel converts shameful secrets into not only wealth but power, enabling Cohen to bully with impunity any Dubliner who crosses her threshold.[24] Clearly neither the police nor Anglo-Irish Brahmans stand outside her sphere of influence.

Bloom, seeing this, shifts tactics, "urgently" inquiring, "And if it were your own son in Oxford?" and "warningly" telling her, "I know" (15.4306). Cohen backpedals instantly, agreeing to Bloom's proposed payment: one shilling, the real cost of the damage. Cohen's son's presumptive identity as an Irish Jew makes him, as Bloom himself knows, particularly vulnerable to scandal charges and particularly powerless to defend against them. But whereas scandalous misappropriations are, throughout Joyce's oeuvre, associated with overpayment, double payment, and outright theft, in this transaction Bloom weighs the worth of one "son's" reputation against another and protects them both from scandal, throwing his own shilling on the table to pay what

Stephen owes (15.4312–13). He will go on to lead Stephen back out of the Nighttown's labyrinthine "house of shame," fending off further scandal threats by means of adroitly wielded scandal fragments.

Bloom thus uses the threat of scandal homeopathically to prevent actual scandal by reemphasizing the continually forgotten point that scandal is a double-edged sword, as much a danger to vulnerable scandalmongers as to their intended victims. In securing Joyce/Stephen's liberty, Bloom's defensive scandal work also ensures a future for the incipient strategies of onanistic complicity that began with an act of voluntary mutual masturbation that took place in Dublin on or around June 16, 1904. In saving Joyce/Stephen from artistic and material pishoguery at the hands of Bella Cohen, Simon Dedalus, and Buck Mulligan, Bloom has, in fact, figuratively ensured the future representation of Dublin's "lost ones" in a register outside of the sentiment/scandal double bind that naturalizes exploitation as the fundamental human relationship.

Perhaps in an artistic act of gratitude for real kindnesses—for Joyce was in fact looked after and perhaps kept from incarceration by Bloom's original, Alfred H. Hunter—Joyce vouchsafes to the fictional Bloom an extraordinary vision of his own lost one, Rudy (15.4956–60). In terms that Vicki Mahaffey has rendered with particular power and sensitivity, Rudy's numinous appearance at the end of "Circe" represents art's capacity to supply imaginative restitution of our deepest desires, specifically those of the heartscalded Bloom but also those of the young Joyce as Stephen Dedalus, the stricken youth of Ireland.[25] In this vision, Rudy materializes as a "fairy boy of eleven, a changeling, kidnapped," a figure for Joyce's own lost brother, George, and for any number of Irish children senselessly dead (15.4957).[26] Embodying the restitution of two other senseless losses, Rudy is also connected to Shakespeare's lost son Hamnet and explicitly to Oscar Wilde, poet of *Salomé*, who, as Joyce argued in 1909, was martyred because he caused a scandal. Rudy's imagined age of eleven years, while technically inaccurate (given his birth date of December 29, 1893), is both the same age as that of Shakespeare's only son, whose childhood death is a cornerstone of Stephen's performance in "Scylla and Charybdis," and the time that passes between Joyce's publication of "Oscar Wilde: The Poet of *Salomé*" in 1909 and his careful completion of "Circe" in 1920.[27]

Rudy holds a slim ivory cane, like Wilde's "famous white ivory cane" cited in Joyce's essay on Wilde, and wears glass slippers that evoke the "sandals encrusted with glass" that Herod offers Salomé in Wilde's play ("Oscar Wilde," 149).[28] He also wears a violet bowknot, recalling Wilde's frequent use of violet, both the flower and the color, as an emblem of the aesthetic and a stand-in, as elsewhere in *Ulysses*, for the lapel flower of which Joyce's essay takes note (150–51). The white lambkin peeping out of his breast pocket makes Rudy, like Joyce's Wilde, a Christic figure, but the lambkin's placement in his pocket signifies a restoration of that which scandalmongers, as pishoguerists and simoniacs, have stolen (151).[29] Rudy, thus, is released from the room of foreclosed possibilities, and through him Oscar Wilde is no longer out of pocket. This vision of restitution vouchsafes to Bloom, fictional counterpart of the little-known Hunter, and to us a fantastic glimpse of Joyce's "own soul," to which he had dedicated his first play, *A Brilliant Career.* Over the course of *Ulysses*, a book that tells the story of its own inception, Joyce's tortuous scandal work does indeed rectify matters a little, at least enough to convey this vision of restitution at last, reflected in a momentarily mended mirror.

Coda

Jamming the Imperial Circuitry:
"The Readiest Channel Nowadays"

While you have a thing it can be taken from you . . . but when you
give it . . . no robber can take it from you. It will be yours always.

—James Joyce, *Exiles*

Assassination, never, as two wrongs did not make one right.
Duel by combat, no. Divorce, not now. Exposure by mechanical
artifice (automatic bed) or individual testimony (concealed
ocular witnesses), not yet. Suit for damages by legal influence
or simulation of assault with evidence of injuries sustained
(selfinflicted), not impossibly.

—James Joyce, *Ulysses*

Although Deasy, the unionist, has more success than either Mulligan
or Haines, the bourgeois cultural nationalists, in tangibly subordi-
nating Stephen Dedalus, he ultimately fails to retain his services. In
an exchange that recasts Deasy as the disesteemed jester in the court

of *his* master, Joyce renders his final verdict on Deasy when Stephen offers his teaching position to the truly improvident and unqualified Corley, whose only known area of expertise is in especially brazen techniques for exploiting women (16.157–59). Corley joins Deasy as an example of that rare category in Joyce: the certified fool. For his part, Deasy has demonstrated pale glimmers of insight only twice. One is his recognition that Stephen is not cut out to be a teacher (2.402), to which Stephen has the last word when he implies that the loutish, imperialist Corley is the kind of teacher that Deasy wants and that Stephen himself is not cut out to be. The other plausible advice that Deasy had offered, and that Stephen's arrangement to substitute Corley for himself decisively rebuts, was to urge Stephen to make and save money.

Deasy's remarks to Stephen on the subject of fiscal prudence aptly call attention to Stephen's status as an easy mark, a potential pishogue; in support of this point, however, he unwittingly cites Shakespeare's Iago, who repeatedly advises his own mark, Roderigo, to "put money in [his] purse" (2.239). Deasy's typically boneheaded allusion once again links pishoguery to scandal, recalling a situation in which an interest in others' private effects is ostensibly beneficent but secretly predatory. In this moment and throughout the novel, Deasy serves as Joyce's most explicit example of how imperial scandal culture reflects capitalist power dynamics by complacently dividing the world into those creditable beings who extract surplus value and their discreditable inferiors from whom surplus value is extracted. In sending Corley to Deasy as his replacement, Stephen thus declines to be guided by Iago, the instigator of English literature's most famous political sex scandal, as to what constitutes admirable conduct and sound economic behavior.

Whereas Corley, Gallaher, Mulligan, Haines, and Deasy, like Iago, expend their ingenuity in manipulating the contents of others' purses and pockets, James Joyce countered the scandal logic of the New Journalism with constant acts of symbolic self-sacrifice, actual or seeming shameful self-exposure. Through the complex and evolving web of scandal work examined in this study, Joyce enticed readers with his own sexual secrets and those of others, which he positioned relative to famous scandal fragments from the Maiden Tribute, Parnell, and Wilde sex scandals. He juxtaposed the salacious appeal of sexual scandal fragments against the traumatic galvanization of violent scandals like the Phoenix Park murders so as to force a recognition of newspapers' use of sex scandal as a way to both wound its victims and frighten its consumers into compliance. Using a wide array of tactics derived from the New Journalists' scandal repertoire, Joyce impossiblized the pishogueristic misappropriation of the secrets he exposed, ensuring that they could never be reified for personally, politically, or socially destructive purposes.

In *Ulysses*, his most thorough engagement with scandal, Joyce accomplished this largely by setting up parallactic views of specific sexual acts. Through this multiperspectival treatment, Joyce disabled sex scandal's "one-eyed" treatment of particular, decontextualized fragments. This strategy is reflected in the continual and intensifying blurring of reality and fantasy over the course of the novel. By the time we reach "Oxen of the Sun," for instance, it is virtually impossible to determine whether Bloom's recalled helplessness after his first act of coitus—with the homeless adolescent Bridie Kelly, whom Bloom recalls as having fled into the night at the sound of a foot patrol—gives rise to or is self-servingly produced by the sentimental discourse in which it is conveyed (14.1063–74). In "Circe," simultaneously the most evidentiary and the most fantastic episode of *Ulysses*, we are left to decide for ourselves which of the episode's sexual occurrences and memories are fantasies, exaggerations, or expressions of unconscious drives and which are, for lack of a better word, real. By removing our ability to confidently assign any moral, biographical, or even ontological status to any given sex act, Joyce interrupts the script of the New Journalist sex scandal that demands unthinking outrage with no discussion.

That Joyce's scandal work so effectively produces such impasses is ensured through his persistent juxtaposition of the irregular but unscandalous against the innocent but potentially scandalous. In *Ulysses*, Joyce presents sexual negotiations such as Mulligan's solicitation of

Stephen, which falls outside the vocabulary of the contemporary New Journalist sex scandal and may therefore be depicted openly, as the moral and representational obverse of socially prohibited but ethical sexual transactions such as the one that occurred in the course of James Joyce and Nora Barnacle's first walk. As Vicki Mahaffey has observed, *Ulysses* is a "hand job" commemorating a hand job;[1] the date on which Joyce set *Ulysses*—June 16, 1904—is widely believed to be the date on which Nora Barnacle, in a public, transgressive sex act, "made [him] a man."[2] Thus *Ulysses* functions, like much of Joyce's scandal work, to transmit the "good news" of his sexual "salvation" in a manner quite similar to that employed by the fictional scandalmonger Ignatius Gallaher: by creating a coded text that is legible only if mapped onto a prior, unrelated text. *Ulysses* is the disguise with which Joyce circumvents journalistic controls to serve up his own history on a "hot plate" (7.76).

That we know from multiple sources that the transgressive sex act between Joyce and Barnacle occurred but cannot definitively date it typifies something important about Joyce's scandal work. By publicizing the most salacious aspects of his own scandal fragments but maintaining strict secrecy concerning their more mundane specifics, Joyce makes it impossible to ascertain the empirical status of the incriminating titbits. The success of Joyce's scandal work relied both on what Latham describes as the power of scandalous secrets to trigger viral streams of communication and on Joyce's employment of prophylactic coding that disabled any use of his secrets as scandal fragments. By practicing safe sex scandal, Joyce not only protected himself, his art, and his family but also repeatedly broke the powerful bond between scandal's direct and indirect functions of exposure and discreditation.

In his initial encounter with Barnacle, Joyce was, so far as he knew, debauching a virgin, the Edwardian period's paradigmatic act of scandalous sexual immorality.[3] Yet we can be sure from the sexual attitudes and values Joyce assigns to some of his most inveterate pishoguerists in *Ulysses*—Corley, Mulligan, Lenehan, Boylan, and Bannon—that Joyce had no intention of joining the libertines in declaring a generalized open season on virgins. As we know from his early letters to Nora Barnacle, Joyce viewed their first encounter, because it was mutually desired and conducted without economic, social, or reproductive motives, as a courageous and liberatory act, a benevolent ritual transformation both radical and sacred. This fundamental contradiction between the laws of scandal and the emotional truth of lived experience represents the plinth on which *Ulysses*, as a work both of and against scandal, is built. Joyce broadcast this detail of his "secret life" to future generations with a breadth of communicative ambition and enthusiasm that approaches that of "the peers" in "Circe," who wire the news of Bloom's ascension not only to other countries but to other planets (15.1500–502).

Yet Joyce, as we have seen, was not content to use his scandal work for his own protection and projection only; he sought with equal fervor to renegotiate the aftereffects of the New Journalist sex scandals that have so potently shaped "the whole aftercourse of our lives." In devising a means to accurately and safely depict the inherent scandalousness of the quotidian, and hence to make clear the indirect political discreditation that the sex scandal's direct acts of blustering, morally outraged exposure render uncontestable, Joyce challenged the new bounds of social identification and exclusion that were perhaps the most lasting and destructive legacy of the New Journalism in Ireland. By relentlessly promoting "Dubliner" as an identity, Joyce contested the synonymity of Irishness with an idealized agrarian Catholicism and the middle-class economic, cultural, and gender norms it naturalized. Throughout his work, he wanted to redress the purgation of non-Catholics from constructions of the Irish nation in the wake of Parnell and the political exclusion of the poor, women, children, and socialists in the run-up to Irish independence.[4] As *Ulysses* scholars have widely noted, Joyce's use of "a perverted Jew" to serve as his emblematic Dubliner aggressively contested a range of commonsense identity binaries, even as the centrality of Dublin to Joyce's scandal work remaps both the increasingly middle-class, pastoral, and sexless Ireland of post-Rising nationalism and the scandalized spatiality of the British Isles. Joyce's relentless focus on Dublin as a paradigmatic modern city as well as a microcosm of Ireland simulta-neously exploited and contested the New Journalism's distribution of scandalized sexual anxieties onto dissident political identities across the archipelago. From this viewpoint, *Ulysses* represents an astonish-ingly humane, anomalously effective, and superlatively odd job, and a watershed in the history of modern scandal work.

NOTES

INTRODUCTION

1. A wealth of anecdotal evidence for Joyce's interest in newspapers has been compiled by Herr, *Joyce's Anatomy of Culture*; Donovan, "Dead Men's News"; Rando, "Scandal," chapter 2 in *Modernist Fiction and News*; and Collier, "'Tell a Graphic Lie': *Ulysses*, Reform, and Repression," chapter 4 in *Modernism on Fleet Street*. Joyce's countless notes on articles in both Irish and English newspapers in the nearly fifty notebooks he used in the writing of *Finnegans Wake* are well documented in *"Finnegans Wake" Notebooks*. See also Bixby, "Perversion and the Press"; Kershner, "Newspapers and Popular Culture" and *The Culture of Joyce's "Ulysses"*; and Utell, *James Joyce and the Revolt of Love*.

2. For a detailed history of *Dubliners'* production and publication, see Gabler, "A History of Curiosities." For a discussion of Joyce's early affinities to naturalism or realism in *Dubliners*, see Kelly, *Our Joyce*.

3. As Riquelme argues, the very character of Stephen Dedalus represents a melding of the figures of Oscar Wilde, the mythic Icarus, and Charles Stewart Parnell, which come together "to colour from the outset our sense of the issues and the risks for Stephen" (*Cambridge Companion*, 104).

4. See, for instance, Deane, "Joyce the Irishman," especially 28–32.

5. All references to *Ulysses* and *Finnegans Wake* come from the editions listed in the bibliography.

6. See Fordham, *Lots of Fun at Finnegans Wake*, particularly the summary of the letter/scandal in the park issue (11–12). See also Rando, "Scandal," 55–56, and Brivic, "Reality as Fetish."

7. For a recent, comprehensive review of the Parnell scandal's significance in Joyce's oeuvre, see the second chapter of Utell, *James Joyce and the Revolt of Love*.

8. See, especially, Valente's introduction to *Quare Joyce*; Norris's "A Walk on the Wild(e) Side"; and Levine's "James Joyce, Tattoo Artist." Dettmar's "Vacation, Vocation, Perversion" provides a particularly detailed explication of *Portrait's* Clongowes smugging episode as it recapitulates the Dublin Castle and Cleveland Street scandals in miniature.

9. Rando's *Modernist Fiction and News* is a welcome exception to the lack of research directly engaging Joyce's relationship to scandal, affording an excellent chapter on the subject. Even the late-nineteenth-century's paradigmatic sex scandal, W. T. Stead's "The Maiden Tribute of Modern Babylon," has been oddly unexplored in most Joyce criticism, with the two notable exceptions of Eckley's *Maiden Tribute* and Mullin's *Joyce, Sexuality and Social Purity.*

10. Joyce scholarship's emphasis on Parnell and its concomitant minimization of Wilde may have originated with Joyce's intensely homophobic brother, Stanislaus, who insisted on Parnell's significance for Joyce (*My Brother's Keeper*, 168). In Ellmann's magisterial literary biography of Joyce (*James Joyce*), Parnell appears ten times, usually as an influence on Joyce's writing, while Wilde merits five mentions, only one of which is contingently connected to Joyce's writing. The seeming absence of Wilde in Joyce's writing is especially pronounced in *Ulysses* criticism, as in Brown's declaration that "the Wilde trial appears [in *Ulysses*] hardly at all; there is little more than a hint of it in 'Eumaeus'" (*Joyce and Sexuality*, 81). More attention has been given to Wilde's influence on *Finnegans Wake*, in studies such as Schork's "Significant Names," Conrad and Wadsworth's "Joyce and the Irish Body Politic," Slote's "Wild(e) Thing," and Crispi and Slote's *How Joyce Wrote "Finnegans Wake."*

11. The term "New Journalism," central to the currently bourgeoning study of newspapers in Victorian and modernist studies, originated with Matthew Arnold, who used it pejoratively in 1887 specifically to describe the activist scandalmongering of W. T. Stead in the *Pall Mall Gazette* (Brake, *Print in Transition*, 216).

12. This claim can be found in Malone, "Sensational Stories, Endangered Bodies," 1.

13. See Kaplan, *Sodom on the Thames*, 175, and Dellamora, *Masculine Desire*, 200.

14. Quoted in Eckley, *Maiden Tribute*, 58.

15. Dwan, *The Great Community*, 198.

16. The groundswell of scholarship on the New Journalism over the past twenty-five years includes Wiener, *Papers for the Millions* (1988); Walkowitz, *City of Dreadful Delight* (1992); Cohen, *Talk on the Wilde Side* (1993); Legg, *Newspapers and Nationalism* (1999); Brake, *Print in Transition* (2001) and "Government by Journalism" (2004); Collier, *Modernism on Fleet Street* (2006); Collier and Ardis, *Transatlantic Print Culture* (2008); Hampton, *Visions of the Press* (2004); Barnhurst and Nerone, *The Form of the News* (2001); Soderlund, "Covering Urban Vice" (2002); Potter, *Newspapers and Empire in Ireland and Britain* (2004); de Nie, *The Eternal Paddy* (2004); and Steele, *Women, Press and Politics during the Irish Revival* (2007). Cocks's

Nameless Offences (2003), by placing the late nineteenth-century sex scandal within the expanding field of newspaper studies, adds to our understanding of the stories that were not told, as well as the stories that were, during the New Journalism's heyday.

17. As noted by Bixby, "Perversion and the Press," 113.

18. Stanislaus Joyce recalls that their father, John, "had been among the first to greet the rising star of Parnell. It was a fanatical lifelong devotion which he handed on to his son" (*My Brother's Keeper*, 28). Elsewhere, he notes that his elder brother "was always of the opinion that a dramatist could understand only one or two of life's tragedies, and that he always presented different aspects of the few he understood," and describes the story of Parnell as part of Joyce's fixation on "the tragedy of dedication and betrayal" (168).

19. Whether John Joyce's lifelong claims of political persecution because of his stubborn loyalty to Parnell accurately diagnosed the cause of his family's precipitous economic decline or were merely the alibi of a spendthrift alcoholic remains debatable. Stanislaus Joyce, who loathed his father, believed that his father brought his troubles on himself, accusing him of laziness, shiftlessness, chronic drunkenness, domestic abuse, and embezzlement (*My Brother's Keeper*, 43–44). Costello's study of John Joyce's financial records, however, finds some evidence that his finances and career were indeed sabotaged and concludes that Stanislaus greatly exaggerated his father's faults (*Joyce*, 106–12). In any case, from the vantage point of James Joyce's childhood, the fall of Parnell and the foundering of the Home Rule movement would have been affectively and causally linked to his family's inexorable decline.

20. Joyce's Paris library and his collection of thousands of press clippings pertaining to himself and his work are housed in the special collections at the University of Buffalo.

21. Slote, in "Wild(e) Thing," has carefully traced one such "figural constellation that disturbs the surface of textual referencing" with regard to Oscar Wilde in *Finnegans Wake* (122).

22. For a provocative phenomenological meditation on social exposure and affect, see Koestenbaum, *Humiliation*.

23. See Searle, *Speech Acts*, 64–71.

24. Lakoff and Johnson, *Metaphors We Live By*.

25. See Warner, *Publics and Counterpublics*.

26. Ellmann, *Selected Letters*, 90.

27. For discussions of *Ulysses* as a sucès de scandal, see Arnold, *The Scandal of "Ulysses,"* and Latham, *Art of Scandal*, especially 89–90.

28. In his introduction to the Norris edition of *Dubliners*, Gabler notes that Joyce initially promoted the collection to Grant Richards as notable for

the "special odour of corruption which, I hope, floats over my stories" (xix). Brown discusses the later letter to Richards in which Joyce defended his use of commonplace words such as *bloody* on the grounds that the "enormity" hidden under the surface of "An Encounter" (which had thus far not entered into their already fraught negotiations) was considerably worse (*Joyce and Sexuality*, 54).

29. In *Joyce's Anatomy of Culture*, Herr acknowledges in a general way what I term Joyce's homeopathic use of cultural logics against themselves, 34–37. Rando, while more insistent than I on Joyce's stylistic opposition to newspapers and scandal (*Modernist Fiction and News*, 54–55), persuasively describes Joyce as "strategically interven[ing] in . . . the news culture of scandal" by drawing "scandalous experience out of the empathic and abstract sphere of the news" (48–49).

30. In addition to Herr's *Joyce's Anatomy of Culture* and Donovan's "Dead Men's News," this work also includes Putz, "(De)Pressing the Reader"; Bixby, "Perversion and the Press"; Collier, "'Tell a Graphic Lie'"; Wicke, *Advertising Fictions*; Leonard, *Advertising and Commodity Culture*; Kershner, "Newspapers and Popular Culture"; and Owens, *James Joyce's Painful Case*.

31. See, for instance, studies such as Brown, *James Joyce and Sexuality*, and Mullin, *James Joyce, Sexuality and Social Purity*.

32. As Latham points out, following Joyce's epic battle to get *Dubliners*, with its few nonfictionalized proper names, into print, in *Portrait*, *Ulysses*, and *Finnegans Wake*, he initiated "an even more aggressive assault on the constraints imposed by the restrictions of libel law" (*Art of Scandal*, 96–98).

33. See Morris and Thompson, "Postcolonial Connolly," 3–4.

34. In her chapter on the Dilke scandal in *Names and Stories* ("French Vices"), Israel supplies a detailed analysis of the means by which competing class loyalties divided late Victorian feminists, with many middle-class feminists using the scandal as an occasion for "the flexing of feminist public muscle" (219), while working-class activists accused W. T. Stead and "professional purity people" of using "filthy insinuation and recitals of vices" to "override working-class and Radical voters' freedom" (224–25).

35. Theweleit, *Male Fantasies*, 365.

36. Fanon, *Wretched of the Earth*, 126.

37. In "Oscar Wilde, Lady Gregory, and Late Victorian Table-Talk," Lucy McDiarmid examines the complex, simultaneously familial and sectarian interrelations among British and Anglo-Irish power brokers by approaching the London dinner table as a "crossover zone, with characteristics of both an intimate domestic sphere and a public, often official, one" (49). She notes as an example Lady Gregory's writing about the small, round dinner table

where Gladstone had first met socially with Parnell: "At this round-table Parnell was squared" (quoted in McDiarmid, 52).

38. Kershner, quoted in Utell's *James Joyce and the Revolt of Love*, takes note of the growing gulf between the respective moral purviews of the journalist and the novelist when he observes that the "scandalously explicit divorce trials of the sort that ruined Parnell" were "followed assiduously by a public that professed shock at the idea of reading Zola's yellow-backed novels" (4).

39. Ellmann, *Selected Letters*, 81–82.

40. For a detailed account of newspaper coverage of "intimate things" around the turn of the century, see Leckie, *Culture and Adultery*, particularly the chapter "Columns of Scandal."

41. Ellmann, *Selected Letters*, 129.

42. Collier, in *Modernism on Fleet Street*, faults Joyce's early allusions to a monolithic "British press" as falsely homogenizing, while recognizing that Joyce used the term figuratively. This study traces tensions in Joyce's work between newspapers and scandals as signifiers and as signified to a rapid and previously unremarked shift from an avowedly political sex scandal that was primarily or at least legibly figurative to scandals in which the potent figurative dimension was ferociously disavowed. As it will show, Joyce's frequent use of journalists, newspapers, and scandal as figures within a strata of moral allegory that runs through his work is one means by which the author countered print capitalism's reifying effects.

43. For a detailed analysis of Parnell and Parnellism's relationship to the press, see Dwan, *The Great Community*, 188–99.

44. The intensity of the modern sex scandal's twin public affects of limitless shame and expansive affirmation relies not on the national system of newspapers and mutually aware readers that Benedict Anderson delineates but, as Ed Cohen points out, on a transnational media network made up of multiple, segmented, but mutually conscious readerships (*Talk on the Wilde Side*). With the emergence of what Potter calls the British empire's imperial press system (*Newspapers and Empire*), one group could rejoice in a distant adversary's humiliation at the same moment that their political, cultural, or ethnic opponents were tasting the acute despair of public disgrace.

45. Here I am indebted to Westervelt-Lutz's sensitive and lucid readings of Joyce's protagonists' use of rhetoric and their successes and failures in terms of audience formation and retention ("A Profoundly Human Parable").

46. Like scandal, controversy is a form of public contestation, though a far more populist and participatory one, and both forms gained new vitality through the expansion of newspapers and newspaper audiences. The two genres share similarly public, collective aspirations and similarly

denunciatory tones, but flourish under different political conditions. This would account for scandal's prominence in the intensely polarized late Victorian period, in contrast with the culture of controversy that thrived during the 1908–1913 period when, as McDiarmid points out, change was in the wind (*Irish Art of Controversy*, 3–6).

47. See Callanan, *T. M. Healy*, especially 346–90.

48. Kee, *The Laurel and the Ivy*, 238n.

49. In *My Brother's Keeper*, Stanislaus Joyce recalls that the poem itself may have been untitled and notes—unsurprisingly, given James's age—that it was terrible. Certain of its trite phrases, such as "my dear old shady home," remained bywords for bad poetry between the two brothers into their adulthood (46). But that Stanislaus referred to the poem as "Et Tu, Healy" and James Joyce accepted this title as apt confirms not only that the poem thematized betrayal but that it figured Healy's use of scandalous invective as a political assassination. Given the significance that John, Stanislaus, and undoubtedly James assigned to the poem as the "first timid blossoms" of Joyce's talent, Joyce would have been unlikely to invoke Caesar's assassination in his later work without recalling this early connection.

50. Ellmann, *James Joyce*, 33.

51. In "Parodic Irishness," Burns notes that with this early poem, Joyce began his career with the voice of disillusioned Irish nationalism. For examples of the poem's influence within Irish historiography, see Callanan, *T. M. Healy*, xxiv; and Kee, *The Laurel and the Ivy*, 601.

52. The scandalmonger's characteristic stance of exaggerated innocence is satirized in the "Aeolus" episode of *Ulysses*, in which the middle-aged Parnellite Myles Crawford caricatures the famously pugnacious Tim Healy as "a sweet thing . . . in a child's frock" (116).

53. See Mullin, *James Joyce, Sexuality and Social Purity*.

54. In his Triestene newspaper essay "The Shade of Parnell," Joyce praises Parnell's "mild, proud, silent and disconsolate sovereignty" (*Occasional, Political, and Critical Writing*, 194). In *Portrait of the Artist*, Stephen exults in his own "mild proud sovereignty" immediately after mentally rejecting the priesthood (148), even though he gains this sense of freedom by accepting the inevitability that, unsheltered by the power of the church, he will be vulnerable to scandal and, in choosing to brave "the snares of the world," "he [will] fall" (144).

55. As Brenda Maddox observes, "Joyce, perhaps above all other authors, used his life as the raw material of his art" (*Nora*, xix). For *Ulysses* as libelous roman à clef, see Latham, *Art of Scandal*, 92–105.

56. In *My Brother's Keeper*, Stanislaus Joyce notes his brother's incorporation of an early poem, "The Villanelle of the Temptress," into *Portrait* (85–86). As discussed in chapter 6 in this volume, Joyce included fragments

of his early story "Matcham's Masterstroke" in the "Calypso" and "Circe" episodes of *Ulysses*. See Kenner, "Beaufoy's Masterplaster," and Stanislaus Joyce, *My Brother's Keeper*, 91. Joyce's early poem on the death of Parnell also plays a significant role in Joyce's short story on the same theme, "Ivy Day in the Committee Room," as discussed later in this volume.

57. *My Brother's Keeper*, 33.

58. The London press's longstanding hostility toward the Irish gained potency through the New Journalism's introduction of new sensationalizing and distorting conventions into mass-scale newspaper writing. Indeed, it could be said that ethnic and national insults that earlier had been expressed visually through the distortions conventional to newspaper illustrations were, after the mid-nineteenth century, increasingly encoded in words. Particularly in coverage of events at the colonial periphery, where libel protections were weakest, news stories were sensationalized through the "spice" supplied by the sensational, decontextualized details I term "scandal fragments." Throughout the second half of the nineteenth century, fragmentary details of Irish experience were used in the pages of the London newspapers as ammunition on one side of an escalating representational war. As Lloyd notes, Irish violence, especially of a sort that could be played up as primitive or bestial, particularly merited attention in the British Press (*Anomalous States*, 125).

59. Joyce, *Occasional, Critical, and Political Writing*, 147.

60. In most editions of *Ulysses*, the episodes are numbered but untitled, as in the original edition. The episode titles generally used by scholars and *Ulysses* enthusiasts and referred to in this volume are taken from the Linati schema, which Joyce supplied for his Italian translator, Carlo Linati. For a history of the Linati schema, a list of the episode titles, and an overview of *Ulysses*, see Norris, *A Companion to James Joyce's "Ulysses,"* 21–27.

61. Cheng, in *Joyce, Race, and Empire* (152), catches the general point but does not note the specific allusion to "the Irish Tempest," which is important because of the strong connection Joyce's citation of this particular image forges among Shakespeare, Wilde, and the role of the British press in the production of a monstrous Irish identity in the course of the Land Wars and subsequent Home Rule debates.

62. As often noted in discussions of Joyce's nationalism, early in his career he expressed respect for the policies of Sinn Fein, which supported Irish-grown materials and industries, policies of which Joyce approved. In a much-quoted letter to Stanislaus from Trieste, he claimed that he would have embraced Sinn Fein wholeheartedly if not for its emphasis on the Irish language (Ellmann, *James Joyce*, 237).

63. In "The Manliness of Parnell," Valente explicates the "double-bind of Irish manhood" that underlies the oscillating treatment of the Irish to

which I allude, schematizing the impossible positioning of Irish nationalists between "weakness and barbarism," with any deviation from one pole lapsing immediately into the other (76–77).

Chapter 1
UNORTHODOX METHODS IN THE HOME RULE NEWSPAPER WARS

1. See, for instance, Walkowitz, *City of Dreadful Delight*; Eckley, *Maiden Tribute*; and Andrews and Taylor, *Lords and Laborers of the Press.* Even the outstanding work of such eminent scholars as Laurel Brake (*Print in Transition)* and Patrick Collier (*Modernism on Fleet Street*), who closely attend to the complex circuitry through which various fin de siècle newspaper stories and conventions came into being, nonetheless view Fleet Street as the center and site of origin of the New Journalism. The preeminent scholar of Irish journalism, Marie-Louise Legg, also seems to overlook the full implication of her discovery that Parnell and the Land League had been honing the tactics of the New Journalism in the pages of the provincial and advanced nationalist press in Ireland well before W. T. Stead's earliest forays into what he called "Government by Journalism" (*Newspapers and Nationalism*, 124).

2. One early study of the role of regional newspapers relative to the New Journalism is Aled Jones's "The New Journalism in Wales." While treating the New Journalism as emanating outward from London through syndicated news reports and the news agencies, Jones notes that "individual lines of connection between English and Welsh journalism may also be drawn in the other direction" (171). The first chapter of Taussig's *Shamanism, Colonialism and the Wild Man* illustrates the role that small, partisan newspapers in colonial settings could play in producing the scoops that the metropolitan press sometimes disseminated. Simon Potter's edited collection, *Newspapers and Empire in Ireland and Britain* (2004), and his *News and the British World* (2003) represent the larger shift in newspaper studies toward an interactive transnational framework in which this study participates.

3. The phrase "government by journalism," often used to invoke the aspirations of the New Journalism, first appeared in May 1886 as the title of an article by W. T. Stead in the *Contemporary Review.* The economic and technological developments underpinning the New Journalism in the late nineteenth century grew out of a longer-term interpenetration of capitalism and the print industry that resulted in what is generally termed "print capitalism." See Underwood, *Journalism and the Novel.*

4. For the most comprehensive account of the factors influencing the rise of modern journalism in Ireland, see Legg, *Newspapers and Nationalism.*

5. As quoted in Bew, *Parnell*, 31.

6. See de Nie, *The Eternal Paddy*, 204.

7. Bew, *Parnell*, 31. At the same time, Parnell's public persona was a masterful media creation, as argued by Legg, *Newspapers and Nationalism*; Loughlin, "Constructing the Political Spectacle"; and Dwan, *The Great Community*. As Loughlin aptly describes it, "the public entity of 'Parnell' itself was the creation of the leader, his lieutenants and the nationalist press" (221).

8. See Legg, *Newspapers and Nationalism*, 72–73. For an overview of the central role of provincial newspapers in producing the creole nationalisms of which Parnell and the Land League were certainly an instance, see Anderson, *Imagined Communities*, 47–65.

9. See Kane, *Constructing Irish National Identity*.

10. For more on structures of feeling, see Williams, *Culture and Society*, esp. 72.

11. Steele, *Women, Press, and Politics*, 7–8. See also de Nie, *The Eternal Paddy*.

12. Cited in Donovan, "Dead Men's News," 30.

13. In his essay on *Ulysses* (*Modernism and Imperialism*), Fredric Jameson insightfully describes Joyce's mode of modernism as reflecting the increasingly fragmentary, opaque fields of social apprehension that the British empire's growth and intensifying economic and material bonds were precipitating in the British metropolis. This study argues that Dublin's position on an unstable fault line between the imperial metropolis and the colonial periphery rendered the postmodern fragmentation of an accelerating, globalizing capitalist order particularly visible in *this* imperial urban center.

14. Obstructionism's combativeness was of particular historic importance for the attractions that it held for many advanced nationalists, or Fenians, who ordinarily would have avoided any form of political activity within the framework of a union they considered invalid. Yet Parnell's position relative to the Fenians was fraught. Too close a relationship with them threatened to undermine his credibility as a good-faith constitutionalist with the Liberals and moderate Irish nationalists. Yet too much compromise or moderation on his part threatened to drive away the Fenian end of his coalition, including many of his movement's most energetic activists. By taking political action that spectacularly resisted the constitutional framework within which it was waged, Parnell and his cohort were able to attract many bright and energetic proponents of physical force into a broad nationalist front without driving out the moderates.

15. In *The Myth of Manliness*, Valente lays out a detailed and persuasive argument for the precise nature of Parnell's unifying appeal (see especially 27–52).

16. Theweleit, *Male Fantasies*, 366.

17. As Larkin notes in his history of the *Freeman's Journal*, nationalists in the 1880s saw Gray as "pandering and flattering" Parnell, with whom he had been in open and heated conflict until the Land League's weekly journal, the *United Ireland*, began to pose a potential threat to the *Freeman's Journal*'s circulation ("'A Great Daily Organ,'" 47). As Larkin observes, Joyce seems to have shared the opinion that Gray's avowed positions lacked conviction; one of the characters in his short story "Grace" describes Gray as "blathering."

18. For a good discussion of the Ladies Land League's ambivalent position within the Parnellite front, see Valente, *The Myth of Manliness*, 47–51.

19. For a detailed if nonscholarly account of the Phoenix Park Murders, see Molony, *The Phoenix Park Murders*, especially 20–28.

20. See de Nie, 241–45.

21. For the best-known images of the British public's horror in response to the Phoenix Park murders and the crime's generalization to the Irish as a whole, see Curtis, *Nothing but the Same Old Story*, and Curtis, *Apes and Angels*.

22. As Valente argues in *The Myth of Manliness*, Irish nationalism had long suffered from the impossible relationship between Irish Catholic men and the English model of manliness, from which Irish males were definitively excluded. As Valente demonstrates, Parnell's complicated subject position and distinctive personal mannerisms offered nationalists an unprecedented opportunity to negotiate with the British from a standpoint of relative equality. The Phoenix Park murders constituted a horrific setback, throwing nationalists as a group back into the abject position of purported bestiality that had been one of their established positions in the English symbolic order dating all the way back to the writings of Geraldis Cambrensis in the twelfth century.

23. For a rigorous, comprehensive study of British newspaper representations of the Irish and of Irish nationalists during this period, see de Nie, "The Land War."

24. The only exceptions to the general horror with which the Phoenix Park murders were greeted among Irish nationalists were among some North American Fenians, most notably Jeremiah O'Donovan Rossa. In this and many other instances, the independent stance of North American Fenians, who had their own newspapers and lecture circuits, further suggests the significance of newspapers and audiences in the creation of collective affects.

25. Waldron, *Maamtrasna*, 17.

26. Irish rage over Maamtrasna was expressed virtually wherever nationalists encountered British officials. In May 1885, British Radical MP Charles Dilke—who was to become another casualty of the Home Rule scandal wars—observed the citizens of Dublin routinely shouting, "Who killed

Myles Joyce?" at Dublin Castle officials going about their business. According to Jenkins, Dilke had gone to Dublin to promote a conciliatory scheme enlisting the Irish Catholic Church as the Liberal government's mouthpiece, but what he saw during his visit converted him to the Parnellite cause (*Victorian Scandal*, 178–83).

27. Latham, *Art of Scandal*, 33.

28. Partial and sometimes misleading accounts of the 1883–1884 Dublin Castle scandal abound, complicated by the fact that two different homosexual scandals are often referred to as the Dublin Castle scandal, and authors alluding to one seldom note the other's existence. The most detailed account of the first Dublin Castle scandal discussed in this study is in Lacey, *Terrible Queer Creatures*, 135–45, which clarifies the confusion caused by scholars' tendency to date the scandal to the first libel trial in 1884 rather than to the first *United Ireland* article in August 1883. Lacey also includes a chapter on the second Dublin Castle scandal, which involved the theft in 1907 of the Irish Crown Jewels (never recovered) by someone connected to a circle of crown appointees in the "mini-court" in Dublin (165–79). As some of these aristocratic men and their sometimes raffish friends were known or believed to engage in homosexual practices, the theft was rapidly sexualized in such headlines as "Abominations of Dublin Castle Exposed" (167).

29. For a detailed overview of the shifting laws, practices, and values governing the publication of private details prior to 1843, see chapter 2 of McKeon, *Secret History*. See also Leckie, *Culture and Adultery*.

30. McKeon's *Secret History* offers several examples of the powerful feelings that threats to individuals' public reputations aroused in the same eighteenth-century journalists and satirists who posed those threats. Andrew Marvell, for instance, describes libel as a form of theft whereby "all that stock of Credit, which an honest Man perhaps hath all his age been toyling for, is in an hour or two's reading plunder'd from him by a Freebooter" (87).

31. Latham, *Art of Scandal*, 33.

32. For an excellent reading of the connection between public exposure, shame, and homosexuality, see Munt, *Queer Attachments*.

33. McKeon, *Secret History*, 57.

34. See Clark, *Scandal*.

35. See Stallybrass and White, *The Politics and Poetics of Transgression*. For a detailed account of the ways in which Edmund Burke's Irish Catholic origins magnetized such humiliating attacks, see O'Donnell's "Edmund Burke's Political Poetics."

36. As Callanan notes, Healy first began to use details from the private lives of Castle officials as political weapons while still suffering physical and emotional distress from his period of incarceration (*Healy*, 89).

37. Indeed, their motivations could even be described as similar to those of the radical gay activists in the 1980s and 1990s who advocated outing closeted gays, lesbians, and bisexuals who used positions of public influence to harm them as a class.

38. Quoted in Callanan, *Healy*, 92.

39. Quoted in Callanan, *Healy*, 88.

40. Quoted in Kaplan, *Sodom on the Thames*, 176–77.

41. Callanan, *Healy*, 88–89.

42. For detailed information on divorce court coverage in the press, see chapter 2 of Leckie, *Culture and Adultery*.

43. Quoted in Kaplan, *Sodom on the Thames*, 177.

44. In the first two chapters of *Nameless Offences*, Cocks supplies extensive evidence that nineteenth-century British police, barristers, judges, and journalists truly did, as Joyce claims in his 1909 essay on Oscar Wilde, refrain from bringing charges against or publicly naming "known" sexual deviants until they were involved in a scandal. Cocks points out that the very naming of such offenses posed significant risks, since both legal and written charges could so easily backfire (50). A key impediment inhered in the problem of how one could safely admit to knowledge of a sin about which decent people supposedly know nothing so as to avoid becoming scandal's object oneself. Slote describes this booby trap within the symbolic order as the "isomorphism of sin and sign," a paradox captured in the Wildean insight that "to recognize sin is to be sinful" ("Wild(e) Thing," 107–8).

45. Kaplan, *Sodom on the Thames*, 177.

46. Before the term "unspeakable crime" first appeared in press coverage of the "Dublin scandal" trial, which opened on Tuesday August 5, 1884, similar euphemisms were already appearing in reference to the scandal, using language taken directly from the *United Ireland*. For instance, on Saturday, October 13, 1883, the *Aberdeen Weekly Journal* cites the *United Ireland* in an allusion to James Ellis French's "detestable crime." A little more than a week before those accused in the *United Ireland* were to stand trial, the *Freeman's Journal* covered a National League demonstration marking the two hundredth anniversary of the Battle of Aughrim, at which speakers used language that subtly but powerfully incorporated the scandal into calls for decolonization. Michael Davitt in particular used phraseology similar to that of Healy and O'Brien, denouncing England as the "father of unmentionable crimes" and denouncing Dublin Castle as an architectural and moral synecdoche for the British state.

47. Abraham Lincoln's assassination, for instance, was considered an unspeakable crime. Unspeakable crimes often involved a high death toll and took place in colonial settings.

48. Cited in Walshe, "The First Gay Irishman?" 42.

49. Dettmar, "Vacation, Vocation, Perversion," 141.

50. The personal interview and its important contribution to the New Journalism's characteristic investigative reporting is a nexus of particular interest and debate within newspaper studies. In "Women's Periodicals and the New Journalism," Rosemary VanArsdel has already noted debates in the field concerning the interview's introduction into the New Journalism (245). My argument here is that personal interviews and firsthand investigative reporting became potential news sources when William O'Brien and the *United Ireland* were absolved of libel.

51. When Parnell backed William O'Shea as an "unpledged" parliamentary candidate for the open seat of Galway City, he put his standing within his own party at risk, violating the principle of absolute party unity on which his political success was based. Parnell's own lieutenants agonized about whether to make the Parnell/O'Shea affair public so as to stave off any further such deals.

52. See Kee, *The Laurel and the Ivy*, 494.

53. Ibid., 497. Understandably goaded in the course of the Galway by-election, Callan (according to Kee) "turned on Parnell in public and asked what there was in Captain O'Shea's political character and private history that was superior to that of Phil Callan and his wife" (494). Parnell put down the rebellion in his own ranks through brute political muscle, but the break this episode precipitated with Tim Healy and the strain it placed on his relations with other top party leaders was what Bew calls "a harbinger of the fatal crisis to come" (*Parnell*, 77).

54. Kee, *The Laurel and the Ivy*, 497–98.

55. Jenkins, *Gladstone*, 478; reported in the *Times*, October 8, 1881, 7.

56. Bew, *Parnell*, 58.

57. At a distance, all the back-channel communication going on between aristocratic English MPs associated with Gladstone's Liberal Party and Irish MPs like Captain William O'Shea appears puzzling and improbable. In fact, the Irish William O'Shea and his English wife, Katharine, had close familial and social connections among the British aristocracy; see Kee, *The Laurel and the Ivy*, 238. That Parnell's growing intimacy with this couple from 1881 should have occasioned periodic outbreaks of evident blackmail and incipient scandal along with periods of advantageous détente between Irish Home Rulers and powerful Liberals is as much to be expected as the regular social gatherings and conversations with fellow power brokers that both William and Katharine, by right of birth, marriage, and rank, participated in as a matter of course.

58. Kee, *The Laurel and the Ivy*, 58.

59. Ibid., 494.

60. In "James Joyce Composing a Chapter," Deppman notes that on June 7, 1926, Joyce wrote to Harriet Shaw Weaver that the misspelled word "hesitency," which recurs in *Finnegans Wake*, is a catchword by which "Irishmen usually remember the Piggott trial" (339n20).

61. Hampton, *Visions of the Press in Britain*, 90.

62. Ellmann, *James Joyce*, 32.

63. Only a single Irish newspaper article of which I am aware covered Wilde in the fashion originated by the Dublin Castle scandal. Unlike the London papers, which (as Walshe paraphrases Ed Cohen's argument in *Talk on the Wilde Side*) "avoided direct mention of same-sex activities by displacing the unnamable sin onto Wilde's body," the Irish press, Walshe dryly notes, "maintained a more discreet distance from both Wilde's sin *and* from his body" ("First Gay Irishman?" 46).

Chapter 2
INVESTIGATIVE, FABRICATED, AND SELF-INCRIMINATING SCANDAL WORK

1. The consolidating effects of this new form, noted in the previous chapter's discussion of Parnellism and anti-Parnellism, is evident in Walkowitz's description of Stead's newly unified audience: "Although he opened his pages to new social constituencies, the editorial and reportorial tone of the *Pall Mall Gazette* addressed a 'unified general public' that submerged class, age, ethnicity, and any particularity into a single moral entity" (*City of Dreadful Delight*, 85).

2. In *City of Dreadful Delight*, Walkowitz supplies a detailed account of this transformation as it specifically played out among women's rights advocates.

3. Ibid., 84.

4. See Sedgwick, *Epistemology of the Closet*, 91–181. For a more detailed discussion of aspects of this process, see Backus, "'The Children of the Nation?'" and "'Odd Jobs.'"

5. Although Dettmar ("Vacation, Vocation, Perversion," 138) and Kaplan (*Sodom on the Thames*, 176) have acknowledged the first Dublin Castle scandal's probable contribution to the Labouchere Amendment, and subsequently to the Wilde trials, the scandal's substantial legal and conventional expansion of scandal discourse has hitherto gone largely unnoticed by scholars.

6. Andrews and Taylor, *Lords and Laborers of the Press*, 2.

7. See Ferriter, *Occasions of Sin*, 28–29, and Walkowitz, *City of Dreadful Delight*, 86–94.

8. Eckley, *Maiden Tribute*, 56. It could be said that Eliza Armstrong's first gynecological exam ritually founded the social purity movement that Joyce so loathed. In acceding to it, the sexually radical feminism of the 1870s and early 1880s made its first discernible shift toward the antisex fanaticism of the 1890s. In campaigning against forced gynecological examinations of prostitutes, Josephine Butler and her comrades argued that such examinations are sexually abusive and stigmatizing of poor women as a class. In the moment that an "expert" forcibly penetrated Armstrong to produce scandalous evidence for Stead's articles, the values of Butler's movement were palpably transformed.

9. Eckley, *Maiden Tribute*, 50.

10. Israel, *Names and Stories*, 221.

11. Andrews and Taylor, *Lords and Laborers of the Press*, 3. For an alternate reading of rituals in the Maiden Tribute scandal, see McDiarmid on Shaw's adaptation of Eliza Armstrong's abduction/reformation in *Pygmalion* in *The Irish Art of Controversy*, 154–56.

12. Bloom's rapidly mutating personas in "Circe" invoke Stead's vacillations in "The Maiden Tribute of Modern Babylon," while Bloom's multiple and incoherent motivations toward Stephen appear to parody Stead's pursuit of a young virgin into the red-light district, prompted by motives ranging from the purely altruistic to the shockingly selfish.

13. In *Joyce, Sexuality and Social Purity*, Mullin provides a bravura explication of the vulnerable position of the slumming social purity activist whose normalizing gaze could unexpectedly be mistaken for or even revealed as prurient (172–80). See also Koven, *Slumming*.

14. Despite Eckley's extensive and invaluable work on Joyce, Stead, and the overlap between the two men's oeuvres in her *Maiden Tribute*, Mullin's *Joyce, Sexuality and Social Purity* and Joyce's work itself seem to challenge her assumption that Stead, the fin de siècle's most ardent and aggressive promoter of sexual purity, was a hero to Joyce.

15. Stead, *Maiden Tribute*, 7.

16. For a striking comparison to Stead's London brothel-world, see O'Conaire's modernist tour de force, *Exile*. Originally written and published in Irish in 1901, *Exile*'s Galwegian narrator describes London as a monstrous maw, devouring enslaved, conquered peoples from around the world. O'Conaire's London makes for a stark contrast with Stead's: the decent, daytime London that obstructs Stead's efforts to document the brute realities of class exploitation on the lower rungs of "the London inferno" is not even detectable to O'Conaire's immigrant protagonist, who perceives only the insatiable creature at the labyrinth's core.

17. In an oft-quoted passage in a letter to Stanislaus, Joyce proclaims "my opinion is that if I put down a bucket into my own soul's well, sexual

department, I draw up Griffith's and Ibsen's and Skeffington's and Bernard-Vaughan's and St. Aloysius' and Shelley's and Renan's water along with my own" (Ellmann, *Selected Letters*, 129).

18. Walkowitz in *City of Dreadful Delight* gives a persuasive account of Stead as slipping into states of manic exhilaration similar to those that Callanan ascribes to Healy. She describes him, for instance, as having slipped "over the edge" (101) and as unable to resist the sense of "playing with fire" that his scandal work aroused (113).

19. Eckley, *Maiden Tribute*, 58.

20. Brake, "'Government by Journalism,'" 229.

21. Eckley, *Maiden Tribute*, 33.

22. Walkowitz briefly but elegantly makes this point, noting "the deliberate suppression of the youth tribute was also a suppression of the homosexual theme (particularly homosexual prostitution) in his exposé of criminal vice—a suppression that nonetheless resurfaced in the margins of Stead's text, and more significantly in the legislative response it evoked" (*City of Dreadful Delight*, 98).

23. Ohi, "Molestation 101," 236.

24. As Brake notes in "'Government by Journalism,'" Stead's writing in "The Maiden Tribute of Modern Babylon" is "self-consciously literary," in effect displacing fiction by drawing on its pleasures (215).

25. Fanon, *The Wretched of the Earth*, 33–43.

26. See Gibson, "'That Stubborn Irish Thing,'" 91–96.

27. Jenkins, *Victorian Scandal*, 182–83.

28. Ibid., 189.

29. Ibid., 317–18.

30. For a detailed and comprehensive explication of the various morally outraged political stances to which the Dilke scandal gave rise, see Israel, "French Vices," chapter 6 in *Names and Stories*.

31. As Walkowitz notes, Stead often "boasted" of how easily he could have raped Armstrong (*City of Dreadful Delight*, 113).

32. Israel, *Names and Stories*, 211.

33. Quoted in ibid.

34. As Israel astutely notes, Dilke's neutralization as Gladstone's successor "can also be mourned in relation to lost feminist possibilities," as Dilke had proven himself, unlike Asquith, a strong and active supporter of women's suffrage (*Names and Stories*, 220).

35. Ohi, "Molestation 101."

36. In Adut's words, for scandal to work, there must be "a strong possibility from the public's perspective that the alleged transgressions might be true." As an example, he cites Christopher Hitchens's allegations that

Mother Theresa was a fraud as an incipient or attempted scandal that never gained traction owing to the public's disinclination to believe such charges of such a person (*On Scandal*, 16).

37. See Norris, *Virgin and Veteran Readings*, 263.

38. See Brake, "Government by Journalism," for a detailed exposition of the process by which the details of the Cleveland Street proceedings became public, 222–28.

39. Quoted in Kaplan, *Sodom on the Thames*, 168.

40. Brake, in "Government by Journalism," makes an argument that is complementary with the argument I am making here but emphasizes the institutional pressures that muffled rather than silenced the period's top radical editors: Labouchere, T. P. O'Connor, and especially Stead (226–27). My reading finds a newly visible and politicized scandal discourse of homosexuality in phrases such as "hideous subject," "horrible thing," and "terrible scandal," to say nothing of "foul loathsome slimy things that are hidden out of sight" (*Star*, November 25, 1889, quoted in Brake). Brake, with equal legitimacy, treats such phrases as demonstrating the ongoing suppression of homosexuality in response to converging pressures connected with gendered discourse and pressures brought to bear on newspapers and their editors in response to governmental and judicial oversight and by vigilant newspaper owners.

41. As Israel notes, Virginia Crawford amassed a surprising fund of moral credibility as the result of her public exposure as a sexual transgressor, becoming a "New Woman saint by converting to Roman Catholicism by 1889 and embarking on a career of religion, feminism, and social reform." Interestingly, Crawford began her self-reinvention as a social purity activist by working as a journalist for Stead's *Pall Mall Gazette* (Israel, *Names and Stories*, 210). Crawford's public transformation to public saint by way of scandalous sexual exposure constitutes an intriguingly symmetrical mirror image to Wilde's trajectory from popularly misconstrued self-exposure to moral martyrdom.

42. In *The Secret Life of Oscar Wilde*, McKenna traces Wilde's pattern of artful self-exposure all the way back to an 1874 contribution to the study *Social Life in Greece*, written with his input by his "first and best teacher," John Pentland Mahaffy, in which McKenna aptly notes a distinctively Wildean voice "raised . . . in defence of Greek love in the sentence: 'As to the epithet unnatural, the Greeks would answer probably, that all civilization was unnatural'" (5–6).

43. It could be argued that the circuitous evasiveness of Wilde's apologia was hardwired into public discourse prior to the New Journalism's consolidation, which upheld a legally and conventionally absolute distinction

between that which is publicly speakable and that which is not. If so, it could be argued that Wilde was being as explicit as possible.

44. See McDiarmid, "Oscar Wilde's Speech from the Dock."

45. McKenna, *The Secret Life of Oscar Wilde*, 136–37. See also Aldington and Weintraub, *Portable Oscar Wilde*, 24.

46. See Cocks, *Nameless Offences*, on the trope of homosexual unspeakability in nineteenth-century England. Cocks argues that homosexuality was demonstrably not invisible during this period and points to a wide array of strategies by which Victorians could be persuaded to think of it as undetectable regardless of the insistence with which it presented itself to the public.

47. Cohen, *Sex Scandal*, 20.

48. Latham, *Art of Scandal*, 20.

49. Cohen, *Talk on the Wilde Side*, 178.

50. Joyce, "Oscar Wilde," in *Occasional, Critical and Political Writing*, 150.

51. The mishandling of scandal even on the part of a lord might, as Wilde himself mischievously suggests when he describes Dorian Gray's grandfather's suspected role in the murder of his daughter's penniless husband, leave one eating one's chop "alone at the club for some time afterwards" (*The Picture of Dorian Gray*, 176).

52. Backus, "'Odd Jobs.'"

53. Mullin, *James Joyce, Sexuality and Social Purity*.

54. Wilde, "The Decay of Lying," quoted in Castle, *Reading the Modern Bildungsroman*, 138.

55. At the level of the textual symbol, the unstable coalescence of a series of historical and symbolically laden events, persons, and social dynamics within the figures of Parnell and Wilde closely resembles the logic of portmanteau words described by Attridge in *Peculiar Language* (206): signifiers whose exfoliation of incongruent and unstable meanings renders any claim to perfect and neat explication back into their neatly fixed and hierarchized component parts unprovable and impossible.

56. Lacey, *Terrible Queer Creatures*, 1.

57. This builds on Valente's observation that rituals of national purification such as the sex scandal and its counterpart, reports of political atrocities, can "never resolve nor significantly reconfigure" the terms of the struggle in which they engage; instead such strategies of scandalous reversal "necessarily reinforc[e] the existing terms of engagement in the process of reversing them" ("The Novel and the Police," 9).

58. Conrad's *Locked in the Family Cell* gives the fullest discussion of the ongoing effects of this representational exclusion of queerness from nationalism at the same time that, paradoxically, revolutionary Ireland was saturated

with male homoeroticism, as Harris in her study *Gender and Modern Irish Drama* and Jamie O'Neill in his novel *At Swim, Two Boys* have in their own ways indicated.

Chapter 3
JAMES JOYCE'S EARLY SCANDAL WORK

1. Saree Makdisi (*William Blake*) has compellingly described stereotypes of the time regarding the urban poor of which Joyce, as a sometimes literally starving urban Irishman, would have been acutely aware and to which he would have felt vulnerable. As a superliterate Dublin slum-dweller whose writing is anchored, if not among the poor, certainly in an urban, lower-middle class distinguishable from Dublin's working poor primarily by its pretensions, Joyce would naturally have viewed all conventions, whether "historical, religious, aesthetic," as Castle puts it in "Ousted Possibilities," as "anathema to the artist" (306).

2. In *Modernism on Fleet Street*, Collier provides an excellent overview of critical debates concerning Joyce's attitude toward newspapers and popular culture more generally. In "Newspapers and Popular Culture," Kershner supplies a more detailed account of this critical terrain.

3. Ellmann, *Joyce*, 163, 165. In "*Dubliners*," Leonard gives an especially persuasive reading of precisely how and to what end Joyce violated the expectations of *Irish Homestead* readers (93–95).

4. The phrase "mild proud sovereignty" is from Joyce, *Portrait*, 149.

5. Ellmann, *Joyce*, 139. See Mullin, *James Joyce, Sexuality and Social Purity*, especially 11–18, for an account of Joyce's consistently combative attitude toward editors.

6. For more information on Joyce's association with *Il Piccolo della Sera*, see Barry's introduction to Joyce, *Occasional, Critical, and Political Writing*.

7. *Stephen Hero* could sustain a chapter charting Joyce's evolving engagement with scandal during this period in its own right. Very notably, for instance, one specific way in which the hero of *Stephen Hero* demonstrates his heroism is in his refusal to engage with the scandal culture that pervades the University College Dublin circles in which he moves. While committing to "disentangle his [own] affairs in secrecy," he simultaneously refrains from prying into the private lives of others. This "reluctance to debate scandal" was "not without a satisfactory flavor of the heroic" (29).

8. Kershner elegantly summarizes this trajectory, revealed in Collier's *Modernism and Fleet Street*, as "the young writer's progression from aspiring social reformer to diagnostician of the newspaper as a mode of social control" ("Newspapers and Popular Culture," 306).

9. Quoted in Donovan, "Dead Men's News," 2.

10. Joyce's passionate and inherently political concern about words as personal objects vulnerable to misappropriation might explain the statement that so mortified his antifascist brother, Stanislaus, when, during World War II, he coolly pronounced that he had no concerns other than style. Ellmann, "Introduction," in Stanislaus Joyce, *My Brother's Keeper*.

11. Foster, *Irish Novels*, 38. For a detailed cultural history of Joyce's adoption by Pound and the "Men of 1914" see Brooker, *Joyce's Critics*, 9–51.

12. Ellmann, *James Joyce*, 609.

13. Regarding his view of the politics of writing, the extent to which Joyce retained his early socialism into later life remains a matter of debate, one this study does not aim to settle, although it does turn on one distinction that Joyce repeatedly made between words as commodities or exchange values and words as use values. In the fierce economic materialism that Joyce brought to this question, at least, he was as good a socialist as even Karl Marx could have wished.

14. Ellmann, *Joyce*, 22n.

15. While Joyce certainly wanted to make money by publishing his work in newspapers, this reading views his unwillingness to tailor his writing in order to do so—which Collier interprets as a kind of failure—as principled. As Collier notes, "no one wishing to make a living in the years 1914 to 1945 could stay out of what T. S. Eliot called 'the journalistic struggle'" (*Modernism on Fleet Street*, 3). Yet, as Collier acknowledges, Joyce's forays into newspaper publication were over forever by 1914, and his early attempts to earn money by newspaper writing—even a brief plan to start up an alternative Dublin newspaper (115)—petered out or blew up. To be sure, Joyce was willing to accept money for his writing, but he adamantly refused to sell his craft for pay.

16. Joyce, *My Brother's Keeper*, 107.

17. See Rice, *Cannibal Joyce*.

18. For a reading challenging the presumed incommensurability between Joyce's nationalist lectures and newspaper essays and his literary representations of Irish nationalism, see Nolan's *James Joyce and Nationalism*, particularly 96–100.

19. One among a chorus of grotesques lining the byways of Nighttown, the Croppy Boy, a sentimental figure from a well-known nationalist ballad, struggles to choke out his confession of a minor doctrinal lapse—forgetting to pray for his mother's rest—as he asphyxiates at the end of a hangman's noose (Joyce, *Ulysses*, 15.4547).

20. McClintock, *Imperial Leather*.

21. These developments reflect an early stage in what Mahaffey describes as Joyce's "two logically incompatible forms of authority." In one mode, "the

authoritative Joyce" is hidden, inaccessible, or, in Stephen Dedalus's terms, "invisible, refined out of existence"; alternately, he asserts or protects his authority by showing himself as "a human being practically interested in the circumstances of his environment." Significantly, every tactic that Mahaffey lists through which Joyce sought to preserve his personal authority to produce his corpus entails a mode of silence or withdrawal: Joyce was nonviolent, he boycotted marriage, and he "escaped the fetters of nationalism through exile and the Church through apostasy" (*Modernist Literature*, 26).

22. Joyce, *Occasional, Critical, and Political Writing*, 99, 310n3.

23. As Nessa Cronin and Louis De Paor, my colleagues at the National University of Ireland–Galway Irish Studies Centre, pointed out in response to my early work on this chapter, this community is, in fact, "silent" only because the English-speaking writer cannot understand Irish. For discussions of the trope of Irish as dying, see McKibben, "Born to Die . . . and Live On," and Ní Dhomhnaill, "Why I Choose."

24. As Valente succinctly puts it, if Irish nationalists asserted their independence, they were bestialized, whereas if they accepted British rule, they were emasculated ("The Manliness of Parnell," 73).

25. Leonard describes this effect of the Joycean epiphany in similar terms, as "not so much a moment of insight as a point where hitherto disparate observations, thoughts, and desires rearrange themselves into an unsuspected pattern that shatters often long held ideas about one's self and one's surroundings" ("*Dubliners*," 91). In "Epiphany as Scene of Performance," Bazargan reaches a similar conclusion, defining Joyce's epiphanic moments as creating an effect through their "presentation of cognition as a dialectical blending of seeing/not seeing in which multiple perspectives are at work," that is, through their invocation of a sort of multiperspectival irony (51). Examining Joyce's early use of the epiphany in his newspaper writing to create a sense of closure that shockingly abuses the conventions of the newspaper scandal offers another influence on his much-noted capacity for shattering long-held ideas and presenting cognition as a dialectical blending of seeing and not seeing.

26. See Sedgwick, *Epistemology of the Closet*, 67–70.

27. As further evidence of Joyce's strong identification with Wilde as an Irish artist, in the midst of the applause that followed the English Players' first production of *The Importance of Being Earnest* (Zurich, February 27, 1918), which Ellmann describes as "a minor triumph," Joyce burst out, "Hurray for Ireland! Poor Wilde was Irish and so am I!" (Ellmann, *Joyce*, 426).

28. Sam Slote (like R. J. Schork) has shown that "the outline Joyce gave of Oscar Wilde's life and career in the 1909 lecture . . . anticipates the complexity of Oscar Wilde's appearance in *Finnegans Wake*" ("Wild(e) Thing," 101). As we shall see in the fourth chapter, the same passage to which Slote

and Schork trace the terms of Joyce's incorporation of Wilde into *Finnegans Wake* also prefigures a Wildean metaphor sequence that pervades much of *Ulysses*. Joyce conflates Oscar Wilde with the Oscar of MacPherson's famously dodgy Ossian cycle, a nephew of King Fingal treacherously killed by his host at a feast. This figure of Wilde as a vine-crowned prince assassinated by his dining companions reframes Wilde's "moral assassination" at the hands of the dangerous but desirable "panthers" with whom he liked to feast by way of a dubious account of ancient Irish nobility, with decorative touches (the vine leaves, the philosophical discussion) lifted from Plato's *Symposium*. To note the specific linkage this vignette posits between flamboyant self-fashioning, feasting, scandal, and political assassination at the hand of an ally is to shed new light on Stephen's internal debate throughout much of *Ulysses* concerning whether or not to "feast" with Haines and Mulligan.

29. In this early fiction, Joyce registers the anxieties that the new relations between public and private life created for those whom Pierre Bourdieu terms "the subordinated fraction of the dominant classes," or those whose class capital is largely or exclusively symbolic (*Distinction*, 125). According to Fanon, the whole of the colonial middle class is of this type (*The Wretched of the Earth*, 149).

30. An example of the centrality of a celebrated political sex scandal in the early *Dubliners* stories is the invocation of Caroline Norton's popular and beloved poem "The Arab's Farewell to His Steed" in "Araby." As Harry Stone has elucidated, Caroline Norton (as the protagonist of "A Little Cloud" aspires to do) converted colonial power relations' dehumanizing effects into a sentimental idiom that converts the pain of exploitation into a masochistically pleasurable mode of literary art (Stone, "'Araby'").

31. As was marriage; see Fairhall, *Joyce and the Question of History*, 54.

32. See chapter 2 of Mullin's *James Joyce, Sexuality and Social Purity* and Walkowitz's tracing of a "dynamic that circulated and amplified stories of sexual danger in a market culture with contradictory political effects" through 1880s newspaper culture (*City of Dreadful Delight*, 244).

33. Stallman, "'Suddenly Someone Else.'"

34. In the "Cyclops" episode, we find Bob Doran in the midst of a multiday drinking binge of a sort to which, as we learn, he succumbs rarely but spectacularly. As described in a later chapter, Bob is described as having engaged, while blind drunk, in a semipublic ménage à trois with two streetwalkers in an account that pointedly invokes the Dilke scandal. Polly, now his wife, continues to be the subject of the hostile gossip that her mother originally married her off in order to silence. "Cyclops's" nameless principal narrator includes in his steady flow of gossip a spiteful description of Polly having inadvertently publicly exposed herself while sleepwalking.

35. See Leonard, "*Dubliners*," 88.

36. Eide offers a particularly elegant reading of the meaning of "gnomon" in "The Sisters," which also views the gnomon as figuring a lack of predetermined closure, in her *Ethical Joyce*, 34–40.

37. Backus and Valente, "'An Encounter.'"

38. In "The Sisters," the dead priest had "something wrong" with him, an unspecifiable but centrally important something that obtrudes almost frantically into the polite if threadbare narrative that the adults surrounding the story's juvenile protagonist labor to sustain. In "Araby" and "Eveline," surface narratives describing innocent if failed courtships are troubled by subtextual suggestions that the young protagonists' love objects are motivated by economic rather than romantic interests, thus introducing the theme of prostitution as simony's sexual correlative that recurs over the course of the collection.

39. In *Dubliners*, in contrast, Joyce deploys story components that solicit particular scandalized understandings that are then disabled. For instance, according to scandal discourses of the time, with their genealogical relationship to the eighteenth-century anti-Catholic gothic, the priest in "The Sisters" "should" have tertiary-stage syphilis, with its characteristic general paralysis of the insane (GPI). Yet, as J. B. Lyons has argued, the medically trained Joyce took care to show that whatever had "gone wrong" with the priest, tertiary-stage syphilis was not it (*Thrust Syphilis Down to Hell*, 60–67).

40. The final image in "The Sisters" of the broken chalice, like the image of the slaughtered horses at the end of "Ireland at the Bar," supplies an emphatic non sequitur, confronting the reader with the powerful overdetermination of journalistically conventional expectations that become tangible only when they are thwarted.

41. For an excellent analysis of Little Chandler's relationship with and reaction to Ignatius Gallaher, see Senn, "Clouded Friendship."

42. See Bixby, "Perversion and the Press."

43. Ibid.; Valente, "The Manliness of Parnell."

44. I would like to credit Matthew Walker's independent study of *Portrait of the Artist* ("The Wilde Rose") as being very helpful in pulling together in one place all the published evidence for a queer reading of *Portrait* and establishing that such a reading is no longer marginal, fragmentary, and speculative but an established and well-defined understanding of the novel as a whole.

45. For a more detailed reading of this scene in connection to Stephen's psychosexual development, see Valente and Backus, "'An Iridescence Difficult to Account For.'"

46. Ibid., 533.

47. Costello, *Joyce*, 63.

48. See also Stanislaus Joyce's account in *My Brother's Keeper*, 10. As Ellmann notes, Joyce gave up the study of Irish with one of the Easter Uprising's future leaders, Patrick Pearse, when Pearse cited the word "thunder" as an instance of the English language's inadequacy (*Joyce*, 61). While Joyce's eventual failure to see eye to eye with the famously romantic and militaristic Pearse was inevitable, that he broke with him over this particular word suggests that Joyce already felt it to be indispensable within his own English-language lexicon.

49. This connection of Simon's warning not to "peach" to the discourse of newspaper sex scandal, which can often involve testimony in which one friend dishonorably impeaches another, dovetails with Mahaffey's observation that an archaic meaning of the word "peach" is to pant or hyperventilate, making Simon's caution not to peach on a fellow into a prudent paternal caution against homosexual activities at boarding school ("Perversion/Im(mere)sion"). Together, these readings interpret Simon's caution as a double-edged, all-purpose warning against the dangers of sex scandal, in which one should play no role, either as a witness or as the accused.

50. In "'An Encounter,'" Valente and I give a detailed description of this process of the homocolonial off-loading of shame.

51. Mahaffey, *Reauthorizing Joyce*, 61.

52. While Joyce's early penchant for cadging money from friends and acquaintances can be seen as a rudimentary, self-created patronage system, for Joyce to attract patronage at the level that would enable him to produce works on the grand scale that his alter ego, Stephen Dedalus, was in 1904 already envisioning in the "Proteus" episode of *Ulysses*, he needed to establish himself within existing literary hierarchies. Newspapers were inevitably the first rung on this ladder, the first step toward making a name for himself. Of Joyce's early writing, from 1900 to 1912, most was either written specifically for newspapers or published in periodicals. Perhaps as a result, in various ways this work was insistently *about* newspapers: the impact of newspapers and specifically the work of scandal within a broader social epistemology.

53. Riquelme is the first critic I am aware of to have noted the intriguing ambiguity of "fly by the nets" ("*Stephen Hero*").

Chapter 4
REINVENTING THE SCANDAL FRAGMENT

1. To point to Parnell's relatively pervasive presence in *Portrait*, from its beginning to its end, is not to suggest that Parnell is the only important

scandal figure in *Portrait*. The significant co-presence in *Portrait* of other turn-of-the-century sex scandals and scandalmongers has been established, for instance, by Valente (introduction, *Quare Joyce*), Dettmar ("Vacation, Vocation, Perversion"), and Riquelme ("*Stephen Hero*"), among others. In addition, Eckley argues that Joyce took the spelling "Dedalus" from Stead (*Maiden Tribute*, 211) and suggestively connects *Portrait*'s sequence of metaphoric rises and falls specifically to Stead's own (292).

2. By far the most extensive folkloric and anthropological work on pishoguery has been done on the topic of cows and dairy farming, which have a particularly rich lore concerning the use of stolen domestic items by witches to appropriate milk or milkfat. See especially Glassie's *Passing the Time in Ballymenone* (548).

3. See Callanan, *T. M. Healy*, 346–90.

4. Further evidence of the particular role into which Joyce was casting Gogarty during this period may be found in the remaining manuscript pages of *Stephen Hero*, on which Joyce continued to work through 1906. In a passage in which the Joyce alter ego, Stephen Hero, reflects on the "deadly chill" brought on by the "plague of Catholicism," he likens Catholic ideology to vermin and locusts and condemns it for spreading a pathological "fear of day and joy, . . . the body burdened and disaffected in its members by its black tyrannous lice. . . . every natural impulse towards health and wisdom and happiness had been corroded by the pest of these vermin." As Slocum and Cahoon note, Joyce had "scrawled" the word "Gogarty" across these sentences "in red crayon" (*Stephen Hero*, 194).

5. Ellmann, *Selected Letters*, 96.

6. Ibid.

7. Bixby, "Perversion and the Press," 113.

8. Cheng observes that the description of Mulligan as "equine" and "grained and hued like pale oak" (3) suggests "the treacherous qualities of the wooden horse" (*Joyce, Race, and Empire*, 152).

9. Platt, "The Buckeen and the Dogsbody," 77.

10. John Gordon ("Haines") lays out abundant evidence that Stephen is viewed by Haines as a stalking black panther, persuasively connecting the image of the black panther with Stephen's colonial/racial/class alterity. In Gordon's words, as Haines sees it, he is "'camping out' among the 'wild Irish' (U1.731), locked in a tower with Mulligan and this perfectly frightful cad" (587). Yet, though he directs us to "innuendoes of homosexual tastes in Haines and his set, see U9.1210–12, U15.4704–06" (593n2), Gordon misses the obvious implication that if Stephen *is* the black panther and the *bullawarrus* Haines fears, this is not only because Stephen's colonized position links him to Africans, but because as a poor urban youth, his proximity activates, for Haines, the ambivalent predator/prey relationship that Wilde and

Douglas evoked when they referred to rent boys as panthers (see Ellmann, *Oscar Wilde*, 389). See, for instance, Dowling, *Hellenism and Homosexuality* (104–54), and Taddeo, *Lytton Strachey* (51–76).

11. Fairhall has a detailed reading of the knife in *Ulysses* as emblematic of the violent historical rupture of the Phoenix Park murders (*James Joyce*, 28).

12. Mulligan's comment in "Scylla and Charybdis," when first hinting to Stephen about Bloom's purported sexual interest in him, that Bloom is "Greeker than the Greeks" verifies that "Greek" can be a coded term for homosexuality in Mulligan's lexicon (*Ulysses*, 165).

13. For a wide-ranging reading of the slang term "touch" in *Ulysses* as related to homosexual and/or commercial sex, see McDonald, "Who Speaks for Fergus?," esp. 504.

14. Cheng reads Mulligan as attempting to prostitute himself, but also as pandering his "semi-willing specimen of study"—Stephen—to Haines as an authentic native object of special interest to the discerning Celticist (*Joyce, Race, and Empire*, 152).

15. In "'A Little Trouble about Those White Corpuscles,'" Leonard elegantly captures the significance of Haines's depiction as a practitioner of imperial pishoguery when he notes, "One purpose of the Oxford 'style,' in the halcyon days of British imperialism, is to obscure the various exploitative ways people 'make their tin'" (5).

16. These early transactions concerning cream and milk between Stephen, Mulligan, and Haines suggestive of pishoguery are echoed in "Ithaca" and "Penelope" in imagery connected with Leopold and Molly's relationship. In "Ithaca," Bloom serves "extraordinarily to his guest [Stephen] and, in reduced measure to himself the viscous cream ordinarily reserved for the breakfast of his wife Marion [Molly]" (17.467–68). Again during their courtship, when Molly is "tasting the butter" in the Lucan dairies Bloom reenacts Paris's choice, telling Molly that "she could give 9 points in 10 to Kathy Lanner and beat her," but Molly doesn't take in his meaning, distracted by the "stoppress edition." When Molly is weaning Milly, Bloom sucks milk from her breasts to relieve the painful pressure of her excess (18.589/596), and of Stephen she thinks, "I suppose he'd like my nice cream too" (18.1558). Of course, critics have noted that Bloom fails Molly when he forgets to pick up and bring home her cream from the chemist.

17. See Valente, "The Perils of Masculinity," 128. Stephen recalls this juxtaposition again in "Proteus" and in "Scylla and Charybdis." For a reading of this phrase's recurrence, see chapter 7, 188–90.

18. We also have a source for Leopold Bloom in an impoverished Dubliner named Alfred H. Hunter who was well outside of Joyce's circle. See Ellmann, *Joyce*, 161, and Costello, *Joyce*, 19.

19. As Ellmann notes, "The conso that they were all characters in his drama annoyed some of his friends, especially Gogarty, who did not much care for the role of culprit in a court where Joyce was both judge and prosecuting attorney. . . . Without perhaps saying so directly, [he] threatened some of them with the punishments he would mete out for slights suffered at their hands. . . . His art became a weapon" (*Joyce*, 149). Of Gogarty in particular, Ellmann writes, "Gogarty and Joyce . . . took part in a lifelong battle in which Gogarty was severely worsted" (207).

20. As in the *Odyssey*, *Hamlet*, and Irish nationalist allegories such as that of Diarmuid and Devorgilla, in this episode the rightful transmission of national sovereignty is interrupted owing to a sexual betrayal; Mulligan's symbolic infidelity with Haines dispossesses the man who in Middle Irish would have been called his *aoin-leapthadh*, or bedfellow (See Palmer, *Language and Conquest*, 142). Mulligan, like the Anglicized Irish lords whom Sarah McKibben shows some far-sighted early modern Irish poets excoriating (*Endangered Masculinities*), is "gaily betraying" Mother Ireland by replacing her worthy son, Stephen, with the unworthy English interloper, Haines. Mulligan's betrayal, however, is distinctly neocolonial. Whereas earlier generations of Irish lords who sold out to the English knowingly risked vilification at the hands of Ireland's poets, Mulligan, as a cultural nationalist operating within a transnational, post-Parnellite print capitalist economy, expects and indeed feels entitled to his betrayed compatriot's continued allegiance and material support.

21. Valente, "Joyce's (Sexual) Choices," 11.

22. For an extended exposition of the central role played by the discourse of English manliness in maintaining this representational cleavage, see Valente's *The Myth of Manliness*.

23. Ellmann, *Joyce*, 265.

24. See Cheng, *Joyce, Race, and Empire*, 27.

25. Deane, "Joyce the Irishman," 41.

26. Joseph Valente, private conversation.

27. In "Deceptive Picture," Alex Ross reflects on Wilde's process of deliberate self-exposure, pointing out that "the multiple versions of 'Dorian Gray' . . . show Wilde deciding, sentence by sentence, just how far he would go" (E1). Concerning Joyce's extension of Wilde's dangerous, deliberate self-revelations in his own complex imbrications of fact and fiction, Patrick Mullen, in *The Poor Bugger's Tool*, directs our attention to Joyce's early theory of drama. As Mullen argues, for the young Joyce, drama "encodes the biographical (that is, the intersection of life and writing) disarticulated from the discursive anchor of the individual" (95). By the time he was writing the "Cyclops" episode, Joyce had established an array of prose-writing strategies allowing for the impersonal integration of fact and fiction he had originally

ascribed only to drama. By means of these, he could intensify Wilde's shameless self-exposure while dispersing the vast array of potentially actionable evidence he discloses into "a drunken web of misnomers, slippages, jokes, and allusions" that burdens both pub patrons and readers with "a constant task of adjudication and orientation" (99).

28. Bourke, *Burning of Bridget Cleary*, 92–93.

Chapter 5
THE PROTRACTED LABOR OF THE NEW JOURNALIST SEX SCANDAL

1. Importantly, in *Stephen Hero*, Stephen recognizes the possibilities of the jester or clown as a figure for representational license. After Stephen's professor of English composition, who works for the *Freeman's Journal* (27), has reported Stephen's freewheeling essays to Father Butt, Stephen buys himself some room to maneuver by calling attention in class to bawdy songs in *Twelfth Night*, asking "very gravely" whether the songs of the clown "were to be learned by heart or not" (28). The flustered Father Butt, forerunner of *Portrait*'s Dean of English (and also, indirectly, of Garrett Deasy), falls back on the empty assertion that because the songs are only a customary amusement, they have no significance (29). Thus Stephen, in defense of his own shocking writing, treats the father's own assigned text as supplying a precedent for artistically valuable representations of sex and other improper matters. Stephen's use of the clown's songs in Shakespeare turns on the same logic that Wilde invoked in his famous defense of pederasty and that Bloom will invoke on behalf of Judaism in "Cyclops"; as Allison Bechdel, in *Fun Home*, recalls of her youthful epiphany that homosexuality was all around her in 1970s American society, "You're soaking in it" (190). This early treatment of the jester as a figure for license is crucial to a full understanding of Stephen's later deprecations, as in "Nestor," of Wilde and other Irish authors who sought English audiences as "jesters." Because while Joyce does, in his private letters and in *Ulysses*, dismiss both Wilde and Gogarty/Mulligan as indulged and disesteemed jesters, he retained, in words from *Stephen Hero*, the jester's "boldnesses," using them throughout his career as "defence-works" behind which he might construct "the enigma of a manner" (27).

2. In *Inventing Ireland*, Kiberd takes a rosier view of Wilde's antics, describing Wilde as countering the destructive effects of the stock stage Irishman by transitioning, personally and in his plays, from "stage-Ireland" to "stage-England" and thereby parodically asserting the "shallowness of such categories" (36).

3. Howes notes the association of the epithet "the seas' ruler" with both Haines and Deasy, arguing that the threat represented by Haines and Deasy

and their providential view of history "cannot be neutralized by sheer parody and mimicry; it must be countered by alternative collective visions of
the Irish" ("Joyce, Colonialism, and Nationalism," 265).

4. When paying Stephen his wages, Deasy proudly if inaccurately
identifies himself with the English, who, he asserts, always pay their debts.
Since "Telemachus" has shown Haines showered with Irish largesse on the
assumption that such gifts will open channels of reciprocity between Irish
entrepreneurs and Haines's wealthy father, we already know how effortlessly
this laudable freedom from debt is sustained. Casting the Irish in general
and Stephen in particular as improvident by citing England's wealth as proof
of "an Englishman's" inherent superiority (2.245), Deasy chides Stephen
about his spending, comparing him disadvantageously to Shakespeare, who
"knew what money was" and amassed wealth by writing: "A poet, yes, but
an Englishman too." Rejecting as false the popular boast that the sun never
sets on the British Empire because (he wrongly claims) the phrase originated
with a French Celt, he in effect denies the benefits that their extensive imperial holdings confer on the English (2.248–49). The enormity of the British
Empire is not, he argues, an Englishman's "proudest boast," but rather his
claim that "*I paid my way.*" When Stephen has to answer no when Deasy
asks if he can say the same, his answer delights Deasy, who sternly informs
Stephen that to be a gentleman he must be financially independent even as
the rest of his speech aggressively denies the economic, political, and cultural arrangements that, in the previous episode, have made the gainfully
employed Stephen an unwilling benefactor to the Oxonian sponger Haines
(2.261–62).

5. As Gifford points out, Deasy once again has gotten his historical
facts wrong ("*Ulysses*" *Annotated*, 39).

6. It is Haines who first introduces the theme of anti-Semitism when
at the end of "Telemachus" he tells Stephen that "European jews" are colonizing England just as England once colonized Ireland. Haines's scapegoat-
ing of Jews works just as Deasy's does, to claim an advantageous unity with
Stephen at the expense of a scandalized other. In both Haines's and Deasy's
claims that the Jews are colonizing England, Joyce points to what Stephen
Arata has termed "fantasies of reverse colonization" ("Occidental Tourist"),
as these circulated in everyday thought and conversation through the mechanism of scandal.

7. An English venture capitalist puts anti-Semitism to the same use
when attempting to recruit a supposed Irish underling in the first scene of
George Bernard Shaw's *John Bull's Other Island*, also set in 1904.

8. In "Vocation, Vacation, Perversion," Dettmar argues that "'smugging' is precisely a non-word that the other boys won't know and yet must
pretend they do" (144).

9. Deasy is, however, again in obvious error when he implies that Ireland's sex scandals have all been heterosexual and claims that Ireland never admitted the Jews (2.442). In *Portrait*, Stephen, as he goes to confess his sins after the hellfire and brimstone retreat, wishes fervently that what he had to confess were only not "the one sin." The specific dangers of this unspeakable and to some extent unspecifiable "one sin" with respect to scandal are specified by the priest who hears his confession and tells him, "'You cannot know where that wretched habit will lead you or where it will come against you.'" He goes on to depict this sin as literally and catastrophically "discrediting": "'As long as you commit that sin, my poor child, you will never be worth one farthing to God'" (*Portrait*, 130).

10. Caraher, "Trieste, Dublin, Galway," 142.

11. Deasy turns next to the geographical English/Irish cleavage that recurred in the Triestene essays as a trope for scandal-skewed representation, "the narrow waters of the channel" (2.327–28), to describe grain supplies running across this rift, recalling Joyce's interest in transnational networks—conduits of information, money, loyalty, and resources—that serve, like London's transnational wire service in "Ireland at the Bar," both to bridge and to sustain the "crack" that differentially empowers the two nations.

12. Whereas Gifford interprets "thank you job" as "sure to bring substantial reward" (7.546), the term itself seems to suggest the insubstantial reward of a mere thank-you, a reading further endorsed by the account that follows of a prince's long forestalled and ultimately misplaced expression of gratitude.

13. This instruction may also be a pun on the phrase "agenbite of inwit"; in other words, Joyce may be having Crawford instruct Joyce/Stephen to put the "bite," or guilt and rage he is feeling over his mother's destruction, into his writing. Certainly it plays on the vampire imagery in Stephen's draft stanza, urging Stephen to create something capable of "biting back" so as to defend itself against imperial vampirism.

14. Throughout the episode, Lenehan, an exaggerated version of the scandalmongering "Irish jester" more generally, has kept up a stream of absurdities. Here, as Crawford speaks proudly of having witnessed Gallaher's triumph, Lenehan unwittingly satirizes the ways in which newspapers reduce momentous events to pithy nonsense, "announcing—Madam, I'm Adam. And Able was I ere I saw Elba" (7.683).

15. Most nationalist papers, led by the *Freeman's Journal*, despairingly accepted blame for the murders on behalf of Ireland as a whole, a position that ignored the assassins' lack of standing in any known nationalist organizations. On the other hand, a handful of North American Fenians, most notably Jeremiah O'Donovan Rossa, further complicated matters by lauding

the assassinations. The *Freeman's Journal*'s craven assumption of guilt on behalf of all nationalists in contrast with some American Fenians' enthusiasm for the assassinations marked the beginning of a split in the powerful coalition between physical force and constitutional nationalists that Michael Davitt, Charles Stewart Parnell, and the Land League had painstakingly built, and hence the beginning of Parnell's fall.

16. The *New York World*, in supplying its readers with privileged, secret details fresh from Dublin, enhanced their sense of importance and privileged insight, exacerbating the factionalization that would ultimately destroy both Parnell and his movement. As argued in chapter 1, the aftermath of Phoenix Park was so politically devastating that the Parnellites themselves, particularly O'Brien and Healy, pioneered the use of sexual exposure as a political weapon, and the scandal wars that ensued "tore away" until the fabric of Parnellite nationalism ripped.

17. Fairhall, *Joyce and the Question of History*, 16–17. As Fairhall has argued, Joyce was struck not only by the assassinations' brutality but by their foreclosing of "certain historical possibilities," a closure symbolized throughout *Ulysses* by the knife, the Invincibles' chosen instrument (33).

18. See Lloyd, *Anomalous States*.

19. For Joyce on Parnell as the Irish Moses, see Joyce's Triestene essay, "The Shade of Parnell," in *Occasional, Critical, and Political Writing*, 193.

20. Healy, through his association with Fitzgibbon (7.800), is figured as part of a group seeking to crush the new or "young" Irish language movement, which it assesses as, like Stephen, "weak, therefore worthless" (7.807–8). The "vials of [Fitzgibbon's] wrath" are reminiscent of Healy's famous oratorical vitriol (7.806).

21. Stephen's status as the addressee of Taylor's speech is pointed up again and again in wording that has far more significance for Stephen himself than for the Irish in general. Stephen, having "but emerged from primitive conditions" in a disintegrating family, repeatedly conceives of himself, in *Portrait* as well as *Ulysses*, as set against "a literature, a priesthood, a history and a polity," and his uncertain vocational status in Ireland's weak economy is once again noted in the phrase "vagrants and daylabourers are you called" (117).

22. As suggested earlier, Joyce had, on Bloomsday or another day close to it, handed the palm of beauty to Nora Barnacle, who famously returned the favor. That Joyce continually conflates writing and masturbation through hand imagery is well established. The decision Stephen weighs here, whether or not to "try his hand" at the work of Moses—that is, to lead "a turbulent and volatile people out of the house of shame" ("The Shade of Parnell," 193)—unites masturbation and writing in a particularly significant way. Having decided toward the end of "Aeolus" that he *will* "try his

hand," Stephen presents an oddly unshaped account of two Dubliners out for a stroll, turning his hand to the scandal work that Joyce would develop throughout his oeuvre. When Stephen reappears in "Oxen" after a lengthy absence, Lenehan announces that he has "defiled the lily virtue of a confiding virgin," indicating that between "Scylla and Charybdis" and "Oxen," Joyce/Stephen and Nora Barnacle have together tried their hands and, in a public sex act, led each other out of the house of shame.

23. Gifford, *"Ulysses" Annotated*, 153.

24. Latham, *Art of Scandal*, 97.

Chapter 6
JAMES JOYCE'S SELF-PROTECTIVE SELF-EXPOSURE

1. For a discussion of Wilde's description of the conventions of realism as a prison-house, see Latham, *Art of Scandal*, 57. Literary realism became treacherous and double-binding as literary conventions were increasingly hemmed in on one side, as Latham shows, by libel law, and on the other, as Mullin shows (*Joyce, Sexuality and Social Purity*), by the social purity movement.

2. In "Beaufoy's Master Plaster," Kenner lays out evidence that Beaufoy's prizewinning 1897 *Tit-Bits* story "For Vera's Sake" was published in favor of fifteen-year-old James Joyce's thematically similar story, which he retroactively titled "Matcham's Masterstroke" (11).

3. In fact, as we have seen in "Aeolus," both the archbishop of Dublin and Deasy have their pronouncements put directly into the newspaper without editorial vetting, and in "Scylla and Charybdis" revivalist poet A.E. provisionally accepts Deasy's letter, and Mulligan and Haines are invited to a gathering of Ireland's promising younger poets, while Stephen is not.

4. Kershner, *The Culture of Joyce's "Ulysses,"* 133.

5. Ellmann, *Selected Letters*, 26.

6. John Eglinton, one of the revivalist gatekeepers who rejected Joyce's early prose fiction as scandalously self-revelatory, would receive his comeuppance by name in "Scylla and Charybdis" (Ellmann, *James Joyce*, 144–47).

7. Ibid., 148.

8. Gorman, *James Joyce*, 116.

9. Joyce, "Oscar Wilde," 151.

10. A story in "Scylla and Charybdis," for instance, has Shakespeare beating Dick Burbage into the bed of a "burgher's wife" as the pretext for a historical pun: "William the Conqueror came before Richard III" (9.637). Then again in "Oxen of the Sun," Joyce elaborately stages a woman's loss of her virginity as a horse race (14.1126–36), noting of the defeated filly, with

words echoing a description of Lily the caretaker's daughter in "The Dead," "Poor Sceptre. . . . She is not the filly that she was" (14.1140–41).

11. See especially "Sirens" (11.158–61, 11.555–58) and "Cyclops" (12.807–8).

12. Ellmann, *Selected Letters*, 25.

13. My suggestion that Joyce and Nora Barnacle's first sexual encounter was mutual is based on a range of suggestive details in Joyce's early letters to and concerning Barnacle. Hand imagery abounds in the early letters to Barnacle, as when Joyce tells her, "your glove lay beside me all night— unbuttoned—but otherwise conducted itself very properly" (22). In another letter Joyce expresses concern that Barnacle is "sorry for something which had *not* happened" and tells her he has "been trying to console [his] hand ever since but can't" (23), suggesting an act of failed manual stimulation. Soon after arriving in Trieste with Barnacle, Joyce writes to Stanislaus with evident pride that "Nora . . . admits the gentle art of self-satisfaction" (45), indicating not only that Joyce and Barnacle talked about female manual stimulation but that Joyce considered this shared knowledge important, exhibiting it to Stanislaus as a sort of prize.

14. Joyce sets up his few subtextual references to his first encounter with Barnacle (in "Calypso," "Nausicaa," and "Oxen") in contradistinction to his many representations of sexual pishoguery and simony. Implicitly, this experience is made sacred and transformative through its mutuality and nonprocreativity, a rite of passage corresponding to Stephen's boyish dreams of a "holy encounter . . . at which weakness and timidity and inexperience were to fall from him" (*Portrait*, 95). Because it is sacred and transformative, however, this transgressive act of public sexual exchange is also paradigmatically ripe for simony, and as such it seems to constitute Joyce's central, germinative scandal fragment, the simultaneous protection, celebration, and elaboration of which energizes the whole of *Ulysses*.

15. Another Joycean "masterstroke" in this sense of an abrupt and catastrophic public fall occurs just prior to the opening moments of the short story "Grace," in which a catastrophic and humiliating public fall attracts an audience, a small group of Dubliners who gather around the fallen man to decide whether to involve the police. As Bloom will do for Stephen, a good Samaritan appears and persuades those gathered to treat the episode as a harmless accident, radically shifting the audience's stance in favor of protecting rather than ostracizing Mr. Kernan; Kernan, rescued from scandalous public exposure, is instead driven into the waiting jaws of the Catholic Church, which snap shut in the story's final sentence.

16. In "Cyclops," the knockout punch in a boxing match alluding (among other things) to the Wilde trials is described in similar language, as "clean and clever" (12.983).

17. As Kershner notes, "these allusions are in some degree occult: they both do and do not bear the signature of the author, and readers must take their own positions regarding their significance" (*The Culture of Joyce's "Ulysses,"* 13).

18. Ellmann, *James Joyce,* 448–52.

19. "I am awfully angry with you. I do wish I could punish you for that. . . . Remember if you do not [write a long letter and tell me more] I will punish you" (5.251–52).

20. In each case, any reader who knows enough to decode any given sexual content knows too much to turn informer without incurring substantial personal risk. In "Lestrygonians," Bloom thinks approvingly of James Stephens's use of a similar strategy, which also distributed dangerous knowledge so as to equalize an otherwise hopelessly disadvantageous power ratio: "James Stephens' idea was the best. He knew them. Circles of ten so that a fellow couldn't round on more than his own ring. Sinn Fein. Back out you get the knife. Hidden hand. Stay in. The firing squad" (8.458–59). In other words, while the sex scandal threatens those bound together by scandalous secrets with moral assassination or even less figurative execution if they don't "round on their own ring," Joyce, like Stephens, evens the odds by placing anyone wanting out in such a position that folding to scandal's moralizing pressures by exposing him would inevitably reveal their own onanistic vulnerability to the "hidden hand."

21. Joyce is again both calling attention to and making use of the interactive and incremental qualities of seduction/initiation, as Valente and I have described in "The Sisters" and in *Portrait* ("'An Iridescence Difficult to Account For'").

22. Joyceans have long noted that "potted meat" is slang for sexual intercourse, so that the tasteless parallelism that Bloom deprecates between meat in a pot and a corpse in a coffin has typically been read as ironically paralleled by Bloom's own purportedly unhappily "meatless" ménage. As Martha Stallman has noted in a private conversation, however, to put meat into the pot was Edwardian sex slang not just for intercourse but specifically for anal sex, so that the death/food/sex toward which the Plumtree's signifier gestures might be not the "incomplete" status of the Bloom's "abode," but rather the sustaining but not completely savory diet of nonprocreative practices on which their marriage has been subsisting.

23. In his essay, "Interpretations of Parnell," historian R. F. Foster recalls that in Waterford in the early 1970s he was "told categorically from the audience, 'Parnell was never in that box!'" (349). In "Hades," Hynes muses on a rumor that Parnell isn't really buried in Glasnevin, and in "Lestrygonians," when Bloom sees Parnell's brother, he recalls Simon Dedalus's prediction that when the opponent who beat Parnell's brother tried to take Parnell's old

seat, "Parnell would come back from the grave and lead him out of the house of commons by the arm" (8.517–19). Those gathered in the cab man's shelter in "Eumaeus" also speculate on the whereabouts of the still living Parnell, now a figure for the long-absent king, Odysseus.

24. Early in "Hades," Bloom muses on the laying out of a corpse, based on memories of Rudy's death, imagining that "they clip the nails and hair" and that the women doing this job might "keep a bit in an envelope." This casual "huggermugger," or secret pillaging of the dead, recalls pishoguery, a subterranean tradition of malevolent magic that Bloom believes might be passed on among the women who take on the laying out of the dead.

25. As Lamson points out in "Orpheus Descending," Glasnevin Cemetery is, like Night Town in "Circe," a depiction of the city of Dublin itself as "a kind of corpse that has been partially exhumed" (256–57).

26. For more on how Parnell's fall destroyed this alliance, see Jenkins, *Gladstone*, 576.

27. Cotter, *James Joyce and the Perverse Ideal*, 100.

28. For a detailed consideration of Joyce's "mingling of genres," see Eide, "Authority of Form."

Chapter 7
(RE)FUSING SENTIMENTALISM AND SCANDAL

1. In "Circe," Bloom, at the height of his political stature and popularity, declares an end to the "patriotism of barspongers and dropsical imposters," a clear reference to the citizen's and the Nameless One's use of rigid nationalism as a sort of protection racket in "Cyclops," forcing money for drinks out of others by threatening to expose their purported political or moral deviance (15.1692).

2. As Latham points out, the names of more real people are invoked in "Scylla and Charybdis" than anywhere else in *Ulysses* (*Art of Scandal*, 102). As Nash observes, "The introduction of 'Best,' 'Eglinton,' Lyster,' and 'AE,'— not to mention all those others, including Synge, Lady Gregory, Wilde, 'WB,' 'Moore,' 'Martyn,' and 'Dowden,'—heightens the self-conscious fictionality of the episode. By alluding to these figures under their actual names or accepted pseudonyms, Joyce draws attention to the relationship between his writing and the particular people and episodes to which it refers" (*Joyce and the Act of Reception*, 82).

3. Ellmann, *Selected Letters*, 129.

4. Latham describes Stephen's performance as "a dazzling yet defamatory attempt to deduce historical fact from otherwise apparently fictional works," and notes that Stephen's scandal work drives away A.E., who

complains that Stephen is "prying into the family life of a great man" (*Art of Scandal*, 103).

5. Nash, *Joyce and the Act of Reception*, 82.

6. See Latham, *Art of Scandal*, 98.

7. Ibid., 103.

8. That Stephen ascribes this strategy to Shakespeare's oeuvre so as to call attention to it in *Ulysses* seems all the more probable given Joyce's further development of his work along precisely these lines in *Finnegans Wake*, which elaborates an illegible "crime in the park" into a vast, opaque web of interrelated scandals, transgressions, and embarrassments. See, e.g., Crispi and Slote, *How Joyce Wrote*, 8–9, 11, 13–14.

9. Clearly, Molly and Leopold Bloom are also using an array of complex and creative stratagems so as to hold onto their marriage through an extended period of emotional and economic tumult, a circumstance that could be read alternately as Joyce's gently satirical, naturalist depiction of the difficulties attending any garden-variety marriage or as his epic rendering of modern marital heroics equivalent to those of Penelope and Odysseus.

10. See Lamos, *Deviant Modernism*, 148.

11. Given the importance that Stephen has earlier accorded to his having refrained from giving "all" to any of his male admirers, as well as the parallel importance Joyce understandably placed on the nonprocreative nature of his first sex act with Nora as it is elaborated in "Matcham's Masterstroke," in Gerty's encounter with Bloom, and in Molly and Bloom's sex life, Stephen's assertion that he is a virgin in "Oxen," as Bloom is found to be in "Circe," suggests that one definition of male virginity in circulation in *Ulysses* is predicated on the absence of anal penetration.

12. Stephen provides his own translation of the Italian term *buonaroba* as "a bay where all men ride" when describing the "scandalous" dark woman of the sonnets to whom Shakespeare sent a surrogate, as the mature Joyce has sent Haines to Gogarty as Mulligan. Both authors send attractive, mercenary, undiscriminating objects of desire "a lordling to woo" (in their stead), presumably knowing that their attractive but untrustworthy beloveds can be counted on to throw over a poet in favor of a lord (9.453).

13. This point was inspired in a conversation with Martha Stallman.

14. Stephen's plan to replace Mulligan's deforming footwear, with its subtle invocation of Stephen's Parisian experience of comfort and delight upon donning a woman's slipper, has obvious implications relating to artistic patronage as well as sexual intercourse, particularly since the majority of Joyce's most important patrons, champions, and, of course, *Ulysses*'s courageous publishers, Sylvia Beach and Adrienne Monnier, were all women.

15. Gifford, *"Ulysses" Annotated*, 245.

16. Ibid.

17. See Dellamora, *Masculine Desire*, 147–66.

18. See Ellmann, *Oscar Wilde*, 84–85. Concerning Joyce's impressions of Pater as reluctantly celibate, Dellamora finds in Pater's essay on Winckelmann a symbolic opposition of the sort Joyce would readily have noted, dividing Winkelmann's homoerotic bodily desire into masturbation, associated with "friendship and cultural inquiry," and sodomy, associated with "casual assignation and murder" (*Masculine Desire*, 68). Such public distancing of himself from physical sex acts with men, along with his well-known efforts to distance himself from Wilde even well before Wilde became notorious, would have associated Pater in Joyce's mind with unhappy, absolute self-denial.

19. Martha Stallman first pointed out to me that Ovid's story of the lapwing casts Stephen's fall as self-inflicted.

20. Stephen envisions both Best and Eglinton as adopting a misogynist, antimarriage stance because they do not desire women and satirically conflates their supposedly repetitive readings of *The Taming of the Shrew* with nightly masturbation, each "fingerponder[ing] nightly . . . his variorum edition" (9.1062–63). When Eglinton alludes to the beloved "lord" of Shakespeare's sonnets as Shakespeare's "dearmylove," Stephen thinks, "Love that dare not speak its name" (9.659). Mulligan's jokes about masturbation throughout the episode indicate that he and Stephen share a standing joke concerning Best and Eglinton's presumably unsuccessful but isolated struggles to suppress their homoerotic desires, a supposition made explicit in the final couplet to Mulligan's last bit of doggerel, "Being afraid to marry on earth/they masturbated for all they were worth" (9.1151–52), to which Stephen silently retorts, "Jest on. Know thyself" (9.1153).

21. Both Dettmar ("Vacation, Vocation, Perversion") and Riquelme ("*Stephen Hero*") have explicated ways in which the scandalization of an explicitly artistic (Wildean) homosexuality at the end of the nineteenth century led in Joyce's writing to textual anxieties amounting at times to homosexual panic as Stephen struggles to claim a literary/artistic vocation.

22. For more on Joycean triangles, see Castle, "Confessing Oneself"; Lamos, *Deviant Modernism*, 148; and Valente, "Thrilled by His Touch."

23. Stephen's suspiciously vague recollections in "Oxen" of a purported ménage à trois—one wonders whether he is perhaps unsure about the doxy—furthermore explicitly recall the theme of homosexual triangles in "Telemachus" and "Scylla and Charybdis" by repeating the words with which Buck Mulligan launched his playful but seductive turn as catamite: "to the best of his remembrance they had but the one doxy between them and she of the stews to make shift with in delights amorous *for life ran very high in those days*" (14.359–60; emphasis added).

24. Ellmann dates this episode to "June 20, four days after [Joyce's] memorable first evening with Nora" (*Joyce*, 160). In contrast with his specific withholding of full corroboration of many other personal "falls," Joyce explicitly corroborated this event in a poem written, Ellmann notes, "as soon as he recovered his wits. Joyce describes himself as he: ' . . . lay in my urine/ While ladies so pure in/White petticoats ravished my gaze'" (160–61).

25. Ellmann, *Selected Letters*, xxiv.

Chapter 8
DUBLIN'S TABLOID UNCONSCIOUS

1. Gifford, *"Ulysses" Annotated*, 452.

2. Indeed, it would not be overstating the case to describe "Oxen" and "Circe" as framed respectively by the two central tropes of the Maiden Tribute scandal. "Oxen's" symbolic focus is on simoniacal rituals through which the sacred is brutally, carelessly, or self-righteously profaned in pursuit of profits and temporal power. "Circe," on the other hand, transposes W. T. Stead's London-based "Modern Babylon," the sinister labyrinth in which such sacrifices occur, to Dublin's Monto District, a modern-day Circe's Island where every activity, object, and aspect of human relations is magically transformed into simultaneously irresistible and damning scandal evidence.

3. Bloom's interest in exploiting Stephen for personal or economic gain is at its most explicit in "Eumaeus." In this episode, well known for its adoption of tabloid discourse, Bloom considers managing Stephen's prospective singing career; that is, he envisions taking relative to Stephen the influential position that Blazes Boylan holds relative to Bloom's wife, Molly. Bloom also momentarily adopts the stance of a modern-day tempter, urging Stephen to take up a career as a journalist, since it is "the readiest channel nowadays." Privately, he entertains the possibility that were Stephen to move in with himself and Molly, Stephen's presence might help to separate Molly from Boylan. Bloom envisions Stephen teaching Molly correct Italian pronunciation, which, he might hope, would upgrade her status to that of classically trained vocalist, an "artiste" whose career would require a better class of manager. Certainly Bloom recalls William O'Shea's apparent early pandering of Katharine O'Shea to the young Parnell when he approvingly foresees that Stephen's youthful good looks might divert Molly's erotic energies away from Boylan.

4. In "Penelope," Molly further connects Bloom with the conventions of the New Journalist sex scandal by repeatedly using the scandal term

"unnatural" to describe Bloom's sexual desires. As Mullin argues, Gerty MacDowell also stands in "ironic proximity" to the stock figures of tabloid scandal, as the "young person" "purity reformers like Stead . . . sought to protect" (*Joyce, Sexuality and Social Purity*, 174–75).

5. These words come from Joyce's poem, "Gas from a Burner," spoken from the perspective of Grant Richards, the editor who held up the publication of *Dubliners* for ten years, expressing his fear of the dark powers that might be unleashed by Joyce's use of business and place names.

6. In his 2011 *New Yorker* essay, "Deceptive Picture," Alex Ross notes that Joyce "evidently drew on the [Wilde] trials of 1895 in creating the hallucinogenic persecution of Leopold Bloom in the "Circe" chapter (E5). In *The Poor Bugger's Tool,* Mullen, while focusing on *Ulysses's* incorporation of Roger Casement's trial and execution, also contributes to a rapidly emerging awareness of Bloom's serial entanglements with Wilde. He notes that in "Cyclops" Joyce "emphasizes the queer polyvalence in [the episode's] figure of love by linking Bloom's declaration of love to Lord Henry's theorization of love for a young Dorian in *The Picture of Dorian Gray*." (115).

7. The late-nineteenth-century British press saw a rapid shift in the application of the terms "pervert" and "perversion" from the realm of the confessional to that of the sexual. In 1904, the phrase "perverted Jew" might have been either only mildly and inadvertently pejorative or very ugly indeed, depending on whether Cunningham is explaining Bloom's religious background or engaging in scandal-speak. It is almost certain that the rather formal Cunningham means the term in the slightly anachronistic sense that Bloom was born a Jew but converted to Catholicism; by using the term "pervert" instead of "convert," Cunningham probably means to suggest openmindedness by treating Bloom's Christianization as a turning away from the point of view of Judaism rather than describing it more approvingly as conversion. A more detailed examination of the slippery status of the term "perversion" during this period would undoubtedly afford further insight into the term's status in Joyce's scandal work.

8. See especially Brake's "Government by Journalism and the Silence of the *Star*."

9. In *Joyce and the Art of Reception*, Nash notes that Joyce was so interested in newspaper coverage of the rioting of Dublin audiences in response to Synge's *Playboy of the Western World* (January 1907) that he sent clippings about the riots to family members in Dublin. These riots broke out in response to Synge's supposed treatment of Irish female virgins as inadequately sexually reticent, especially in Christy Mahon's invocation of a chorus line of Irish virgins ranging "from here to the western world, and they in their shifts." Joyce's interest in the *Playboy* riots was undoubtedly prompted

by the ferocity of this spontaneous public expression of outrage toward a perceived violation of Irish female innocence, which dramatically registered the dangers that the scandalization of virgins posed not only for Irish girls and women but for Irish artists.

10. The exact history of the fifteen-year-old Joyce's rejected *Tit-Bits* submission, known only through an account from Stanislaus Joyce, is unascertainable. Stanislaus recalled the main character's reverie about his beloved, which included the phrase "laughing witch," as "not without grace" (Ellmann, *Joyce*, 50). Joyce revised it as a burlesque "three or four years later," or around 1901 (ibid.). Sometime close to Joyce's submission of the first version of the story to *Tit-Bits*, a story by Philip Beaufoy that, like Joyce's, was also about romance and intrigue among the Russian nihilists, "For Vera's Sake," was published as the "Prize Tit-Bit for May 1897." Whether the young Joyce had merely emulated Beaufoy or "chanced independently to hit on the same theme," we cannot know (Kenner, "Beaufoy's Masterplaster," 11). However, Joyce's double incorporation into *Ulysses* of words from his early writing ascribed to the actual Beaufoy, who, like the fictional Deasy, beat him into print, certainly retroactively encodes an act of public sex that Joyce sincerely prized and is indeed a "masterstroke" of scandal work.

11. See Bristow, *Effeminate England*.

12. For instance, Bloom's guilty hallucinations reflect his fear that he had launched Bridie Kelly, his first sexual partner, into a life of prostitution, although both were presumably equally young and feckless (15.361–64). At the end of "Sirens," Bloom recalls having sex with the aging whore of the lane and his mortification when, in mid-coitus, she revealed that she would prefer doing Molly's laundry to doing her husband, uncomfortably revealing the depth of her economic desperation (11.1255–59). Bloom's pent-up desire certainly had led him to approach Mary Driscoll, the family maid, possibly grabbing and bruising her (15.879–88). Even if Mary's claims in "Circe" that Bloom used force merely reflect his unconscious guilt at having desired her at all, his sexual interest in her did constitute a sort of sexual, domestic theft: as Molly's memories in "Penelope" confirm, Bloom's too evident attentions cost Driscoll her job (18.68–70). Bloom has, moreover, put his daughter Milly, another "maid," in harm's way by sending her off to Mullingar, whether unconsciously to protect her from his own wayward passions or consciously, as Molly believes, to spare her knowledge of her mother's (18.1004–8). Finally, the marital moratorium into which Bloom and Molly have fallen following Rudy's death has certainly contributed to both Molly and Bloom's vulnerability to Blazes's encroachments.

13. In "Lestrygonians," Bloom reflects on the politics of food within post-Parnellian Irish nationalism in which the hunger of the urban poor,

and even of the nominally middle class, makes them vulnerable to cooptation by well-to-do nationalists. Joyce here elaborates on the web of connections that make the knife an apt emblem for scandal: as a weapon, as in the Phoenix Park murders; as an emblem of social influence in the hands of middle-class "carvers"; and as an emblem of rhetorical or analytical cuts determining how an issue will be approached.

14. The monstrous sexual crime of trans-species miscegenation figured by the Minotaur is again invoked in "Circe" in reference to a sex scandal involving the famed operatic tenor Caruso, in which Bloom, adopting the position of Caruso following scandalous accusations in the press, tries to explain away the charge that he has pinched a young woman's bottom in the New York City Zoo's monkey house. Trying to defend himself in parodic scandal fragments, Bloom makes the unnamed offense sound considerably worse than the original claim (15.1188–90).

15. Valente, *Myth of Manliness*, 58.

16. Gifford, *"Ulysses" Annotated*, 480.

17. The theme of pishoguery is reinforced in "Circe" through the importance ascribed to Zoe's appropriation of Bloom's talisman, a loss that leaves Bloom, unlike Odysseus, at the mercy of hostile magical transformations. In addition to Corley's gold coin, the coin Gabriel forces on Lily, Ursula's purloined mirror, Deasy's cache of Stuart coins, and other metonymic figures for pishoguery occur across Joyce's oeuvre. While space limitations forbid a full discussion of these, an overview of a few more will make clear how many such metonyms appear among the treasures the wealthy American collects on Bloom's behalf. The invocation in "Araby" of Caroline Norton's "An Arab's Farewell to His Steed," as Harry Stone has shown, links the short story's proceedings to another famous nineteenth-century sex scandal by way of a poem that climaxes in a young man reclaiming the beloved horse he ill-advisedly sold and flinging the coins he received in payment back at his pursuers ("Araby," 396–97). Bloom's Parnell-like care not to sign documents that might be entered into evidence contrasts with Stephen's signatory incontinence, figured not only when others suggest that he smears shit on his sheets but also by his IOU to A.E., making IOUs another kind of detachable, appropriable folly that might be taken hostage and deployed against one. The most significant pishogueristic theft I have excluded, however, occurs in "Oxen of the Sun," in which Alec Bannon's proud display of Milly Bloom's locket as a sexual trophy parallels Mulligan's earlier display of Ursula's stolen mirror (14.761). As if to emphasize this parallel, Bannon and Mulligan have walked together to the National Maternity Hospital after meeting up at the door of "the Rt. Hon. Mr Justice Fitzgibbons," a man whose position on the Trinity Estates Commission sets him (as Joyce repeatedly reminds us)

literally and figuratively alongside Tim Healy, O'Brienite scribe and anti-Parnellite scandalmonger (7.800–801, 14.493, 15.4343).

18. These offspring are not merely metallic, but preciously metallic: each son bears a name referencing either silver or gold. The octuplets' specific metallurgy, coupled with their immediate ascension to "positions of high public trust" that connote varying degrees of status, calls to mind a passage from Plato's *Republic*: "but the god who made you mixed some gold into those who are adequately equipped to rule, because they are the most valuable. He put silver in those who are auxiliaries and iron and bronze in the farmers and other craftsmen" (*Republic*, 3:415a–b).

19. This pattern recurs in "Eumaeus," when Bloom recalls of the Parnell scandal, "The fact, namely, that he had shared her bedroom which came out in the witnessbox on oath when a thrill went through the packed court literally electrifying everybody in the shape of witnesses swearing to have witnessed him on such and such a particular date in the act of scrambling out of an upstairs apartment with the assistance of a ladder . . . a fact the weeklies, addicted to the lubric a little, simply coined shoals of money out of" (16.1372–80).

20. In "Lestrygonians," Bloom recalls the essence of Healy's accusation that Parnell "used men as pawns" and "let them all go to pot" (8.511). The connections between the press, Parnell's tactics for mobilizing his "pawns," and the ensuing disaster after which his followers were left to "go to pot" are also suggested when he overhears a reference to a two-headed octopus by Revivalist poet A.E. (8.520). By the time Joyce composed "Lestrygonians," the term "octopus" had been used by Labor leader James Larkin to describe the many interwoven forms of influence, power, and appropriation that newspaper owner William Martin Murphy, who was also Parnell's literal replacement at the head of the *Irish Independent*, used to quash the expansion of trade unions into Dublin. Murphy, Larkin charged, controlled "an industrial octopus" whose tentacles strangled workers through starvation and the flow of critical perspectives through his inexpensive, widely circulating newspapers. Joyce ascribes this octopus metaphor to A.E., who knew and worked with Larkin, edited a militantly regional newspaper, loathed industrialism, and promoted his own agrarian alternatives to the capitalist mode of production to invoke imperial networks of influence. Certainly the image of newspapers as networks extending outward from a powerful two-headed octopus, one head located in the seemingly indestructible heart of the empire, London, and the other in Edinburgh, supplies one apt overview of the beast that strangled Parnell, leaving his adherents to stew. See Kenner (*Ulysses*, 74) for a different reading of this reference.

21. Interestingly, Foster and Jackson argue that Parnell's memory itself was infused by the Siegfried myth. They cite Joyce's one-time Irish-language

instructor Patrick Pearse recalling Parnell as "an embodied conviction; a flame that seared, a sword that stabbed" and contend that here and elsewhere Parnell was "remembered as a Siegfried who had tried to wrest the sacred weapon from the stone" ("Men for All Seasons?," 421).

22. As Valente has persuasively argued in "The Novel and the Police (Gazette)," the sensationalizing gaze is readily reversible, making attempts to counter it directly, like decapitating a hydra, an understandably attractive but hopelessly counterproductive strategy.

23. That this sum is just what Stephen has left is hinted at when Bloom demands of Bella, "Haven't you lifted enough off him?" and is explicitly indicated when Stephen, early in "Eumaeus," drunkenly hunts in his pockets for some pennies to give to the down-and-out Corley and hands him one of the only two coins he finds there, which are two half-crowns, or ten shillings (16.191–94).

24. In one of several passages in which Joyce draws parallels among the church, the press, and prostitution, with the threat of scandal as the underlying, unifying theme, in "The Lotus Eaters" Bloom, standing at the "open backdoor of All Hallows" (5.318), muses that the Catholic Church "goes like clockwork" because of confession, a "great weapon in their hands." His thoughts about the confessional, however, invoke newspaper headlines: "Husband learn [sic] to his surprise . . ." He reflects that the Salvation Army is a "blatant immitation," raking in money by using the "lovely shame" of reformed prostitutes—"How I found the Lord"—to draw an audience (5.425–35).

25. Mahaffey, "Joyce and Sexuality," 124–26; see also Ellmann, *Joyce*, 161–62.

26. See ibid., 93–94.

27. As Stallman notes, "Many readers have noted the care Joyce takes with dates and ages in Circe, particularly with Stephen and Bloom: While Bloom is Joyce's age as it was when he was writing Circe, Stephen is 22, Joyce's age as it would have been in 1904. In that light, it might be interesting to note that the date *Ulysses* is published—1922—is 22 years after Wilde's death in 1900" ("'Suddenly Somebody Else,'" 14).

28. Ibid., 13.

29. According to Stallman, "While Rudy's reading from right to left can easily be seen as a reference to Bloom's Jewishness, it might take on an additional layer of meaning when one considers Joyce's comment about Wilde in a letter to Stanislaus, that: 'Quite the reverse is/The style of his verses' [Ellmann, *Selected Letters*, 96]). If Wilde reverses his verses (so to speak), then having this tiny avatar of him read in the reverse direction makes a great visual pun" (ibid., 13).

CODA

1. Mahaffey, "A Portrait of the Artist."

2. Ellmann, *James Joyce*, 156.

3. Joyce himself seems to have remained sometimes agonizingly and sometimes titillatingly uncertain on the question of Barnacle's prior virginity for a long time, which suggests that Joyce very much needed this sense of uncertainty, allowing him to envision both himself and Nora Barnacle as, by turns, the more experienced ravisher and the innocent virgin, "the willer with the willed" (14.1069–70). See Ellmann, *James Joyce*, 279–81.

4. See Backus, "'More Useful Washed and Dead,'" and "'The Children of the Nation?'"

BIBLIOGRAPHY

Adut, Ari. *On Scandal: Moral Disturbances in Society, Politics, and Art.* Cambridge: Cambridge University Press, 2008.

Aldington, Richard, and Stanley Weintraub. "Introduction." In Aldington and Weintraub, *The Portable Oscar Wilde.*

———, eds. *The Portable Oscar Wilde.* Rev. ed. New York: Penguin, 1981.

Allen, Nicholas. *Modernism, Ireland and Civil War.* Cambridge: Cambridge University Press, 2009.

Anderson, Benedict. *Imagined Communities: Reflections on the Origin and Spread of Nationalism.* London: Verso, 1991.

Andrews, Linton, and Henry Archibald Taylor. *Lords and Laborers of the Press: Men Who Fashioned the Modern British Newspaper.* Carbondale: Southern Illinois University Press, 1970.

Arata, Stephen D. "The Occidental Tourist: *Dracula* and the Anxiety of Reverse Colonization." *Victorian Studies* 33, no. 4 (Summer 1990): 621–45.

Arnold, Bruce. *The Scandal of "Ulysses."* New York: St. Martin's, 1991.

Attridge, Derek, ed. *The Cambridge Companion to James Joyce.* Cambridge: Cambridge University Press, 1990.

———. *Peculiar Language.* 2nd ed. London: Routledge, 2004.

Attridge, Derek, and Marjorie Howes, eds. *Semicolonial Joyce.* Cambridge: Cambridge University Press, 2000.

Austin, J. L. *How to Do Things with Words.* Cambridge, Mass.: Harvard University Press, 1962.

Backus, Margot Gayle. "'The Children of the Nation?': Representations of Poor Children in Mainstream Nationalist Journalism, 1882 and 1913." *Éire-Ireland* 44, nos. 1/2 (2009): 118–46.

———. *The Gothic Family Romance: Heterosexuality, Child Sacrifice, and the Anglo-Irish Colonial Order.* Durham, N.C.: Duke University Press, 1999.

———. "'More Useful Washed and Dead': James Connolly, W. B. Yeats, and the Sexual Politics of Easter 1916." *Interventions: International Journal of Postcolonial Studies* 10, no. 1 (2008): 67–85.

———. "'Odd Jobs': James Joyce, Oscar Wilde and the Scandal Fragment." *Joyce Studies Annual* (2008): 105–45.

Backus, Margot Gayle, and Joseph Valente. "'An Encounter': James Joyce's Humiliation Nation." In *Collaborative Dubliners: Joyce in Dialogue*, edited by Vicki Mahaffey, 48–68. Syracuse, N.Y.: Syracuse University Press, 2012.

Balzano, Wanda. "'Eveline,' or the Veils of Cleaning." In Frawley, *A New and Complex Sensation*, 81–93.

Barnhurst, Kevin, and John Nerone. *The Form of News: A History*. New York: Guilford, 2001.

Barry, Kevin. "Introduction." In *James Joyce: Occasional, Critical and Political Writing*, edited by Kevin Barry. Oxford: Oxford World Classics, 2000.

Bazargan, Susan. "Epiphany as Scene of Performance." In Frawley, *A New and Complex Sensation*, 44–54.

Bechdel, Alison. *Fun Home: A Family Tragicomic*. Boston: Houghton Mifflin, 2006.

Berlant, Lauren Gail. *The Queen of America Goes to Washington City: Essays on Sex and Citizenship*. Durham, N.C.: Duke University Press, 1997.

Bew, Paul. *Charles Stewart Parnell*. Dublin: Gill & Macmillan, 1991.

———. "Parnell and Davitt." In Boyce and O'Day, *Parnell in Perspective*, 38–51.

Bhroimeil, Una Ni. "The South African War, Empire and the Irish World, 1899–1902." In *Newspapers and Empire in Ireland and Britain: Reporting the British Empire, c. 1857–1921*, edited by Simon James Potter, 195–216. Dublin: Four Courts, 2004.

Bixby, Patrick. "Perversion and the Press: Victorian Self-Fashioning in 'A Painful Case.'" In Frawley, *A New and Complex Sensation*, 112–21.

Blamires, Harry. *The New Bloomsday Book: A Guide through Ulysses*. 3rd ed. London: Routledge, 2004.

Bourdieu, Pierre. *Distinction: A Social Critique of the Judgment of Taste*. Trans. Richard Nice. Cambridge, Mass.: Harvard University Press, 1984.

Bourke, Angela. *The Burning of Bridget Cleary: A True Story*. London: Pimlico, 1999.

Boyce, D. G., and Alan O'Day, eds. *Parnell in Perspective*. London: Routledge, 1991.

Boyce, George. "'The Portrait of the King Is the King': The Biographers of Charles Stewart Parnell." In Boyce and O'Day, *Parnell in Perspective*, 284–309.

Brake, Laurel. "Government by Journalism and the Silence of the *Star*." In *Encounters in the Victorian Press: Editors, Authors, Readers*, edited by Laurel Brake and Julie F. Codell, 213–35. New York: Palgrave, 2004.

———. *Print in Transition: 1850–1910*. New York: Palgrave, 2001.

Breatnach, Liam. "On Satire and the Poet's Circuit." In *Unity in Diversity: Studies in Irish and Scottish Gaelic Language, Literature, and History*, edited by Cathal G Ó Háinle and Donald Meek, 25–35. Dublin: School of Irish Trinity College, 2004.

Bristow, Joseph. *Effeminate England: Homoerotic Writing after 1885*. New York: Columbia University Press, 1995.

Brivic, Sheldon. "Reality as Fetish: The Crime in *Finnegans Wake*." *James Joyce Quarterly* 34, no. 4. (Summer 1997): 449–60.

Brooker, Joseph. *Joyce's Critics: Transitions in Reading and Culture*. Madison: University of Wisconsin Press, 2004.

Brown, Richard. *James Joyce and Sexuality*. Cambridge: Cambridge University Press, 1985.

Bull, Philip. "The Fall of Parnell: The Political Context of His Intransigence." In Boyce and O'Day, *Parnell in Perspective*, 129–50.

Burns, Christy. "Parodic Irishness: Joyce's Reconfigurations of the Nation in *Finnegans Wake*." *NOVEL: A Forum on Fiction*, 31, no. 2 (1998): 237–55.

Callanan, Frank. *T. M. Healy*. Cork, Ireland: Cork University Press, 1996.

Caraher, Brian G. "Trieste, Dublin, Galway: Joyce, Journalism, 1912." In *Joyce on the Threshold*, edited by Ann Fogarty and Timothy Martin, 132–50. Gainesville: University Press of Florida, 2005.

Casanova, Pascale. *The World Republic of Letters*. Translated by M. B. DeBevoise. Cambridge, Mass.: Harvard University Press, 2004.

Castle, Gregory. "Confessing Oneself: Homoeros and Colonial *Bildung* in *A Portrait of the Artist as a Young Man*." In Valente, *Quare Joyce*, 157–82.

———. "Ousted Possibilities: Critical Histories in James Joyce's *Ulysses*." *Twentieth Century Literature* 39, no. 3 (1993): 306–28.

———. *Reading the Modernist Bildungsroman*. Gainesville: University Press of Florida, 2006.

Chalaby, Jean K. *The Invention of Journalism*. New York: St. Martin's, 1998.

Chauncey, George. *Gay New York: Gender, Urban Culture, and the Making of the Gay Male World, 1890–1940*. New York: Basic Books, 1994.

Cheng, Vincent. *Joyce, Race, and Empire*. Cambridge: Cambridge University Press, 1995.

Clark, Anna. *Scandal: The Sexual Politics of the British Constitution*. Princeton, N.J.: Princeton University Press, 2004.

Cocks, H. G. *Nameless Offences: Homosexual Desire in the Nineteenth Century*. London: I. B. Tauris, 2003.

Cohen, Ed. *Talk on the Wilde Side: Toward a Genealogy of a Discourse on Male Sexualities*. New York: Routledge, 1993.

Collier, Patrick. *Modernism on Fleet Street*. Aldershot, U.K.: Ashgate, 2006.

Collier, Patrick, and Ann Ardis, eds. *Transatlantic Print Culture, 1880–1940*. New York: Palgrave Macmillan, 2008.

Conboy, Martin. *The Press and Popular Culture*. London: SAGE, 2002.

Conrad, Kathryn A. *Locked in the Family Cell: Gender, Sexuality, and Political Agency in Irish National Discourse.* Madison: University of Wisconsin Press, 2004.

Conrad, Kathryn A., and Darryl Wadsworth. "Joyce and the Irish Body Politic: Sexuality and Colonization in *Finnegans Wake.*" *James Joyce Quarterly* 31, no. 3 (1994): 301–13.

Costello, Peter. *Joyce: Years of Growth.* New York: Pantheon, 1993.

Cotter, David. *James Joyce and the Perverse Ideal.* New York: Routledge, 2003.

Crispi, Luca, and Sam Slote. *How Joyce Wrote "Finnegans Wake": A Chapter-by-Chapter Genetic Guide.* Madison: University of Wisconsin Press, 2007.

Cullingford, Elizabeth Butler. "Phoenician Genealogies and Oriental Geographies: Joyce, Language, and Race." In Attridge and Howes, *Semicolonial Joyce,* 219–39.

Curtis, L. Perry. *Apes and Angels: The Irishman in Victorian Caricature.* Washington, D.C.: Smithsonian Books, 1979.

Curtis, Liz. *Nothing but the Same Old Story: Roots of Anti-Irish Racism.* London: Sasta, 1984.

Cvetkovich, Ann. *An Archive of Feelings: Trauma, Sexuality, and Lesbian Public Cultures.* Durham, N.C.: Duke University Press, 2003.

Deane, Seamus. "Dead Ends: Joyce's Finest Moments." In Attridge and Howes, *Semicolonial Joyce,* 21–36.

———. "Joyce the Irishman." In Attridge, *Cambridge Companion to James Joyce,* 28–48.

Dellamora, Richard. *Masculine Desire: The Sexual Politics of Victorian Aestheticism.* Chapel Hill: University of North Carolina Press, 1990.

Demoor, Marysa. *Marketing the Author: Authorial Personae, Narrative Selves, and Self-Fashioning, 1880–1930.* Hampshire: Palgrave Macmillan, 2004.

de Nie, Michael. *The Eternal Paddy: Irish Identity and the British Press, 1798–1882.* Madison: University of Wisconsin Press, 2004.

Deppman, Jed. "James Joyce Composing a Chapter: *Finnegans Wake* 2.4." In Crispi and Slote, *How Joyce Wrote "Finnegans Wake,"* 304–46.

Dettmar, Kevin. "Vacation, Vocation, Perversion: Stephen Dedalus and Homosexual Panic." In *European Joyce Studies 11: James Joyce and the Fabrication of An Irish Identity,* edited by Michael Patrick Gillespie, 132–50. Amsterdam: Rodopi, 2001.

Devine, Paul. "Fact or Fiction: Material Evidence in *Dubliners.*" In Frawley, *A New and Complex Sensation,* 94–103.

Devlin, Kimberly. "En-Gendered Choice and Agency in *Ulysses.*" In Gillespie and Fargnoli, *"Ulysses" in Critical Perspective,* 70–87.

———. "'I Saw That Picture Somewhere': Tracking the Symptom of the Sisters of Lazarus." In Norris, *Companion to James Joyce's "Ulysses,"* 187–202.

Devlin, Kimberly J., and Marilyn Reizbaum, eds. *"Ulysses" En-gendered Perspectives: Eighteen New Essays on the Episodes*. Columbia: University of South Carolina Press, 1999.

Dobbins, Gregory. "Where-ever Green Is Red: James Connolly and Postcolonial Theory." *Nepantla: Views from the South* 3 (2000): 605–48.

Doherty, Gerald. *Pathologies of Desire: The Vicissitudes of the Self in James Joyce's "A Portrait of the Artist as a Young Man."* New York: Peter Lang, 2008.

Donovan, Stephen. "Dead Men's News: Joyce's 'A Painful Case' and the Modern Press." *Journal of Modern Literature* 24, no. 1 (2000): 25–45.

Douglas, Mary. *Purity and Danger: An Analysis of Concepts of Pollution and Taboo*. New York: Praeger, 1966.

Dowling, Linda. *Hellenism and Homosexuality in Victorian Oxford*. Ithaca, N.Y.: Cornell University Press, 1997.

Downing, Gregory. "Joycean Pop Culture: Fragments toward an Institutional History and Futurology." In Gillespie and Fargnoli, *"Ulysses" in Critical Perspective*, 117–34.

Dudgeon, Jeffrey. Review of "'Terrible Queer Creatures': A History of Homosexuality in Ireland." *History Ireland* 17, no. 2 (2009): 63.

Duffy, Enda. "Disappearing Dublin: *Ulysses*, Postcoloniality, and the Politics of Space." In Attridge and Howes, *Semicolonial Joyce*, 37–57.

———. "Interesting States: Birthing and the Nation in 'Oxen of the Sun.'" In Devlin and Reizbaum, *"Ulysses" En-gendered Perspectives*, 210–28.

Dwan, David. *The Great Community: Culture and Nationalism in Ireland*. Dublin: Field Day, 2008.

Eckley, Grace. *Maiden Tribute: A Life of W. T. Stead*. Philadelphia: Xlibris, 2007.

Eide, Marian. *Ethical Joyce*. Cambridge: Cambridge University Press, 2002.

———. "Joyce, Genre, and the Authority of Form." In Rabaté, *Palgrave Advances in James Joyce Studies*, 97–120.

Ellmann, Richard. *James Joyce: The First Revision of the 1959 Classic*. Oxford: Oxford University Press, 1983.

———. *Oscar Wilde*. New York: Knopf, 1988.

———, ed. *Selected Letters of James Joyce*. New York: Viking, 1975.

Fairhall, James. *James Joyce and the Question of History*. Cambridge: Cambridge University Press, 1995.

Fanon, Frantz. *The Wretched of the Earth*. Translated by Constance Farrington. New York: Grove, 1963.

Ferriter, Diarmaid. *Occasions of Sin: Sex and Society in Modern Ireland*. London: Profile Books, 2009.

———. *The Transformation of Ireland*. Woodstock, N.Y.: Overlook, 2005.

Fordham, Finn. *Lots of Fun at Finnegans Wake: Unravelling Universals.* Oxford: Oxford University Press, 2007.

Foster, John Wilson. *Irish Novels, 1890–1940: New Bearings in Culture and Fiction.* Oxford: Oxford University Press, 2008.

Foster, R. F. "Interpretations of Parnell." *Studies: An Irish Quarterly Review* 80, no. 320 (1991): 349–57.

———. *Modern Ireland: 1600–1972.* New York: Penguin, 1988.

Foster, R. F., and Alvin Jackson. "Men for All Seasons? Carson, Parnell, and the Limits of Heroism in Modern Ireland." *European History Quarterly* 39 (2009): 414–38.

Foucault, Michel. *The History of Sexuality.* Vol. 1, *An Introduction.* Translated by Robert Hurley. New York: Pantheon Books, 1986.

Frawley, Oona, ed. *A New and Complex Sensation: Essays on Joyce's "Dubliners."* Dublin: Lilliput, 2004.

Frehner, Ruth. "Textile *Dubliners.*" In Frawley, *A New and Complex Sensation,* 197–211.

Gabler, Hans Walter. "Introduction: A History of Curiosities, 1904–1914." In James Joyce, *Dubliners: Authoritative Text, Contexts, Criticism,* Norton Critical Edition, ed. Margot Norris, xv–xlii. New York: Norton, 2006.

Gagnier, Regenia. *Idylls of the Marketplace: Oscar Wilde and the Victorian Public.* Stanford, Calif.: Stanford University Press, 1986.

Gamson, Joshua. "Normal Sins: Sex Scandal Narratives as Institutional Morality Tales." *Social Problems* 48, no. 2 (2001): 185–205.

Gibbons, Luke. "'Have You No Homes to Go To?': Joyce and the Politics of Paralysis." In Attridge and Howes, *Semicolonial Joyce,* 150–71.

Gibson, Andrew. *Joyce's Revenge: History, Politics, and Aesthetics in "Ulysses."* Oxford: Oxford University Press, 2002.

———. "'That Stubborn Irish Thing': A Portrait of the Artist in History." In *Joyce, Ireland, Britain,* edited by Andrew Gibson and Len Platt, 85–103. Gainesville: University Press of Florida, 2006.

Gifford, Don. *"Ulysses" Annotated: Notes for James Joyce's "Ulysses."* Berkeley: University of California Press, 1989.

Gillespie, Michael Patrick, and A. Nicholas Fargnoli, eds. *"Ulysses" in Critical Perspective.* Gainesville: University Press of Florida, 2006.

Glassie, Henry. *Passing the Time in Ballymenone: Culture and History of an Ulster Community.* Philadelphia: University of Pennsylvania Press, 1982.

Gordon, John. "Haines and the Black Panther." *James Joyce Quarterly* 27, no. 3 (Spring 1990): 587–94.

Gorman, Herbert. *James Joyce.* New York: H. Wolff, 1939.

Groden, Michael. "Before and After: The Manuscripts in Textual and Genetic Criticism." In Gillespie and Fargnoli, *"Ulysses" in Critical Perspective,* 152–70.

Hampton, Mark *Visions of the Press in Britain, 1850–1950.* Urbana: University of Illinois Press, 2004.

Harris, Susan. "Clearing the Stage: Gender, Class, and the 'Freedom of the Scenes' in Eighteenth-Century Dublin." *PMLA* 119 (2004): 1264–78.

———. *Gender and Modern Irish Drama.* Bloomington: Indiana University Press, 2002.

Herr, Cheryl. *Joyce's Anatomy of Culture.* Urbana: University of Illinois Press, 1986.

———. "Old Wives' Tales as Portals of Discovery in 'Proteus.'" In Devlin and Reizbaum, *"Ulysses" En-gendered Perspectives,* 30–41.

Howes, Marjorie. "Joyce, Colonialism, and Nationalism." In Attridge, *Cambridge Companion to James Joyce,* 254–71.

Hurts, Michael. "Parnell in the Spectrum of Nationalisms." In Boyce and O'Day, *Parnell in Perspective,* 77–128.

Israel, Kali. *Names and Stories: Emilia Dilke and Victorian Culture.* New York: Oxford University Press, 2002.

Jackson, Kate. *George Newnes and the New Journalism in Britain, 1880–1910: Culture and Profit.* Aldershot, U.K.: Ashgate, 2001.

Jameson, Fredric. *Modernism and Imperialism.* Nationalism, Colonialism and Literature: Field Day Pamphlet 14. Derry, Northern Ireland: Field Day, 1988.

JanMohamed, Abdul R. "Rehistoricizing Wright: The Psychopolitical Function of Death in *Uncle Tom's Children.*" In *Richard Wright,* edited by Harold Bloom. New York: Chelsea House, 1987.

Jenkins, Roy. *Gladstone: A Biography.* New York: Random House, 1997.

———. *Victorian Scandal: A Biography of the Right Honorable Gentleman Sir Charles Dilke.* New York: Pyramid Books, 1969.

Jones, Aled G. "The New Journalism in Wales." In Wiener, *Papers for the Millions,* 165–81.

Joseph, Betty. *Reading the East India Company, 1720–1840: Colonial Currencies of Gender.* Chicago: University of Chicago Press, 2004.

Joyce, James. *Dubliners.* New York: Dover, 1991.

———. *The "Finnegans Wake" Notebooks at Buffalo.* Edited by Vincent Deane, Daniel Ferrer, and Geert Lernout. Turnhout, Belgium: Brepols, 2001.

———. "Ireland at the Bar." In *Occasional, Critical, and Political Writing,* 145–47.

———. "Ireland: Island of Saints and Sages." In *Occasional, Critical, and Political Writing,* 108–26.

———. *Letters of James Joyce.* Edited by Richard Ellmann. London: Faber and Faber, 1966.

———. *Occasional, Critical, and Political Writing.* Edited by Kevin Barry. Oxford World's Classics. Oxford: Oxford University Press, 2000.

———. "Oscar Wilde: The Poet of *Salomé*." In *Occasional, Critical, and Political Writing*, 148–51.

———. *A Portrait of the Artist as a Young Man*. Edited by R. B. Kershner. New York: Bedford Books, 1993.

———. *Stephen Hero*. Edited by John J. Slocum and Herbert Cahoon. Norfolk, Conn.: New Directions, 1963.

———. *Ulysses: The Corrected Text*. Edited by Hans Walter Gabler. New York: Vintage Books, 1986.

Joyce, Stanislaus. *My Brother's Keeper: James Joyce's Early Years*. Edited by Richard Ellmann. 1958. Reprint, Cambridge, Mass.: Da Capo, 2003.

Kane, Anne. *Constructing Irish National Identity: Discourse and Ritual during the Land War, 1879–1882*. New York: Palgrave Macmillan, 2011.

———. "The Ritualization of Newspaper Reading and Political Consciousness: The Role of Newspapers in the Irish Land War." In *Reading Irish Histories: Texts, Contexts, and Memory in Modern Ireland*, edited by Lawrence McBride, 40–61. Dublin: Four Courts, 2003.

Kaplan, Morris. *Sodom on the Thames: Sex, Love, and Scandal in Wilde Times*. Ithaca, N.Y.: Cornell University Press, 2005.

Kee, Robert. *The Laurel and the Ivy: The Story of Charles Stewart Parnell and Irish Nationalism*. London: Hamish Hamilton, 1993.

Kelly, John. "Parnell in Irish Literature." In Boyce and O'Day, *Parnell in Perspective*, 242–83.

Kelly, Joseph. *Our Joyce: From Outcast to Icon*. Austin: University of Texas Press, 2010.

Kenner, Hugh. "Beaufoy's Masterplaster." *James Joyce Quarterly* 24, no. 1 (1986): 11–18.

———. *Joyce's Voices*. Berkeley: University of California Press, 1978.

———. *Ulysses*. Rev. ed. Baltimore: Johns Hopkins University Press, 1987.

Kershner, Brandon. *The Culture of Joyce's "Ulysses."* New York: Palgrave Macmillan, 2010.

———. "Family Resemblances in *Dubliners*." In Frawley, *A New and Complex Sensation*, 168–73.

———. *James Joyce in Context*. Cambridge: Cambridge University Press, 2009.

———. "Newspapers and Popular Culture." In McCourt, *James Joyce in Context*, 299–308.

Kiberd, Declan. *Inventing Ireland*. Cambridge, Mass.: Harvard University Press, 1996.

Kidd, John. "Filling in the Portrait." *Washington Post*, May 23, 1993.

Knowles, Sebastian D. G. "Introduction." In Gillespie and Fargnoli, *"Ulysses" in Critical Perspective*, 1–8.

Koestenbaum, Wayne. *Humiliation*. New York: Picador, 2011.

Koss, Stephen E. *The Rise and Fall of the Political Press in Britain.* Chapel Hill: University of North Carolina Press, 1984.

Koven, Seth. *Slumming: Sexual and Social Politics in Victorian London.* Princeton, N.J.: Princeton University Press, 2004.

Lacey, Brian. *Terrible Queer Creatures: Homosexuality in Irish History.* Dublin: Wordwell, 2008.

Lakoff, George, and Mark Johnson. *Metaphors We Live By.* Chicago: University of Chicago Press, 1980.

Lamos, Colleen. *Deviant Modernism: Sexual and Textual Errancy in T. S. Eliot, James Joyce, and Marcel Proust.* Cambridge: Cambridge University Press, 1998.

———. "The Double Life of 'Eumaeus.'" In Devlin and Reizbaum, *"Ulysses" En-gendered Perspective,* 242–53.

Lamson, Brandon. "Orpheus Descending: Images of Psychic Descent in 'Hades' and 'Circe.'" *Joyce Studies Annual* (2010): 254–61.

Larkin, Felix M. "'A Great Daily Organ': *The Freeman's Journal*, 1763–1924." *History Ireland* 14, no. 3 (2006): 44–49.

Latham, Sean. *The Art of Scandal: Modernism, Libel Law, and the Roman à Clef.* New York: Oxford University Press, 2009.

———. "The 'Nameless Shamelessness' of *Ulysses*: Libel and the Law of Literature." In *Scandalous Fictions: The Twentieth-Century Novel in the Public Sphere,* edited by Jago Morrison and Susan Watkins, 27–47. Hampshire, U.K.: Palgrave Macmillan, 2006.

Leckie, Barbara. *Culture and Adultery: The Novel, the Newspaper, and the Law, 1857–1914.* Philadelphia: University of Pennsylvania Press, 1999.

Lee, Alan J. *The Origins of the Popular Press in England, 1855–1914.* London: Croom Helm, 1976.

Legg, Marie-Louise. *Newspapers and Nationalism: The Irish Provincial Press, 1850–1892.* Dublin: Four Courts, 1999.

Leonard, Garry Martin. *Advertising and Commodity Culture in Joyce.* Gainesville: University Press of Florida, 1998.

———. *"Dubliners."* In Attridge, *Cambridge Companion to James Joyce,* 87–102.

———. "'A Little Trouble about Those White Corpuscles': Mockery, Heresy, and the Transubstantiation of Masculinity in 'Telemachus.'" In Devlin and Reizbaum, *"Ulysses" En-gendered Perspectives,* 1–19.

Levine, Jennifer. "James Joyce, Tattoo Artist." In Valente, *Quare Joyce,* 101–20.

Lloyd, David. 1993. *Anomalous States: Irish Writing and the Post-Colonial Moment.* Durham, N.C.: Duke University Press.

———. "Counterparts: *Dubliners*, Masculinity, and Temperance Nationalism." In Attridge and Howes, *Semicolonial Joyce,* 128–49.

Loughlin, James. 1987. "Constructing the Political Spectacle: Parnell, the Press, and National Leadership 1879–1885." In Boyce and O'Day, *Parnell in Perspective*, 221–41.

———. *Gladstone, Home Rule, and the Ulster Question, 1882–93*. Atlantic Highlands, N.J.: Humanities Press International, 1987.

Lowe-Evans, Mary. *Crimes Against Fecundity*. Syracuse, N.Y.: Syracuse University Press, 1989.

———. "Sex and Confession in the Joyce Canon: Some Historical Parallels." *Journal of Modern Literature* 16, no. 4 (Spring 1990): 563–76.

Lull, James, and Stephen Hinerman. *Media Scandals: Morality and Desire in the Popular Culture Marketplace*. New York: Columbia University Press, 1997.

Lyons, J. B. *Thrust Syphilis Down to Hell and Other Rejoyceana: Studies in the Border-Lands of Literature and Medicine*. Dun Laoghaire, Ireland: Glendale, 1988.

Maddox, Brenda. *Nora: The Real Life of Molly Bloom*. Boston: Houghton Mifflin, 1988.

Mahaffey, Vicki. "Joyce and Gender," in Rabaté, *Palgrave Advances in James Joyce Studies*, 121–43. New York: Palgrave Macmillan, 2004.

———. "Love, Race, and Exiles: The Bleak Side of *Ulysses*." *Joyce Studies Annual* (2008): 92–108.

———. *Modernist Literature: Challenging Fictions*. Malden, Mass.: Blackwell, 2007.

———. "A Portrait of the Artist as a Sympathetic Villain: Forgery, Melodrama, and Silent Film." Keynote address, North American James Joyce Conference, University of Texas, Austin, June 2007.

———. *Reauthorizing Joyce*. Cambridge: Cambridge University Press, 1988.

———. "Sidereal Writing: Male Refractions and Malefactions in 'Ithaca.'" In Devlin and Reizbaum, *"Ulysses" En-gendered Perspectives*, 254–66.

———. *States of Desire: Wilde, Yeats, Joyce, and the Irish Experiment*. New York: Oxford University Press, 1998.

Makdisi, Saree. *William Blake and the Impossible History of the 1790s*. Chicago: University of Chicago Press, 2003.

Malone, Carolyn. "Sensational Stories, Endangered Bodies: Women's Work and the New Journalism in England in the 1890s." *Albion: A Quarterly Journal Concerned with British Studies* 31 (Spring 1999): 49–71.

———. *Women's Bodies and Dangerous Trades in England, 1880–1914*. Woodbridge, U.K.: Boydell, 2003.

Mason, Ellsworth. "James Joyce's Shrill Note: The *Piccolo Della Sera* Articles." *Twentieth Century Literature: A Scholarly and Critical Journal* 2, no. 3 (1956): 115–39.

Maume, Patrick. *The Long Gestation: Irish Nationalist Life 1891–1918*. New York: St. Martin's, 1999.

McClintock, Anne. *Imperial Leather: Race, Gender, and Sexuality in the Colonial Contest*. New York: Routledge, 1995.

McCourt, John, ed. *James Joyce in Context*. Cambridge: Cambridge University Press, 2009.

———. "The News from Home." In Frawley, *A New and Complex Sensation*, 223–32.

McDiarmid, Lucy. *The Irish Art of Controversy*. Ithaca, N.Y.: Cornell University Press, 2005.

———. "Oscar Wilde, Lady Gregory, and Late Victorian Table-Talk." In *Oscar Wilde and Modern Culture: The Making of a Legend*, edited by Joseph Bristow, 46–62. Athens: Ohio University Press, 2009.

———. "Oscar Wilde's Speech from the Dock." *Textual Practice* 15, no. 3 (2001): 447–66.

McDonald, Russell. "Who Speaks for Fergus? Silence, Homophobia, and the Anxiety of Yeatsian Influence in Joyce." *Twentieth Century Literature* 51, no. 4 (2005): 391–413.

McGee, Patrick. "Machines, Empire, and the Wise Virgins: Cultural Revolution in 'Aeolus.'" In Devlin and Reizbaum, *"Ulysses" En-gendered Perspectives*, 86–99.

McKenna, Neil. *The Secret Life of Oscar Wilde*. New York: Basic Books, 2005.

McKeon, Michael. *The Secret History of Domesticity: Public, Private, and the Division of Knowledge*. Baltimore: Johns Hopkins University Press, 2005.

McKibben, Sarah E. "Born to Die . . . and Live On: Terminal Metaphors in the Life of Irish." *Irish Review* 26 (Autumn 2000): 89–99.

———. *Endangered Masculinities in Irish Poetry: 1540–1780*. Dublin: University College Dublin Press, 2010.

Medd, Jodie. "'The Cult of the Clitoris': Anatomy of a National Scandal." *Modernism/Modernity* 9, no. 1 (2002): 21–49.

Miller, Nicholas Andrew. *Modernism, Ireland, and the Erotics of Memory*. Cambridge: Cambridge University Press, 2002.

Molony, Senan. *The Phoenix Park Murders: Conspiracy, Betrayal, and Retribution*. Cork, Ireland: Mercier, 2006.

Morash, Christopher. *A History of the Media in Ireland*. Cambridge: Cambridge University Press, 2010.

Morris, Catherine, and Spurgeon Thompson. "Postcolonial Connolly." *Interventions: The International Journal of Postcolonial Studies* 10, no. 1 (2008): 1–6.

Mullen, Patrick R. *The Poor Bugger's Tool: Irish Modernism, Queer Labor, and Postcolonial History*. Oxford: Oxford University Press, 2012.

Mullin, Katherine. *James Joyce, Sexuality and Social Purity*. Cambridge: Cambridge University Press, 2003.

Munt, Sally R. *Queer Attachments: The Cultural Politics of Shame*. Aldershot, U.K.: Ashgate, 2008.

Nash, John. *James Joyce and the Act of Reception*. New York: Cambridge University Press, 2008.

Ní Dhomhnaill, Nuala. "Why I Choose to Write in Irish: The Corpse That Sits Up and Talks Back." *New York Times Book Review*, January 8, 1995, 3, 27–28.

Nolan, Emer. *James Joyce and Nationalism*. London: Routledge, 1995.

Norris, Margot. *A Companion to James Joyce's "Ulysses": Biographical and Historical Contexts, Critical History, and Essays from Five Contemporary Critical Perspectives*. Boston: Bedford Books, 1998.

——. "Disenchanting Enchantment: The Theatrical Brothel of 'Circe.'" In Devlin and Reizbaum, *"Ulysses" En-gendered Perspectives*, 229–41.

——. "Narratology and *Ulysses*." In Gillespie and Fargnoli, *"Ulysses" in Critical Perspective*, 9–34.

——. *Virgin and Veteran Readings of "Ulysses."* New Directions in Irish and Irish American Literature. New York: Palgrave Macmillan, 2011.

——. "A Walk on the Wild(e) Side: The Doubled Reading of 'An Encounter.'" In Valente, *Quare Joyce*, 19–33.

O'Brien, Eugene. "'You Can Never Know Women': Framing Female Identity in *Dubliners*." In Frawley, *A New and Complex Sensation*, 212–22.

Ó Conaire, Pádraic. *Exile*. Translated by Gearailt Mac Eoin. Indreabhán, Conamara, Ireland: Cló Iar-Chonnachta, 1994.

O'Day, Alan. "Parnell: Orator and Speaker." In Boyce and O'Day, *Parnell in Perspective*, 201–20.

O'Donnell, Katherine. "Edmund Burke's Political Poetics." In *Anáil an Bhéil Bheo: Orality and Modern Irish Culture*, edited by Sean Crosson, Louis de Paor, John Eastlake, and Nessa Cronin. Newcastle: Cambridge Scholars, 2009.

Ohi, Kevin. "Molestation 101: Child Abuse, Homophobia, and *The Boys of Saint Vincent*." *GLQ: A Journal of Lesbian and Gay Studies* 6, no. 2 (2000): 195–248.

O'Malley, Patrick. "Confessing Stephen: The Nostalgic Erotics of Catholicism in *A Portrait of the Artist as a Young Man*." In *Catholic Figures, Queer Narratives*, edited by Lowell Gallagher, Frederick S. Roden, and Patricia Juliana Smith, 69–84. New York: Palgrave Macmillan, 2007.

O'Neill, Jamie. *At Swim, Two Boys*. New York: Scribner, 2001.

O'Rourke, Fran. "Philosophy." In McCourt, *James Joyce in Context*, 320–31.

Owens, Cóilín. *James Joyce's Painful Case*. Gainesville: University Press of Florida, 2008.

Palmer, Patricia. *Language and Conquest in Early Modern Ireland: English Renaissance Literature and Elizabethan Imperial Expansion*. Cambridge: Cambridge University Press, 2001

Pierce, David. *James Joyce's Ireland*. New Haven, Conn.: Yale University Press, 1992.

Platt, L. H. "The Buckeen and the Dogsbody: Aspects of History and Culture in 'Telemachus.'" *James Joyce Quarterly* 27, no. 1 (1989): 77–86.

———. *Joyce, Race, and "Finnegans Wake."* Cambridge: Cambridge University Press, 2007.

Potter, Simon J. *News and the British World: The Emergence of an Imperial Press System, 1876–1922*. Oxford: Clarendon, 2003.

———. *Newspapers and Empire in Ireland and Britain*. Portland, Ore.: Four Courts, 2004.

Putz, Adam. "(De)Pressing the Reader: Journalism and Joyce's 'A Painful Case.'" *European Joyce Studies* 18, no. 1 (2008): 9–19.

Rabaté, Jean-Michel, ed. *Palgrave Advances in James Joyce Studies*. New York: Palgrave Macmillan, 2004.

Rando, David. *Modernist Fiction and News: Representing Experience in the Early Twentieth Century*. New York: Palgrave Macmillan, 2011.

Read, Forrest. "Introduction." In *Pound/Joyce: The Letters of Ezra Pound to James Joyce*, edited by Forrest Read, 1–14. New York: New Directions, 1967.

Reizbaum, Marilyn. "Urban Legends." *Éire-Ireland* 45, nos. 1/2 (2010): 242–65.

Reynolds, Paige. *Modernism, Drama, and the Audience for Irish Spectacle*. Cambridge: Cambridge University Press, 2007.

Rhoades, Georgia. "Decoding the Sheela-na-gig." *Feminist Formations* 22, no. 2 (2010): 167–94.

Rice, Thomas Jackson. *Cannibal Joyce*. Gainesville: University Press of Florida, 2008.

Rickard, John. "Stephen Dedalus among Schoolchildren: The Schoolroom and the Riddle of Authority in *Ulysses*." *Studies in the Literary Imagination* 30, no. 2 (1997): 17–36.

Riquelme, John Paul. "'Preparatory to Anything Else': Joyce's Styles as Forms of Memory—The Case of 'Eumaeus.'" In Gillespie and Fargnoli, *"Ulysses" in Critical Perspective*, 9–34.

———. "*Stephen Hero* and *A Portrait of the Artist as a Young Man*: Transforming the Nightmare of History." In Attridge, *Cambridge Companion to James Joyce*, 103–21.

Ross, Alex. "Deceptive Picture: How Oscar Wilde Painted over 'Dorian Gray.'" *New Yorker*, August 8, 2011, E1–E12.

Schork, R. J. "Significant Names in *Finnegans Wake* 46.20 and 371.22." In *"Finnegans Wake* Issue," *James Joyce Quarterly* 34, no. 4 (Summer 1997): 505–16.

Searle, John. *Speech Acts: An Essay in the Philosophy of Language*. Cambridge: Cambridge University Press, 1969.

Sedgwick, Eve. *Between Men: English Literature and Male Homosocial Desire*. New York: Columbia University Press, 1985.

———. *Epistemology of the Closet*. Updated ed. Berkeley: University of California Press, 2008.

———. "Privilege of Unknowing: Diderot's *The Nun*." In *Tendencies*, 23–51. Durham, N.C.: Duke University Press, 1993.

Senn, Fritz. "Clouded Friendship." In Frawley, *A New and Complex Sensation*, 104–11.

Shloss, Carol. "Milly, Molly, and the Mullingar Photo Shop: Developing Negatives in 'Calypso.'" In Devlin and Reizbaum, *"Ulysses" En-gendered Perspectives*, 42–50.

Slote, Sam. "Wild(e) Thing: Concerning the Eccentricities of a Figure of Decadence in *Finnegans Wake*." In *European Joyce Studies 5, Probes: Genetic Studies in Joyce*, edited by David Hayman and Sam Slote, 101–22. Amsterdam: Rodopi, 1995.

Smith, James, and Maria Luddy. "Editors' Introduction." In "Children, Childhood and Irish Society," ed. James Smith and Maria Luddy, special issue, *Éire-Ireland: An Interdisciplinary Journal of Irish Studies* 44, nos. 1–2 (2009): 5–8.

Soderlund, Gretchen. "Covering Urban Vice: The *New York Times*, 'White Slavery,' and the Construction of Journalistic Knowledge." *Critical Studies in Media Communication* 19, no. 4 (December 2002): 438–60.

Spoo, Robert. *James Joyce and the Language of History: Dedalus's Nightmare*. New York: Oxford University Press, 1994.

———. "'Nestor' and the Nightmare: The Presence of the Great War in *Ulysses*." *Twentieth Century Literature* 32, no. 2 (1986): 105–24.

Stallman, Martha. "'Suddenly Somebody Else': Child Loss and Identity in *Dubliners* and *Ulysses*." Honors thesis, University of Houston, 2007.

Stallybrass, Peter, and Allon White. *The Politics and Poetics of Transgression*. Ithaca, NY: Cornell University Press, 1986.

Stead, William T. *The Maiden Tribute of Modern Babylon: The Report of Our Secret Commission, As Published in the "Pall Mall Gazette" of July, 1885*. Reprint, Swindon, U.K.: Lowood, 2011.

Steele, Karen. *Women, Press, and Politics during the Irish Revival.* Syracuse, N.Y.: Syracuse University Press, 2007.

Stone, Harry. "'Araby' and the Writings of James Joyce." *Antioch Review* 25, no. 3 (1965): 375–410.

Taddeo, Julie Anne. *Lytton Strachey and the Search for Modern Sexual Identity: The Last Eminent Victorian.* Binghamton: Haworth, 2002.

Taussig, Michael. *Shamanism, Colonialism, and the Wild Man: A Study in Terror and Healing.* Chicago: University of Chicago Press, 1987.

Theweleit, Klaus. *Male Fantasies.* Vol. 1, *Women, Floods, Bodies, History.* Translated by Stephen Conway. Minneapolis: University of Minnesota Press, 1987.

Thompson, John B. *The Media and Modernity: A Social Theory of the Media.* Stanford, Calif.: Stanford University Press, 1995.

Thompson, Spurgeon. "Recovering *Dubliners* for Postcolonial Theory." In Frawley, *A New and Complex Sensation,* 186–96.

Thorton, Weldon. *Allusions in "Ulysses": An Annotated List.* Chapel Hill: University of North Carolina Press, 1992.

Thuente, Mary Helen. "United Irish Ideology, Images, and Identity, 1798–1998: The Angel Harp." Keynote address, International Association for the Study of Irish Literatures, University of Limerick, July 1998.

Tymoczko, Maria. *The Irish Ulysses.* Berkeley: University of California Press, 1997.

Underwood, Doug. *Journalism and the Novel: Truth and Fiction, 1700–2000.* Cambridge: Cambridge University Press, 2008.

Utell, Janine. *James Joyce and the Revolt of Love: Marriage, Adultery, Desire.* New York: Palgrave Macmillan, 2010.

Valente, Joseph. *James Joyce and the Problem of Justice: Negotiating Sexual and Colonial Difference.* Cambridge: Cambridge University Press, 1995.

———. "Joyce and Sexuality." In Attridge, *Cambridge Companion,* 213–33.

———. "Joyce's (Sexual) Choices: A Historical Overview." In Valente, *Quare Joyce,* 1–16.

———. "Joyce's Sexual Differend: An Example from *Dubliners.*" *James Joyce Quarterly* 28, no. 2 (1991): 407–43.

———. "The Manliness of Parnell." *Éire-Ireland* 41, no. 1 (2006): 64–121.

———. *The Myth of Manliness in Irish National Culture, 1880–1922.* Urbana: University of Illinois Press, 2010.

———. "The Novel and the Police (Gazette)." *Novel* (1995): 8–18.

———. "The Perils of Masculinity." In Devlin and Reizbaum, *"Ulysses" Engendered Perspective,* 111–35.

———, ed. *Quare Joyce.* Ann Arbor: University of Michigan Press, 2000.

———. "Thrilled by His Touch: The Aestheticizing of Homosexual Panic in *A Portrait of the Artist as a Young Man*." In Valente, *Quare Joyce*, 47–75.

———. "*Ulysses* and Queer Theory: A Continuing History." In Gillespie and Fargnoli, "*Ulysses*" *in Critical Perspective*, 88–116.

Valente, Joseph, and Margot Backus. "'An Iridescence Difficult to Account For': Sexual Initiation in Joyce's Fiction of Development." *ELH: Journal of English Literary History* 76, no. 2 (2009): 523–45.

VanArsdel, Rosemary. "Women's Periodicals and the New Journalism: The Personal Interview." In Wiener, *Papers for the Millions*, 243–56.

Van Boheemen, Christine. "Molly's Heavenly Body and the Economy of the Sign: The Invention of Gender in 'Penelope.'" In Devlin and Reizbaum, "*Ulysses*" *En-gendered Perspectives*, 267–82.

Waldron, Jarlath. *Maamtrasna: The Murders and the Mystery*. Dublin: E. Burke, 1992.

Walker, Matt. "The Wilde Rose and Stagnant Waters: Homosexual Panic in Joyce's *The Portrait of the Artist as a Young Man*." Unpublished paper, University of Houston, Spring 2008.

Walkowitz, Judith. *City of Dreadful Delight: Narratives of Sexual Danger in Late-Victorian London*. London: Virago, 1992.

Walshe, Éibhear. "The First Gay Irishman? Ireland and the Wilde Trials." *Éire-Ireland* 40, no. 3 (2005): 38–57.

———. *Oscar's Shadow: Wilde, Homosexuality and Modern Ireland*. Cork, Ireland: Cork University Press, 2011.

Warner, Michael. *Publics and Counterpublics*. New York: Zone Books, 2002.

Warwick-Haller, Sally. "Parnell and William O'Brien: Partners and Friends—From Consensus to Conflict in the Land War." In Boyce and O'Day, *Parnell in Perspective*, 52–76.

Westervelt-Lutz, Austin T. "A Profoundly Human Parable: Ireland's New Aesthetic Community in the 'Scylla & Charybdis' Episode of James Joyce's *Ulysses*." Thesis, University of Houston, 2005.

Wicke, Jennifer. *Advertising Fictions: Literature, Advertisement, and Social Reading*. New York: Columbia University Press, 1988.

Wiener, Joel, ed. *Papers for the Millions: The New Journalism in Britain, 1850s to 1914*. London: Greenwood, 1988.

Wilde, Oscar. *The Decay of Lying*. 1891. Reprint, Electronic Texts Edition; Cork, Ireland: University College, Cork, 2010. http://www.ucc.ie/celt/online/E800003-009.

———. *The Picture of Dorian Gray*. In Aldington and Weintraub, *The Portable Oscar Wilde*.

———. *The Portrait of Mr. W.H.* London: Hesperus, 2003.

Williams, Raymond. *Culture and Society, 1700–1950.* New York: Harper & Row, 1966.

Wills, Clair. "Joyce, Prostitution, and the Colonial City." *South Atlantic Quarterly* 95, no. 1 (1996): 79–95.

Winston, Greg. "Militarism and 'The Dead.'" In Frawley, *A New and Complex Sensation*, 122–32.

Woods, C. J. "Parnell and the Catholic Church." In Boyce and O'Day, *Parnell in Perspective*, 9–37.

INDEX

Page numbers in italics refer to graphics.